# 40 Strategies for Integrating Science and Mathematics Instruction

## K–8

John Eichinger

*Charter School of Education*
*California State University, Los Angeles*

Merrill
Prentice Hall

Upper Saddle River, New Jersey
Columbus, Ohio

Library of Congress Cataloging-in-Publication Data

Eichinger, John.
    40 strategies for integrating science and mathematics instruction : K–8 / John Eichinger.
        p. cm.
    Includes bibliographical references.
    ISBN 0-13-022516-9
        1. Science—Study and teaching (Elementary)   2. Science—Study and teaching (Middle
    school)   3. Mathematics—Study and teaching (Elementary)   4. Mathematics—Study and
    teaching (Middle school)   I. Title: Forty strategies for integrating science and
    mathematics instruction.   II. Title.

Q181.E48 2001
372.3'5'0973—dc21                                                            00-033919

**Vice President and Publisher:** Jeffery W. Johnston
**Editor:** Linda Ashe Montgomery
**Editorial Assistant:** Jennifer Day
**Production Editor:** Mary M. Irvin
**Design Coordinator:** Diane C. Lorenzo
**Text Design and Production Coordination:** The Clarinda Company
**Cover Design:** Jason Moore
**Cover Art:** SuperStock
**Production Manager:** Pamela D. Bennett
**Director of Marketing:** Kevin Flanagan
**Marketing Manager:** Amy June
**Marketing Services Manager:** Krista Groshong

This book was set in Optima by The Clarinda Company and was printed and bound by
Courier/Kendallville, Inc. The cover was printed by Phoenix Color Corp.

Q
181
.E48
2001

Merrill
Prentice Hall

10 9 8 7 6 5 4 3 2

ISBN: 0-13-022516-9

# *Preface*

*Forty Strategies for Integrating Science and Mathematics Instruction: K–8* was designed to provide elementary and middle school teachers, student teachers, and teaching interns with a thorough, step-by-step, hands-on guide to interdisciplinary instruction. Teachers and teacher educators will find a wide range of engaging, discovery-based, and academically rigorous lessons that balance science and mathematics content with creative inquiry and critical thinking. *Forty Strategies for Integrating Science and Mathematics Instruction: K–8* offers significant connections with the national standards in science and mathematics, and can serve as a supplemental text for graduate level courses in teacher preparation, a reference book for inservice K–8 teachers, or a resource for interested parents.

## *Acknowledgments*

I would like to thank the wonderful people at Merrill Prentice Hall for their guidance and support. These include editor Linda Montgomery, production editor Mary Irvin, and acquisition editor Linda McElhiney, whose vision and expertise were essential in bringing this book to print. Many thanks to production editor Silvia Freeburg and copy editor Kathy Pruno at Clarinda Publication Services for their outstanding efforts in putting the book together. Special thanks to my education students at CSLA, who continue to enlighten and inspire me, and especially to my research assistant, Laura Schmidt, for her invaluable work on references. I also want to express my appreciation to my colleagues for their insights and suggestions, especially Chogollah Maroufi, Elizabeth Viau, Judy Washburn, Norm Unrau, Jean Adenika-Morrow, Webster Cotton, Fred Uy, Frances Lang, and Ken Anderson.

I would like to thank the reviewers of my manuscript for their comments and insights: Helene J. Sherman, University of Missouri–St. Louis; Michael Odell, University of Idaho; M. Dale Streigle, Iowa State University; Brian Murfin, New York University; and Anne G. Dorsey, University of Cincinnati.

I am particulary grateful to my friends and family for their unflagging support, patience, and encouragement. This book is sincerely dedicated to my niece and nephew, Heidi and Alex: May your lives be filled with adventure and inquiry!

# Contents

# Science Disciplines

# Earth Science:

# Organizational Matrix: Science and Mathematics Standards, Listed by Activity Number

## MATHEMATICS STANDARDS

| Page 1 SCIENCE STANDARDS | Numbers and Operations | Algebra | Geometry | Measurement | Data Analysis and Probability | Problem Solving | Reasoning and Proof | Communication | Connections | Representation |
|---|---|---|---|---|---|---|---|---|---|---|
| Abilities Necessary to do Scientific Inquiry | 5, 6, 13, 18, 20, 21, 26–28, 32, 33, 36 | 1, 17, 21, 24, 25, 28 | 2, 6, 7, 9, 16, 27, 28, 36–38 | 2–6, 10, 17, 18, 20–22, 26, 27, 35, 37, 38 | 3, 13, 22, 26, 30, 35 | 2, 4, 6, 9, 10, 15–17, 22, 25–28, 30, 33, 35–38 | 1, 7, 13, 16–18, 20–22, 24–27, 30, 35–38 | 2–4, 6, 8, 15, 16, 18, 20, 21, 23, 26, 30, 32 | 4–6, 8, 9, 13, 15, 17, 21, 23, 25, 28, 30 | 7, 9, 24, 32 |
| Understanding About Scientific Inquiry | 5, 6, 13, 18, 20, 21, 26–28, 32, 33, 36, 39 | 1, 17, 21, 24, 25, 28, 39 | 2, 6, 7, 9, 16, 27, 28, 36–38 | 2, 3, 5, 6, 10, 17, 18, 20–22, 26, 27, 35, 37, 38 | 3, 13, 22, 26, 30, 35 | 2, 5, 6, 9, 10, 16, 17, 22, 25–28, 30, 33, 35–38 | 1, 7, 13, 16–18, 20–22, 24–27, 30, 35–38 | 2, 3, 6, 16, 18, 20, 21, 26, 30, 32 | 5, 6, 9, 13, 17, 21, 25, 28, 30 | 7, 9, 24, 32 |
| Properties of Objects and Materials | 11, 13, 19, 20, 39, 40 | 1, 24, 39, 40 | 19, 37, 38 | 10, 12, 14, 20, 37, 38 | 13, 14 | 10, 19, 37, 38, 40 | 1, 11, 12–14, 20, 24, 37, 38 | 11, 12, 20, 40 | 19, 24 | |
| Position and Motion of Objects | 18 | 17 | | 17, 18 | | 17 | 17, 18 | 18 | | |
| Light, Heat, Electricity, and Magnetism | 5 | | 2 | 2, 3, 5, 22 | 3, 22 | 2, 5, 22 | 22 | 2, 3 | 5, 17 | |
| Properties and Changes of Properties in Matter | 11, 13, 19, 20 | 1 | 19 | 10, 14, 20 | 13, 14 | 10, 19 | 1, 11, 13, 14, 20 | 11, 20 | 13, 19 | 19 |
| Motions and Forces | 18 | 17 | | 17, 18 | | 17 | 17, 18 | 18 | 17 | |
| Transer of Energy | 21 | 21 | 2 | 2–4, 12, 21 | 3 | 2, 4 | 12, 21 | 2–4, 12, 21 | 4, 21 | |
| Characteristics of Organisms | 5, 6, 28, 29 | 25, 28 | 6, 7, 9, 28, 29 | 5, 6, 14 | 14, 30 | 5, 6, 9, 25, 28, 30 | 7, 14, 25, 30 | 6, 30 | 5, 6, 9, 25, 28–30 | 7, 9 |

## MATHEMATICS STANDARDS

| SCIENCE STANDARDS | Numbers and Operations | Algebra | Geometry | Measurement | Data Analysis and Probability | Problem Solving | Reasoning and Proof | Communication | Connections | Representation |
|---|---|---|---|---|---|---|---|---|---|---|
| Organisms and Environments | 40 | 40 | | 12 | | 40 | 12 | 12, 40 | | |
| Structure and Function in Living Systems | 5, 6, 26–29 | 25, 28 | 6, 7, 9, 27–29 | 5, 6, 14, 26, 27 | 14, 26, 30 | 5, 6, 9, 25–28, 30 | 7, 14, 25–27, 30 | 6, 26, 29, 30 | 5, 6, 7, 9, 25, 28, 30 | 9 |
| Regulation and Behavior in Living Systems | 5, 27 | | 7, 27 | 5, 12, 14, 27 | 14, 30 | 5, 27, 30 | 7, 12, 14, 27, 30 | 12, 30 | 5, 7, 30 | |
| Diversity and Adaptations of Organisms | 6, 28, 29 | 25, 28 | 6, 28, 29 | 6, 12 | 30 | 6, 25, 28, 30 | 12, 25, 30 | 6, 12, 29, 30 | 6, 25, 28, 30 | |
| Properties of Earth Materials | 31–33, 36 | | 36 | 35 | 35 | 33, 35, 36 | 31, 35, 36 | 31, 32 | | 31, 32 |
| Structure of the Earth System | 31–33, 36 | | 36 | 34, 35 | 35 | 33, 35, 36 | 31, 34–36 | 31, 32 | 34 | 32, 32, 34 |
| Abilities of Technological Design | 19 | | 19, 37, 38 | 3, 4, 37, 38 | 3 | 4, 19, 37, 38 | 37, 38 | 3, 4 | 4, 19 | 19 |
| Understanding About Science and Technology | 19 | | 2, 19, 37, 38 | 2–4, 37, 38 | 3 | 2, 4, 19, 37, 38 | 37, 38 | 2–4 | 4, 19 | 19 |
| Science and Technology in Society | | | 37, 38 | 3, 37, 38 | 3 | 37, 38 | 37, 38 | 3, 8, 15, 23 | 8, 15, 23 | |

# Introduction

"The solution which I am urging, is to eradicate the fatal disconnection of subjects which kills the vitality of our modern curriculum. There is only one subject matter for education, and that is Life in all its manifestations."

—Alfred North Whitehead
(The Aims of Education, 1929)

## Overview

40 Strategies for Integrating Science and Mathematics Instruction: K–8 (40 SISMI) was written as a hands-on guide for elementary and middle school teachers, student teachers, and interns who want to offer their students more than the traditional, discipline-bound methods of instruction. The book presents 40 engaging, discovery-based, and academically rigorous strategies that connect the various disciplines of science not only to the study of mathematics, but also to the visual arts, social sciences, and language arts. The strategies are aligned with the latest national standards, including the updated standards recently published by the National Council of Teachers of Mathematics (2000). The ideas balance integrated content with the processes of personally relevant inquiry and are designed to promote creative, critical thinking on the part of all students. The lessons are teacher friendly, too. That is, they do not require advanced expertise in any particular subject area, and they use only simple, inexpensive, and accessible materials.

40 SISMI provides a way of deepening students' understanding in science and mathematics by integrating the content in meaningful and dynamic ways. In searching for the common ground between science and math 40 SISMI also offers significant connections with the national standards adopted by both disciplines, which call for an increase in interdisciplinary instruction. 40 SISMI should not be considered simply a peripheral "add on" to the required curriculum—it represents an engaging supplement to the core classroom curriculum.

40 SISMI is of particular value to preservice teachers at the K–8 level, because early preparation in these sorts of strategies is a key to developing effective interdisciplinary classroom instruction. Indeed, as McComas and Wang noted, "If blended science instruction is [to] become a reality, preservice instructional plans must be overhauled to ensure that teachers can gain both the necessary content and experience [that] effective blended science instruction models firsthand" (1998, p. 345). 40 SISMI is an effort to do just that: to model alternative, yet proven, teaching practices for preservice and inservice educators alike. I hope that 40 SISMI will also act as a catalyst to encourage teachers to adapt these lessons to their own needs and especially to develop and implement their own interdisciplinary lesson ideas.

Although the lessons can be applied in any classroom, they are particularly suited to urban schools, where access to natural study sites such as lakes, streams, and forest trails, or even small plots of grass, are limited. 40 SISMI was developed with gender equity, multiculturalism, and multilingualism in mind, relying on students' personal observations and cooperative group work rather than teacher-centered lectures, traditional textbooks, or pencil-and-paper tests as the basis for conceptual understanding.

## Theoretical Foundation

40 SISMI is built on a constructivist foundation, which holds that meaningful learning depends on prior experience (Piaget, 1970). In the constructivist perspective, understanding is mediated by personal and social background, as knowledge is constructed, negotiated, and tested via experience by

active knowers. The only adequate test of knowledge is in its viability when applied to current problems (Tobin, 1993). Constructivism does not delineate a particular methodology, but generally suggests that teachers attend to students' prior understandings, create situations in which students have opportunities to reconceptualize naive notions, and remain flexible and alert to the growth and viability of student knowledge. As von Glasersfeld noted, "successful thinking is more important than 'correct' answers," (1993, p. 33), and to foster motivation the constructivist teacher "will have to create situations where the students have an opportunity to experience the pleasure inherent in solving a problem" (1993, p.33).

*40 SISMI* activities and strategies have been chosen and presented so that they might clearly provide teachers with discovery-based, highly motivating, and student-centered learning opportunities that have been proven in real K–8 classrooms. Effective pedagogic strategies permeate the lessons and include such techniques as hands-on/minds-on instruction, guided discovery, the learning cycle, open-ended challenges, projects, metacognition, attention to the affective domain, and authentic assessment. Four overarching components of the *40 SISMI* lessons, each requiring further explanation below, are *student relevance, interaction/collaboration, problem-based learning,* and *integrated instruction.* Each of these notions is clearly recognized and encouraged by the national standards in science and mathematics (American Association for the Advancement of Science, 1993; National Council of Teachers of Mathematics, 1989; National Research Council, 1996).

The first component, *student relevance,* refers to a focus on student interests, questions, and ideas, and on student-generated solutions and projects. Lessons must reflect the lives of the students involved. Memorization and retention of facts, imposed by the teacher, are insufficient and ineffective. If a deeper and more viable understanding is to be reached, students must be assisted in bridging from the familiar to the unfamiliar.

The second component, *interaction/collaboration,* reminds us that elementary students, as fundamentally concrete thinkers, require a personal and interpersonal experience to learn effectively. Students must, therefore, be actively involved both personally and socially in science/math explorations. Engaging lessons that encourage involvement and provide and provide opportunities for meaningful understanding are optimally motivating for students, especially at the K–8 grade range. Furthermore, we know that to be fully effective, interactive studies must be undertaken in a collaborative manner. Learning depends on socialization, and a deep understanding of science and math depends on an awareness of the interpersonal aspects of those disciplines (Vygotsky, 1978).

The third overarching component of many of the *40 SISMI* lessons, *problem-based learning,* provides a challenging and motivating context for classroom math and science exploration. An essential feature of the current national standards in math and science education is a call for deeper, more active, and more relevant inquiry. Posing realistic, interesting, open-ended, and challenging problems for students to solve is a mainstay of the reform movement. Through problem solving in the classroom, students learn to effectively confront demands encountered in "real life" by applying higher order thinking skills.

The fourth key component of *40 SISMI* activities is *integrated instruction,* or the blending of two or more academic disciplines into a particular classroom lesson. Science and mathematics, although traditionally treated as discrete intellectual entities, are not separated in the world outside the classroom. Integrated instruction not only promotes the presentation of the subjects in a realistic and relevant context, but also provides opportunities for imaginative and personal connections between students and subject matter, which serve to further enhance understanding and motivation, Cross-disciplinary connections deepen understanding by allowing the learner to simultaneously utilize the representational forms of several disciplinary media. That is, the learner has an opportunity to view and comprehend the situation from more than one disciplinary perspective, generating a greater complexity of meaning (Fosnot, 1996). Research into the impact of integrated science/math instruction shows a positive effect on student achievement, problem-solving ability, self-worth, motivation, and interest (Meier, Cobbs, & Nicol, 1998). At a very practical level, integrated instruction, by connecting subjects and thereby condensing teaching time, provides more time to teach science and math in what for many teachers has become a very tight daily teaching schedule.

A few words about nomenclature and the natures of science and mathematics would be appropriate here. Terminology describing simultaneous instruction in multiple disciplines abounds: integrated, unified, blended, interdisciplinary, cross-disciplinary, multidisciplinary, thematic, coordinated, and probably several others. These terms tend to be used inconsistently and therefore lead to a great deal of confusion about the general notion and the specific methods. Lederman and Neiss (1998) wrote that the term *integration* tends to be used in one of two ways. First, it may refer to instructional situations where traditional boundaries are blurred or even lost. Second, it may refer to situations that maintain traditional boundaries, but stress the interaction between the disciplines during instruction. Lederman and Neiss favor the latter definition, explaining that conventions differ between science and mathematics, largely related to the notion that science (and not math) needs to refer to external empirical observations in problem-solving situations. That is, ways of knowing differ significantly between science and mathematics (as well as between other academic disciplines), enabling us to discriminate one discipline from another. Therefore, if students are to gain understanding of how science, math, or any other intellectual discipline functions, the lines demarcating the disciplines should not be erased or even significantly blurred. Rather than dissolving disciplines into incongruous hybrids, Lederman and Neiss argue, teachers interested in integrated instruction should assist the students in finding meaningful interconnections among existing disciplines. Although a certain amount of disciplinary "cloudiness" is bound to exist in any attempt at integrated instruction, *40 SISMI* supports the position of Lederman and Neiss.

*40 SISMI* breaks new ground by integrating math, science, and other disciplines, including the visual arts, into a collage of sorts by embedding the various disciplines into a truly interactive, integrated matrix based on observation, pattern recognition, reflective analysis, and problem solving. By offering a variety of experiences and cognitive "footholds," *40 SISMI* lessons will significantly increase the likelihood that all students will make personally meaningful connections with classroom instruction.

## *General Suggestions for Use*

Whether it is used as a supplemental text for graduate-level courses in teacher preparation, as a reference book for inservice elementary and/or middle school teachers, or as a resource to assist parents in expanding their child's understanding of the world, *40 SISMI* will help clarify the connections between science and other academic fields, especially mathematics. There is no particular sequence in which the lessons should be introduced. They may be utilized in a variety of ways: as an active introduction or dynamic closure to a unit of study; as a motivational, guided inquiry that supplements the core curriculum via application; or as an open-ended and independent investigatory project. Choose *40 SISMI* lessons that reflect and extend your required curriculum, or just try some that look interesting or that you think your students will enjoy. Then as you teach those lessons, watch for opportunities to emerge that allow you and your class to make connections with past or future areas of study.

Remember also that this is not just an "activity book," but a resource offering sensory-based, concrete *investigations embedded in effective instructional strategies*. The lessons are adaptable to individual situations, and the pedagogy may be applied to active teaching scenarios in any discipline.

Readers are enthusiastically encouraged to adapt these lessons to their own classroom needs. Use all or part of the extensive *40 SISMI* lesson plans, as time and interest permit. The book is not meant to be prescriptive—it can serve as a catalyst for teachers to expand and ultimately to develop their own integrated lessons. A practical model for the development of interdisciplinary lessons, by the way, was provided by Francis and Underhill (1969).

Activities may be selected by referring to the Organizational Matrix: Science and Mathematics Standards (based, respectively, on NRC, National Research Council and NCTM, National Council of Teachers of Mathematics standards), or to the Table of Contents Based on Science Disciplines. However, the discipline-based table of contents is offered only to expedite the location of appropriate lesson ideas. In actuality, many activities include aspects of several different science disciplines. For instance, Activity 5, Examining Colors, Color Perception and Sight, is listed as Life Science project, but it also involves a significant amount of physics. Similarly, most activities have a great deal more math embedded in the procedure than is delineated in the lesson's list of concepts. How much science, math, art, literature, and so on, each teacher includes in his or her presentation of the lesson depends on that educator's pedagogic style and curricular direction. The depth and breadth of interdisciplinary connections is entirely up to individual teachers and their students.

Standardized or traditional assessment methods are often inappropriate for evaluating integrated, problem-based tasks such as those that appear in this book. More appropriate means of assessment have therefore been included for each lesson. Those methods are all what may be termed "authentic assessment," i.e., methods of evaluation that are well matched to experiential tasks. Those methods include:

- *Embedded*—This technique blends assessment and instruction into a seamless whole, rather than following the traditional teach, test, teach, test format. In embedded assessment, the teacher observes students as they participate in hands-on activities, looking for mastery of desired skills, processes, and content understanding. This sort of observation is facilitated by asking questions about their experiences as they participate, such as "What if . . . ?" or "Explain how you know. . . ."

- *Performance Tasks*—Students apply their knowledge as they solve concrete problems in a procedure separate from the instruction sequence. For example, in *40 SISMI* Activity 18, students conduct an experiment comparing the jumping abilities of small, medium, and large origami frogs. Their understanding of that experimental procedure may be assessed by evaluating their performance as they test and analyze the jumping ability of a fourth, differently sized frog.

- *Journal Entries*—Journals are an effective means of integrating language arts into the study of science and math. In their journals, students can collect and analyze data, explain what they learned, and reflect on their experiences. Entries could also include illustrations and sketches to allow assessment from a nonverbal angle.

- *Portfolio*—Portfolios are collections of student work, often chosen and reflected on by the students themselves. They can be used to indicate progress over time and may include lab reports, writing samples, graphs, illustrations, and so on.

For each suggested means of assessment in each lesson, the particular type(s) of appropriate authentic assessment(s) is(are) offered (e.g., from Activity 25, "Could students see the value of fingerprints in various jobs and possibly in their everyday lives? [embedded, journal entries]"). To gain a more complete perspective of student progress, one should employ several means of assessment within a given lesson. Whatever means of evaluation one uses, however, the assessment must match the task.

During the implementation of the *40 SISMI* lessons, safety issues are of utmost importance. Teachers are strongly urged to utilize appropriate laboratory procedures while undertaking the activities, not only for the students' immediate safety, but also for the development of lifelong safety habits. Essential safety recommendations include:

1. Keep the work area clean. Clean up all spills immediately. Clean and store equipment and materials after use.

2. Never taste unknown chemicals. Always sniff gases cautiously. Store materials appropriately and safely.

3. Wear protective eyewear when working with hazardous substances or in any hazardous situations.

4. Be especially careful with electricity.

5. Provide constant supervision during individual or group work.

6. Allow sufficient time to complete tasks without rushing.

7. Provide sufficient lighting and ventilation.

8. Keep safety in mind when undertaking any *40 SISMI* or other investigatory activities.

## Specific Suggestions for Use

The *40 SISMI* lessons have a basic structure, which essentially asks the teacher to provide a framework and opportunity for students to do much of their own exploring and discovering. The teacher introduces an idea or concept via a question, demonstration, or simple activity, allowing him/her to check for background knowledge and interest in the topic. Then the teacher and class, often broken into small, cooperative groups, proceed through the lesson, step-by-step. The students collect, analyze, and discuss data, sharing their reactions and insights. There is no particular script for teachers to follow, yet the teachers are encouraged at all times to model inquiry and problem-solving strategies in their own approaches to the activity. The step-by-step directions are specific enough for teachers to easily work through the activity, yet general enough to allow for adaptations as necessary.

A crucial aspect of the *40 SISMI* lessons is the teacher's attention to his or her questioning strategy, utilizing a range of open- and closed-ended questions to stimulate students' critical thinking. Discussion questions are provided within the procedure and in a separate section following the procedure; teachers should also develop their own questions. Be careful not to dwell too much on or to give away "the right answers," however, because an essential aspect of these lessons is that students have a chance to participate in the process of inquiry.

A recommended grade range is provided for each lesson, but the lessons can be easily adapted for either younger or older students. For younger students, generally simplify the use of terminology, eliminate or adapt procedures requiring fine motor skills, break the duration of the inquiry into shorter segments, and be sure that the lesson proceeds in an orderly and sequential manner. For older students, expand on the terminology and concepts, provide deeper connections to other disciplines, and offer opportunities for individual exploration, perhaps extending to investigations that can be undertaken outside the classroom (home, neighborhood, museums, etc.).

The *40 SISMI* activity format is broken into a number of sections, each providing the user with important information at a glance. Before trying the activity in class, it is strongly recommended that the teacher read the entire lesson to facilitate choices of questioning strategies, modifications, assessment, and overall implementation. What follows is an explanation of each section of the activity format, as well as suggestions for use.

**Overview:** Gives a concise description of the activity and helps the teacher decide where it might fit into his or her curriculum.

**Concepts:** Clarifies the particular subject matter concepts emphasized in the activity.

**Processes/Skills:** Clarifies the processes and skills that students can be expected to employ as they participate in the lesson.

**Recommended for:** Offers a general grade range for which the activity is most appropriate, as well as a recommendation for individual, small group, or whole class instruction.

**Time Required:** Offers an approximate time range for completion of the lesson. This will, of course, vary from class to class and should only be considered a rough estimate.

**Materials Required:** Lets the teacher know just what materials are needed for the main activity as well as any pre- or postactivities. Be sure to assemble all materials prior to teaching the lesson—nothing will ruin your well-organized plan as quickly as having omitted a vital item.

**Standards:** Clarifies the NRC and NCTM standards associated with the activity.

**Objectives:** Delineates performance objectives that students can be expected to reach during the lesson.

**Background Information:** Provides the teacher with conceptual information and explanations of terminology, when needed. In some cases, background information is included within the activity's step-by-step procedure.

**Preliminary Activity:** Provides an introductory or anticipatory experience for students and allows the teacher to check on the status of prior experience and knowledge.

**Main Activity, Step-by-Step:** Provides sequential and ready-to-implement steps, which are adaptable to fit the needs of each classroom.

**Follow Up Activity:** Expands on the specific concepts examined in the main activity.

**Questions for Discussion:** Offers several thought-provoking questions to promote the development of higher order thinking skills, synthesis of disciplinary interconnections, and a deeper overall understanding.

**Assessment:** Describes several means of evaluating student progress, and in brackets, lists specific methods of evaluation. Rubrics or other details regarding actual evaluation should be determined prior to doing the lesson so that the teacher's expectations are clearly defined and communicated. Teachers should include aspects of the affective domain in their assessment: are the students having fun and acting interested?

**Connecting Activity:** Offers a connecting activity to expand the basic lesson into another subject area, particularly the visual arts.

**Other Options and Extensions:** Offers further ideas for extension of the basic lesson. These can be pursued with the class as time allows, or they can be made available to individual students as homework or as a foundation for further study.

**Resources and Further Information:** Provides the teacher with citations for books, articles, and other supplementary resources.

When implementing the lesson ideas, plan thoroughly, yet try to remain open to emergent and spontaneous learning opportunities, paying particular attention to student questions, impressions, and proposals. Student-generated ideas are often the keys to establishing meaningful understanding and lasting motivation. Listen carefully to the students as they investigate, think, and grow in confidence and knowledge. Listen for ways to improve instruction. Listen for options and extensions. Try something new. Try something suggested by an enthusiastic student. Prepare thoroughly and enjoy the experience. Share your joy of learning with your students.

## References

American Association for the Advancement of Science. (1993). *Benchmarks for science literacy.* New York: Oxford University Press.

Fosnot, C. T. (1996). *Constructivism: A psychological theory of learning.* In C. T. Fosnot (Ed.), *Constructivism: Theory, perspectives, and practice* (pp. 8–33). New York: Teachers College Press.

Francis, R., & Underhill, R. G. (1996). A procedure for integrating math and science units. *School Science and Mathematics 96,* 114–119.

Lederman, N. G., & Neiss, M. L. (1998). 5 apples + 4 oranges = ? *School Science and Mathematics, 98,* 281–284.

McComas, W. F, & Wang, H. A. (1998). Blended science: The rewards and challenges of integrating the science disciplines for instruction. *School Science and Mathematics 98,* 340–348.

Meier, S. L., Cobbs, G., & Nicol, M. (1998). Potential benefits and barriers to integration. *School Science and Mathematics, 98,* 438–445.

National Council of Teachers of Mathematics. (1989). *Curriculum and evaluation standards for school mathematics.* Reston, VA: Author.

National Research Council. (1996). *National science education standards.* Washington: National Academy Press.

Piaget, J. (1970). *Genetic epistemology.* New York: Columbia University Press.

Tobin, K. (Ed.). (1993). *The practice of constructivism in science education.* Washington: AAAS Press.

von Glasersfeld, E. (1993). Questions and answers about radical constructivism. In K. Tobin (Ed.), *The practice of constructivism in science education* (pp. 23–38). Washington: AAAS Press.

Vygotsky, L. S. (1978). *Mind in society.* Cambridge, MA: Harvard University Press.

# Investigating Textures

 **Overview**

This is a simple but engaging activity for students of all grade levels, K–8. Textures are all around us, and they are important to our everyday activities—consider a piece of sandpaper, a cheese grater, or the soles of your shoes. As students become aware of the details and properties of familiar surroundings, which they do here with their texture rubbings, they learn to more closely observe the conditions around them.

## Concepts

Students investigate textures by making, observing, and comparing rubbings of various objects and surfaces in and around the classroom.

## Processes/Skills

- Observing
- Comparing
- Describing
- Identifying patterns
- Collecting
- Asking insightful questions

## Recommended for

| | |
|---|---|
| K–2 ✔ | Individual ✔ |
| 3–5 ✔ | Small Group ✔ |
| 6–8 ✔ | Whole Class ✔ |

## Time Required

1–2 hours

## Materials Required

**FOR MAIN ACTIVITY**

- Paper
- Pencils (soft lead)
- Other writing utensils (e.g., charcoal, markers)
- A range of objects with varying surface textures

**FOR CONNECTING ACTIVITY**

- All of the above
- Glue or paste

## Standards

**SCIENCE**

- Properties of Objects and Materials
- Properties and Changes of Properties in Matter
- Abilities Necessary to Do Scientific Inquiry
- Understanding About Scientific Inquiry

**MATH**

- Reasoning and Proof
- Algebra

## Objectives

- Students will collect and observe texture rubbings from a variety of surfaces.
- Students will describe specific aspects of their rubbings and will identify differences and similarities between the various rubbings.
- Students will clarify some of the ways that textures are important to us in our daily lives.

## Main Activity, Step-by-Step

1. Begin by asking the class, "Can you think of some ways that the surface of the floor and the chalk-board (or any two surfaces in the room) differ?" Allow for a variety of student answers. Expand and/or explain that one way they differ is in their surface texture. Explain that today we will collect and compare the impressions of several different surfaces.

2. Demonstrate the rubbing process by placing a paper over a flat, textured surface and gently rubbing back and forth over it with the pencil or other writing utensil. An impression of the surface texture will appear in the pencil marks (if not, you may not be using a soft enough pencil, or you may be rubbing too lightly or too heavily). Have everyone make a rubbing and check to see that they all have mastered the technique.

3. With adequate paper supplies and pencils, instruct the students to collect at least ten different rubbings from the objects you have provided (such as pieces of wood, a flower pot, rocks, shells, a cast iron frying pan, and so on) and/or from surfaces in the classroom. Encourage them to investigate as many types of surfaces as possible—some may be easier to collect than others. What sorts of surfaces make the most interesting rubbings? On some surfaces they may want to collect two or more rubbings from different areas (such as pavement, where there is a lot of variation). You may want to allow them to collect rubbings outside the classroom, too, if this is feasible.

4. When all collections are completed, reassemble in small groups to discuss, compare, and analyze the textural collections. The ensuing classwide discussion can focus on student-generated questions and ideas, teacher-generated questions and ideas, and/or the discussion questions offered below.

## Questions for Discussion

1. In your own words, describe three rubbings in detail, paying particular attention to textural patterns.
2. Are any of the rubbings similar to each other? How are they similar?
3. Which rubbings are most different from one another? What makes them different?
4. Are any of the surface textures made that way for a particular reason (such as for added friction, greater smoothness)? How do you know?
5. What are some ways that textures are important to us in our daily lives?

## Assessment

1. Were the students able to collect and describe a variety of textural rubbings? [performance task]
2. Were they able to notice and describe similarities and differences between various rubbings? [embedded]
3. Were they able to identify any patterns in surface texture and/or use? [embedded, journal entries]
4. Were they able to explain how varying textures may be useful for different purposes? [embedded, journal entries]

## Connecting Activity

To connect the texture inquiry to the visual arts, make a collage or mosaic of various rubbings. Cut and paste, using bits and pieces of rubbings. Make it even more interesting by using a variety of writing implements (e.g., softer pencils, harder pencils, charcoal, colored pencils, markers) to create the rubbings. Consider depicting an object or scene, or portray a relationship between the various textures (e.g., alternating rough/smooth).

## Other Options and Extensions

1.  Homework: Ask students to collect interesting rubbings at home. Bring them to class for further comparison, analysis, and discussion.

2.  Mystery rubbings: Have students try to challenge one another with "unknown" rubbings, allowing their classmates to guess the source of the mystery rubbings.

3.  Quantify the analysis by counting or estimating the number of bumps per square inch on several rubbings. Then by using a chart or bar graph format, compare the "feel" of those rubbings with the number of bumps per square inch. For instance, do rough surfaces have more bumps per square inch than smooth surfaces? How do different surfaces compare, quantitatively?

## Resources and Further Information

Jenkins, P. D. (1980). *Art for the fun of it.* New York: Fireside.

McIntyre, M. (1978). Art experiences: Opening the door to science. *Science and Children, 15* (7), 38–39.

Miller, L. (1972). Creative rubbings. *School Arts, 72* (4), 4–5.

Schisgall, J. (1976). Discovering textures with young children. *School Arts, 76* (3), 16–17.

Williams, D. (1995). *Teaching mathematics through children's art.* Portsmouth, NH: Heineman.

# What Do You See?
# Visual Observation

 ## Overview

As Yogi Berra said, "You can observe a lot just by watching." The following activities will help to strengthen your students' skills in a fundamental aspect of mathematics and science: visual observation. In this activity, students carefully examine and sketch a variety of objects, then analyze the sketches for shapes, patterns, and relationships. They will investigate the concept of "field of view" and notice how it can vary depending on distance. As a connecting activity, they can incorporate careful observation, field of view, and shape/pattern recognition into a painting.

## Concepts

Students observe, sketch, and analyze things they see. They identify shapes and patterns in their sketches. They also explore the concept of field of view.

 ## Processes/Skills

- Observing
- Measuring
- Collecting data
- Comparing
- Graphing
- Using compass and ruler
- Using optical instruments
- Recognizing shapes and patterns
- Sketching
- Painting
- Cooperating
- Questioning

## Recommended for

| | |
|---|---|
| K–2 | Individual ✔ |
| 3–5 ✔ | Small Group ✔ |
| 6–8 ✔ | Whole Class |

## Time Required

2–3 hours

## Materials Required

**MAIN ACTIVITY**

- A variety of objects to observe
- Paper
- Pencils and/or other drawing tools
- Optical instruments (which might include hand lenses, binoculars, reversed binoculars, and/or microscopes)
- Drawing compass
- Metric rulers
- Meter sticks
- Index cards

**CONNECTING ACTIVITY**

- Paint
- Paper
- Other drawing materials

## Standards

**SCIENCE**

- Understanding About Science and Technology
- Abilities Necessary to Do Scientific Inquiry
- Understanding About Scientific Inquiry

- Light, Heat, Electricity, and Magnetism
- Transfer of Energy

**MATH**

- Communication
- Geometry
- Measurement
- Problem Solving

- Students will make observations and sketches using one or more optical instruments.
- Students will define *observation* and *field of view* based on their own experiences in this lesson.
- Students will measure field of view and recognize the relationship between field of view and viewing distance.
- Students will identify and describe patterns, colors, and geometric shapes in their observations, sketches, and paintings.

 ## *Objectives*

- Students will observe and sketch a variety of familiar objects.

## *Main Activity, Step-by-Step*

1. Begin by showing the students an array of objects. This miscellaneous collection should include the familiar (e.g., stapler, fast-food containers, rocks) as well as the relatively or totally unfamiliar (e.g., pine cones, sea shells, hand tools). Direct students to just look at these objects for several minutes without speculation as to their use, origin, or impact. Just *look* at them, one at a time, and notice the details. It will be valuable to have students patiently concentrate on a few favorite objects, rather than trying to rush through the entire collection. Ask, "How do these objects differ? How are they similar? What visual characteristics can you observe? Which objects would you like to see more of? Why?" Encourage a discussion about observation: Why do we see some things but not others? What does *observation* mean?

2. Direct students to sketch one or more of the objects using pencil, charcoal, crayon, and/or ink. Make the sketches as detailed as possible. You may want to suggest that they sketch other objects, indoor or outdoor views, and so forth in addition to the objects that you collected. Encourage attention to visual detail, shapes, patterns, and the "not so obvious." Ask them to try to notice something about the object that they've never noticed before. When each student has completed several sketches, ask them to identify patterns, colors, and geometric shapes in their work. Students may then share and discuss their sketches in groups.

3. Using optical instruments, have students look at different objects and views to get the feel of the instruments. Direct them to sketch one or more views, as seen through the instrument of choice. Ask, "Under what conditions might each of these instruments be useful? For instance, which might be good for close work? For distant viewing? How do you know?"

4. Using drawing compass and ruler, students can now make viewfinders from index cards. To construct a viewfinder, simply cut two separate holes, one 2 cm and the other 6 cm in diameter, in the index card. The viewfinder will be used in the next few procedures.

5. Working in pairs or small groups, but with each student using her or his own viewfinder, students should look through the large and the small holes at near and distant objects (keep the other eye closed). Record rough sketches of what they see through the large hole, near and distant, and through the small hole, near and distant. How do the large-hole sketches compare? The small-hole sketches? How do the large-hole observations compare with those through the small holes? Promote a variety of responses, and encourage students to note that what they see through the viewfinder depends also on how far it is held from the eye. Introduce the concept of field of view (the entire area you can see at any given time and under any particular circumstances; the field of view can be relatively wide or narrow), encouraging student definitions.

6.  Next, while using the viewfinders students will measure and compare widths of fields of view. Ask, "How does the field of view change with distance?" Holding the viewfinder 20 cm from the eye and remaining a fixed distance from the object being observed (this can be done by standing 1 m away from the chalkboard and telling a partner where to mark the edges of the field), measure the field of view as seen through the large hole, then through the small hole. Then move 2 m away from the chalkboard while holding the viewfinder 20 cm from the eye and measure the fields as seen through each of the holes again. Repeat at a distance of 4 m. Record all data on Activity Sheet 2. What patterns do the students see in the data (graphing distance versus width of field for each of the holes may help clarify the relationship between these variables). Have students discuss their findings in groups. Engage the entire class in the discussion, using examples of paintings to demonstrate the notion that field of view broadens with distance.

## Questions for Discussion

1.  What have you learned about your own ability to observe?

2.  How can you become a better, more careful observer? How might observation skills affect your life?

3.  Can you name some jobs that require careful observation skills?

4.  How do the optical instruments change your field of view?

5.  How did using the viewfinder affect your ability to observe?

## Assessment

1.  Were students able to notice and sketch or describe details of the objects observed? [embedded, performance]

2.  Were they able to observe and sketch using one or more optical instruments? [embedded]

3.  Did they notice differences between unaided and aided observations, or between the various optical instruments? [embedded, journal entries]

4.  Could students generate working definitions of *observation* and *field of view?* [embedded, journal entries]

5.  Were they able to measure field of view and to recognize the relationship between field of view and viewing distance? [embedded, journal entries]

6.  Were they able to identify and describe patterns, colors, and geometric shapes in their paintings, sketches, and observations? [embedded, journal entries, portfolio]

## Connecting Activity

To connect the lesson to the visual arts, direct the students to sketch several additional views in greater detail (and in color, if they so choose), close or far, through small or large holes of the viewfinder (being sure to record for each sketch the approximate focal distance and whether the large or small hole was used). If possible, allow them to leave the classroom to generate a wider variety of observations. They then choose one view and paint it. Consider using colors other than the "real" colors. Consider substituting shapes, patterns, and textures (e.g., triangle for circle, regular for irregular, rough for smooth). Display the paintings. Discuss how the paintings would be different if they had incorporated a wider or narrower field of view.

## Other Options and Extensions

1. Homework: Make sketches of objects or views at home. Ask parents to suggest objects and make more sketches. Share the sketches in class.

2. Consider Main Activity 6: Challenge pairs or groups of students to use similar methods, or to devise new techniques, to investigate the relationship between width of field of view and distance that the viewfinder is held from the eye. Ask, "How does the field of view change as you move the viewfinder closer/farther from your eye?" Encourage a variety of answers, then direct them to collect data to support or refute your explanation."

3. Create a writing assignment by asking students to describe their connecting activity paintings in words (perhaps a poem, a story, a newscast, or a play).

## Resources and Further Information

Gaylen, N. (1998). Encouraging curiosity at home. *Science and Children, 36* (4), 24–25.

Glatenfelter, P. (1997). Making observations from the ground up. *Science and Children, 34* (8), 28–30.

Glenn, D. (1984). Sight in stereo. *School Arts, 83* (9), 13–14.

Jenkins, P. D. (1980). *Art for the fun of it.* New York: Fireside.

Johns, F., & Liske, K. (1992). Schoolyard adventuring. *Science and Children, 30* (3), 19–21.

Spooner, W., & Bowden, S. (1983). Enlarging science learning with magnifiers. *Science and Children, 20* (7), 12–14.

### Activity Sheet 2.  What Do You See? Visual Observation

Use this table to record the width of the field of view observed through the viewfinder. "How does the field of view change with distance?"

|  | *1 m distance* | *2 m distance* | *4 m distance* |
|---|---|---|---|
| Viewed Through Large Hole (6 cm) |  |  |  |
| Viewed Through Small Hole (2 cm) |  |  |  |

What conclusions can you reach about the effect of distance on the field of view?

# Investigating the Pinhole Camera and Camera Obscura

 **Overview**

In this activity, students from grades 3 through 8 can explore the nature of light, including the fact that it travels in straight lines, by building and using two visual tools. The first is a simple pinhole camera: a box with a pin hole opening. The second is a camera obscura, a tool of historical interest, particularly in the arts. The camera obscura, basically a pinhole camera with a lens, was a forerunner of the modern camera and allowed 17th- and 18th-century artists to make very accurate sketches of their subjects. During the activities, students will explore the operation of these simple instruments, and will learn why, historically, the camera obscura was an important tool for many artists. The entire lesson will also serve as an introduction to the art of photography, which will be explored more fully in Activity 4.

 **Concepts**

Students investigate the behavior of light by using a simple pinhole camera, with particular emphasis on the relationship between distance from the light source and image size. This concept is expanded to make a camera obscura, which will then be used, as it was historically, to make accurate sketches.

 **Processes/Skills**

- Observing
- Constructing
- Measuring
- Graphing
- Predicting
- Describing
- Inferring
- Designing experiments
- Comparing

- Creating
- Sketching
- Appreciating
- Cooperating
- Communicating

 **Recommended for**

| K–2 | | Individual | |
|-----|---|-----------|---|
| 3–5 | ✔ | Small Group | ✔ |
| 6–8 | ✔ | Whole Class | |

 **Time Required**

2–4 hours

 **Materials Required**

MAIN ACTIVITY

- Shoe boxes
- Pin or needle
- Transparent tape
- Paper
- Scissors
- Flashlights
- Meter sticks
- Graph paper
- Hand lenses
- Medium-sized cardboard box(es)
- Large appliance box(es)
- Pencils/charcoal/crayons

*Optional*:

- Small mirrors (metal or plastic, not glass)
- Dark cloth for shrouding

**CONNECTING ACTIVITY**

- A variety of drawing and painting materials
- Paper

 **Standards**

**SCIENCE**

Abilities Necessary to Do Scientific Inquiry

Understanding About Scientific Inquiry

Light, Heat, Electricity, and Magnetism

Transfer of Energy

Abilities of Technological Design

Understanding About Science and Technology

Science and Technology in Society

**MATH**

Communication

Measurement

Data Analysis and Probability

 **Objectives**

Students will successfully construct and operate the pinhole camera and the camera obscura.

Students will be able to explain how they know that light travels in straight lines.

Students will quantify and explain the relationship between the distance from the light source and the size of the image seen, using the pinhole camera.

Students will understand the historical place of the camera obscura.

 **Background Information**

You'll definitely want to make and operate a simple pinhole camera and a camera obscura of your own before asking students to try this. Making them is easy, but it may take a bit of creative "play" to obtain clear images. Remember that the pinholes must be very small and that both instruments work best under *very* dark conditions.

## Main Activity, Step-by-Step

1. Ask students to brainstorm their responses to the question "What do your eyes, a cardboard box, and a camera all have in common?" Encourage a variety of answers.

2. Have students build a very simple pinhole camera (*camera* is from Latin for "room or chamber") using a shoe box. Cut out one end of the box and replace it with a piece of plain white paper. Make the pinhole very small in the center of the other end of the box (see Figure 3–1). Cut a small triangle (equilateral, about 3 cm per side) from the discarded shoe box end and secure it with transparent tape to the center of a flashlight lens, as in Figure 3–2. In a very darkened room, have each group of students shine the light at the pinhole in their camera. This might be easier if the box is held and "adjusted" while the light remains stationery. What image appears on the box's "screen"? Have students explore the properties of this apparatus, then ask them to share what they have discovered and what they would like to know about this camera. Point out that the triangle is projected through the pinhole because light travels in straight lines. How is this camera similar to other cameras they have seen? How is it different?

3. Using the same pinhole and flashlight arrangement, tell the students that their job is to find out what relationship exists between the camera's distance from the light source and the size of the image seen. Have them hypothesize what they think will happen to the size of the image as the box is moved farther from the light. Then they can collect data by measuring the image size at various distances from the light and record their findings on Activity Sheet 3. The data can be made into a line graph (independent variable, i.e., distance, on x axis; and dependent variable, i.e., image size, on y axis), and each student, or group, can explain in writing what the graph shows. That is, what is the relationship between the two variables?

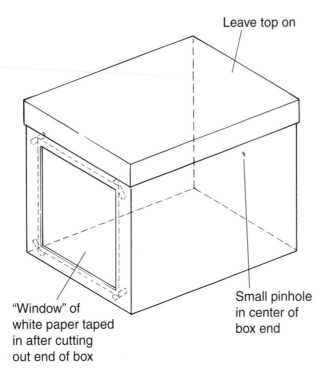

Leave top on          **Figure 3–1.**    Pinhole camera

"Window" of
white paper taped
in after cutting
out end of box

Small pinhole
in center of
box end

4.  Ask, "How might an artist use a camera such as the one you made? How could she or he modify the pinhole camera to be useful in sketching an accurate picture?" Allow time for groups to ponder the question and perhaps make illustrations to explain their proposed modifications. Encourage a variety of answers from groups/individuals, recalling that this is an opportunity for all to engage their imaginations and is not the time to judge or criticize responses.

5.  Introduce the history and use of the camera obscura ("dark chamber"). This forerunner of the modern camera was used by many great 17th- and 18th-century painters, including Jan Vermeer and Paul Sandby, as an aid in making accurate preliminary drawings. It was essentially a modified pinhole camera, i.e., a box fitted with lens and mirror which projected the chosen image onto a piece of paper placed on the base of the box. A curtain was hung over an open side of the box, allowing access to the paper. The artist, shrouded by the curtain, could then easily trace the image that was projected on the paper in the box. Show, examine, and discuss examples of Vermeer's paintings. Notice his careful attention to detail, made possible in large part by the camera obscura.

6.  Have students construct a camera obscura, using one of several pinhole-type designs. The simplest design is nothing more than a box camera arrangement that a student can put his or her head into, thus allowing them to see the image (see Figure 3–3). Use a medium-sized box, and instead of the "screen" at the far end of the chamber, just tape a piece of white paper on the inside of the box. The image comes through the pinhole and falls on the paper. Try varying the size of the pinhole.

**Figure 3–2.**    Flashlight with cardboard triangle taped to lens

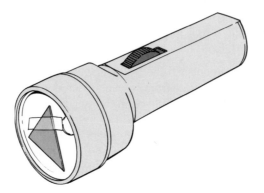

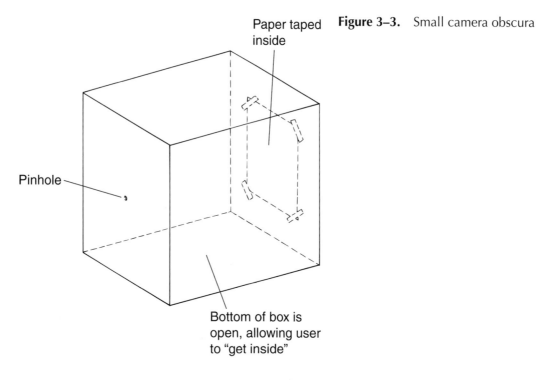

Paper taped inside

**Figure 3–3.** Small camera obscura

Pinhole

Bottom of box is open, allowing user to "get inside"

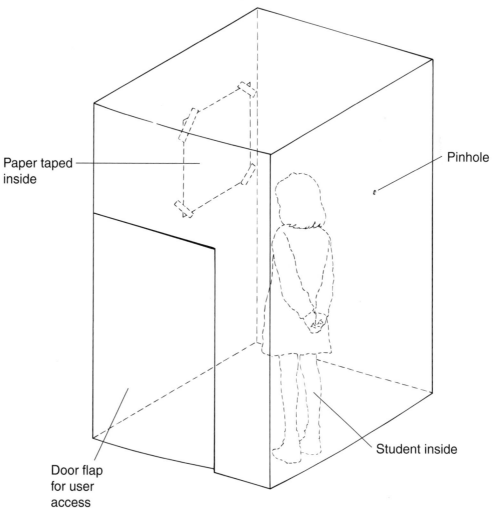

Paper taped inside

Pinhole

Door flap for user access

Student inside

**Figure 3–4.** Large camera obscura

17

The user's head enters from the bottom of the box. Be sure to block any extra light from entering from below by stuffing/shrouding the area around the shoulders with a blanket.

Another possibility is to make the camera obscura so large that students can climb completely inside. This can be done by turning an empty appliance box into an oversized pinhole camera, cutting a door in the side for access (see Figure 3–4). Once inside, it is easy for students to draw the image that falls on the taped up "screen" of white paper.

These designs may be improved by adding one or more components to the camera obscura, such as adjusting the image with a lens, reflecting the image with a mirror, and/or opening the side of the chamber and adding shrouding to keep unwanted light out. Let students explore different ways of modifying the apparatus. The camera obscura will operate best in bright light, especially in sunlight.

7.  Allow each student to make a sketch using a camera obscura. Then have them sketch the same image, without using the apparatus. How do the two drawings compare? Introduce the concepts of "accuracy" (conformity to truth or to a standard or model; exactness) and "precision" (the degree of refinement with which an operation is performed or a measurement stated). That is, *accuracy* refers to the sketch's nearness to the actual view, whereas *precision* refers to the similarity of repeat sketches of the same view. What, then, does it mean to make *accurate* drawings, and how does the camera obscura help? Are all painters interested in accuracy? Under what circumstances would mathematicians or scientists need to be accurate or make accurate drawings? Explain your answers. Students could be asked to explore these questions (and/or others) in a journal writing assignment. What questions do they have about the camera obscura or pinhole camera? What further investigations would they like to undertake?

## Questions for Discussion

1.  What did you enjoy about making and/or using the pinhole camera? The camera obscura?

2.  As you performed these investigations, what did you learn about light? What else would you like to know?

3.  Under what circumstances would a camera obscura be a useful tool for an artist?

4.  How do the pinhole camera and camera obscura differ from a modern camera?

## Assessment

1.  Did students successfully construct and operate the pinhole camera and camera obscura? [embedded]

2.  Were students able to explain how they know that light travels in straight lines? [embedded, journal entries]

3.  Did students effectively use the pinhole camera to quantify (and possibly graph) the relationship between the distance from the light source and the size of the image seen? [embedded, performance]

4.  Were they able to explain the value of the camera obscura to painters, and to see the instrument in historical perspective? [embedded, journal entries]

## Connecting Activity

Students can elaborate on their camera obscura sketches using media of their choice (paint, charcoal, crayons, pastels, collage, etc.). What do the individual student artists like about their own pictures? What aspects would they change? Why? Hang the finished products, with student approval (don't hang a picture if the artist doesn't approve). Encourage a discussion of similarities and differences, especially in regard to the instrument-enhanced perspectives of their work (i.e., How might these depictions differ if you hadn't used the camera obscura? How would you react to those differences?).

## Other Options and Extensions

1. Introduce and encourage student research into the structure and function of the vertebrate eye (see Activities 5, 6, and 7 for more on this topic). Outside reading, diagrams, and illustrations would be appropriate. Consider dissecting cow or sheep eyes to provide hands-on experience.

2. Use the large camera obscura under a variety of lighting conditions to determine its strengths and limitations. Encourage student suggestions regarding relevant modifications in its design.

## Resources and Further Information

Gore, G. (1974). Pinhole photography for young students. *Science and Children, 12* (1), 14–16.

Junger, T. (1971). The pinhole camera. *School Arts, 7* (4), 14–15.

McQueen, R. (1996). Pinhole. *Photo Instructor, 18,* 9–10.

Shull, J. (1974). *The hole thing: A manual of pinhole fotography.* Dobbs Ferry, NY: Morgan & Morgan.

Smith, L. (1985). *The visionary pinhole.* Salt Lake City: Peregrine Smith.

Victor, R. (1984). The return of the sun dragon. *Science and Children, 21* (8), 16–18.

Worne, J. (1984). Pinhole photography—A budget saver. *School Arts, 83* (6), 19–22.

## Activity Sheet 3. Investigating the Pinhole Camera and Camera Obscura

What do you think will happen to the size of the image as the camera is moved farther away from the light source? Explain your answer.

Collect data by measuring the image size at various distances from the light. Record your data in the table below.

| Distance from Light Source to Camera | Size of Image |
|---|---|
|  |  |
|  |  |
|  |  |
|  |  |
|  |  |

What conclusions can you reach, based on your data?

# Recording Images Using a Simple Pinhole Camera

 **Overview**

Students develop and expand their observational skills and technological understanding by building and operating a pinhole camera. The interdisciplinary connections are in the realm of application in this very motivating activity. Designed for grades 6 through 8 but adaptable to lower grades, this lesson provides students with opportunities to connect technology (the camera itself) to its aesthetic product (the photograph).

 **Concepts**

Images of visible light will be captured on photosensitive paper and/or film using a simple pinhole camera, providing students with a background in the fundamentals of camera operation, including mathematical applications such as distance/focus, composition, exposure, and development.

**Processes/Skills**

- Observing
- Constructing
- Measuring
- Creating
- Comparing
- Imagining
- Recognizing shapes
- Predicting
- Inferring
- Analyzing
- Appreciating
- Problem solving
- Cooperating
- Communicating

**Recommended for**

| | |
|---|---|
| K–2 | Individual |
| 3–5 | Small Group ✔ |
| 6–8 ✔ | Whole Class |

**Time Required**

2–4 hours

**Materials Required**

- Black cardboard
- Inexpensive photography paper or sun paper
- Masking tape
- Scissors
- 15- to 25-watt red light bulb and lamp

(Most of these materials should be available from a local photography store or catalog)

**Standards**

**SCIENCE**

- Abilities Necessary to Do Scientific Inquiry
- Transfer of Energy
- Abilities of Technological Design
- Understanding About Science and Technology

**MATH**

- Problem Solving
- Communication
- Connections
- Measurement

## ⦿ *Objectives*

- Students will successfully construct and operate pinhole cameras.

- Students will understand and be able to explain the fundamentals of camera construction, including the importance of exposure time.

- Students will be able to compare photography to the other visual arts, including painting, drawing, and sculpting.

## *Main Activity, Step-by-Step*

1. Ask, "How are the pinhole camera and camera obscura from Activity 3 like a modern camera? How are they different from a modern camera?" [If you haven't done Activity 3, you could demonstrate the basic function of a simple pinhole camera to the class.] A diagram and a camera would be useful as visual aids at this point. Ask, "How would you modify a pinhole camera so that it could record an image itself?." Encourage a variety of responses, possibly having students illustrate their ideas with simple diagrams.

2. Have each group construct a pinhole camera similar to the one used in Activity 3, with several important modifications: (a) instead of using a shoe box, the cube-shaped chamber will be constructed from pieces of black cardboard, as in Figure 4–1, and (b) instead of cutting a "window" of white paper in the end of the chamber, students will secure a piece of photosensitive paper (either sun paper or inexpensive photography paper) to the inside of the end of the box (see Figure 4–2). The camera, of course, can be constructed under normal lighting conditions, but the

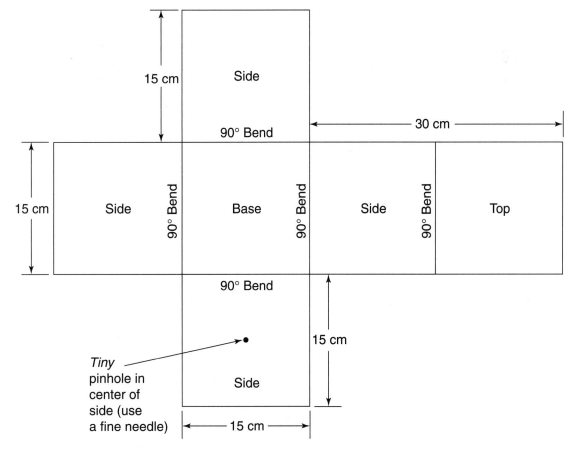

**Figure 4–1.** Construction of pinhole camera

Pinhole
covered
by tape

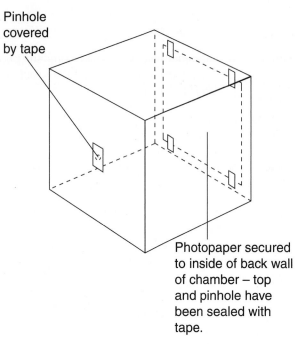

**Figure 4–2.**   Completed pinhole camera

Photopaper secured
to inside of back wall
of chamber – top
and pinhole have
been sealed with
tape.

photosensitive paper will have to be inserted under darkroom conditions (if you use sun paper, you will only need a well-darkened room), which can be accomplished by simply taping the paper in place by feel over the entire inside of the box-end in a completely darkened room, or by using a 15- to 25-watt red light bulb in an otherwise completely darkened room (such as a small, windowless storage room with the base of the door covered). Under darkroom conditions, after securing the photosensitive paper, place a piece of tape over the camera's pinhole to block light from coming in. That piece of tape will be removed when students are ready to record an image.

3.  Discuss with the class what makes an interesting photographic image. Exposure to exemplary photographs, books, and so on at this point will facilitate student analysis, discussion, and creativity in photo esthetics. With the photosensitive paper secured and all camera openings thoroughly sealed (including the pinhole), student groups may find an image outside the classroom that they would like to expose and record. A sunny, bright day is ideal for this activity. Because the camera must be motionless during the exposure, students may want to tape the chamber to a chair or stool in preparation for recording the image. Aim the camera at the desired image, carefully remove the tape from the pinhole, and expose the photosensitive paper (4 to 10 seconds for photography paper in direct sunlight, or at least a minute for sun paper). A group member should keep track of exposure time, and when the exposure is complete, the pinhole tape seal is gently replaced. Cameras should be marked with members' names to facilitate their return to the correct group. The recorded image should be described briefly in writing, including the exposure time and the general environmental conditions under which the photo was made (tape the description to the side of the camera).

4.  If you used photography paper, you will need to have the exposures developed. Due to safety concerns, students shouldn't be directly involved in this process unless your experience in photo developing is substantial (and, of course, safety must then be a primary consideration).

5.  When students receive their developed photos, have the student groups meet to appreciate and analyze their work. Display photos, with student permission, gallery-style. Invite supportive and aesthetic comments. Initially in small groups and then via classroom discussion, compare the products of photography to those of other visual arts (painting, sculpture, drawing, etc.).

6.  If time permits, a second attempt at recording images will be interesting after students have observed, analyzed, compared, and problem solved. For instance, they may want to see what happens

if they set the camera in a stationary position (e.g., on a chair) instead of holding it by hand during exposure. Let them try it again, encouraging imaginative modifications in the exposure process.

7. Here is an alternative to constructing the pinhole camera from scratch: Obtain several inexpensive cameras (a local photo shop may donate these if they are persuaded to see the potential benefits involved with cultivating student interest in this area). Remove the shutter/aperture from each camera and attach (with tape) a piece of black cardboard with a tiny pinhole. This way students can make pinhole photos using normal rolls of film. Problems with developing these images are eliminated as they can be processed anywhere.

## Questions for Discussion

1. What did you expect your group's recorded image, that is, the photograph, to look like? How did it differ from your expectations?

2. How would you do this activity differently if you were to do it again?

3. What problems did you encounter (especially if the image did not turn out quite the way you expected or wanted)? How could you solve those problems?

4. How is photography like drawing? Like painting? Like sculpture? How is it different? Which do you prefer? Why?

5. What skills, talents, characteristics do you have that make you a good photographer? Explain.

6. Why is math important in photography? Science?

## Assessment

1. Were the students able to successfully construct the cameras? [embedded]

2. Were students able to record images with their pinhole cameras? [embedded, performance, portfolio]

3. Did they understand the fundamentals of camera construction and operation, including the importance of exposure time? [embedded, journal entries]

4. Were students able to compare photography with other arts, such as drawing, sculpting, or painting? [embedded, journal entries]

## Other Options and Extensions

1. Homework: Take more photos! Encourage students to try this at home with family members. Make a collection of favorite family pinhole photos.

2. Study photographs, old and new. Bring photos into class to share. Discuss the setting, the equipment and techniques used (if known), and the effect on the viewer.

3. Find out about the history of photography and famous photographers such as Anne Brigman and Alfred Stieglitz.

4. Compare the function of the modern camera to the function of the eye (see Activities 5, 6, and 7). Pay particular attention to the retina/film analogy.

5. Use the Internet to research the chemistry of the film development process.

## Resources and Further Information

Gore, G. (1974). Pinhole photography for young students. *Science and Children, 12* (1), 14–16.

Junger, T. (1971). The pinhole camera. *School Arts, 7* (4), 14–15.

McQueen, R. (1996). Pinhole. *Photo Instructor, 18,* 9–10.

Shull, J. (1974). *The hole thing: A manual of pinhole photography.* Dobbs Ferry, NY: Morgan & Morgan.

Smith, L. (1985). *The visionary pinhole.* Salt Lake City: Peregrine Smith.

Victor, R. (1984). The return of the sun dragon. *Science and Children, 21* (8), 16–18.

Worne, J. (1984). Pinhole photography—A budget saver. *School Arts, 83* (6), 19–22.

# Examining Colors, Color Perception, and Sight

 ## Overview

Students of all ages are fascinated by color and how we perceive it. In the main activity, your class will explore colors and visual perception by mixing colors in several ways. They will find out more about colors, light, vision, and color composition as they mix paints, "magically" spin two or more colors into new colors and make discoveries about color perception in the human eye and brain. The preliminary activity dynamically introduces several important terms related to vision: *refraction, reflection,* and *spectrum.* In the follow-up activity, students will learn about the anatomy of the vertebrate eye, as they build and operate a simple eye model, complete with lens. Finally, in the connecting activity, the class will discover several variables that can affect an individual's sense of color perception.

 ## Concepts

Students discover aspects of vision and perception, including refraction, the color spectrum, and eye anatomy and function. They use ratios, proportions, and/or percentages as they mix colors and solve problems related to vision.

 ## Processes/Skills

- Observing
- Measuring
- Predicting
- Describing
- Inferring
- Experimenting
- Communicating
- Reflecting
- Recognizing patterns
- Problem Solving
- Analyzing

- Inquiring
- Creating
- Cooperating

 ## Recommended for

| | |
|---|---|
| K–2 ✔ | Individual |
| 3–5 ✔ | Small Group ✔ |
| 6–8 ✔ | Whole Class |

## Time Required

2–3 hours

## Materials Required

**PRELIMINARY ACTIVITY**
- Clear jars or glasses
- Flashlights
- Prisms
- Protractors

**MAIN ACTIVITY**
- Food coloring
- Small, clear containers (e.g., plastic medicine cups)
- Tempera paints
- Cardboard
- String or twine

**FOLLOW-UP ACTIVITY**
- White construction paper
- Plastic hand lenses
- Tape
- Paper clips

**CONNECTING ACTIVITY**

- Incandescent and fluorescent light sources
- Paint
- Paper

##  Standards

**SCIENCE**

- Abilities Necessary to Do Scientific Inquiry
- Understanding About Scientific Inquiry
- Light, Heat, Electricity, and Magnetism
- Characteristics of Organisms
- Structure and Function in Living Systems
- Regulation and Behavior in Living Systems

**MATH**

- Connections
- Numbers and Operations
- Measurement
- Problem Solving

## Objectives

- Students will recognize primary and secondary colors, will blend them to create new colors, and will be able to explain how they did so.
- Students will successfully mix colors by spinning a multicolored disk and will be able to explain their predictions for the blended colors that result.

## Background Information

This activity includes a Learning Cycle lesson, a constructivist technique based largely on Piagetian theory. The Learning Cycle is composed of three phases: *exploration* (in which student explorations with concrete materials and problems allow them to make new connections with past experiences), *conceptual invention* (in which meaningful terms and concepts related to the students' exploratory experiences are introduced), and *conceptual expansion* (in which students apply the experiences and concepts to a new, but related, activity, allowing them to grow in their understanding of the subject). The learning cycle is particularly useful in providing students with opportunities to tie their prior experience to new and unfamiliar concepts and terminology.

## Preliminary Activity

1. Before students start exploring color perception, they need to find out about several other phenomena related to light. Give each group of students a clear glass or jar, half full of water. Instruct them to place a pencil or ruler into the water (see Figure 5–1), to look at it from all sides, and to report on what they observed. They will notice that the pencil appeared to be broken or bent as it entered the water. This is because the light rays (which are bouncing off of the pencil and into our eyes, allowing us to see it) move faster in air than in water. Light moves at 186,000 miles per second (300,000 km/sec) in air, and only at about 3/4 that speed in water (calculate light's speed in water in terms of km/sec). That is, the light rays bouncing off the pencil are slowed down by the water and appear to bend. This phenomenon is known as *refraction*. Ask the students where they have seen other instances of refraction.

2. Students should also understand that what they see when they view any object or color is actually the light that is being *reflected* by that object or color. A yellow pencil, for instance, absorbs all colors other than yellow, so that what reaches us, and what we perceive, is yellow.

3. Finally, darken the room and shine a flashlight through a prism, a beaker of water, or a crystal. Ask the students what they see, on the floor, ceiling, or wall. The light passing through the prism, beaker of water, or crystal should create a rainbow, or color *spectrum*. Ask students to think of other times they've seen rainbows or color spectra (maybe after a rain, on a soap bubble, or on the surface of an oily puddle). Here's what's happening: White light is made up of all the various colors (red, orange, yellow, green, blue, indigo, and violet; an easy way to remember the colors in order is to recall the name ROY G. BIV). When the white light passes through the prism, beaker, or crystal, it is refracted (bent). The various colors are refracted differently, with violet being bent

**Figure 5–1.** Refraction

the most and red the least. Therefore, the colors are slightly separated when the light emerges from the prism, and we see a color *spectrum*. If you have enough prisms, beakers, or crystals, you can let each group of students create and observe spectra of their own. As they explore, challenge them to find the angle (using a protractor to measure the angles and a white sheet of paper for a "rainbow projection screen") at which the light leaves the prism (see Figure 5–2). How can such an angle be predicted? At what angles do the various colors travel when they leave the prism? Which colors are bent the least? Which the most? How do you know?

## Main Activity, Step-by-Step

1. Next, the student can try some color mixing, undertaken via a learning cycle lesson format (i.e., in three phases: exploration, conceptual invention, and conceptual expansion), using water tinted with food coloring. Each group of two or three students will need an eyedropper; several small, clear containers (e.g., plastic medicine cups); a larger container of clear water; a small container of blue, yellow, and red (the primary colors); water; and some paper towels. Tell them to use their materials to make a variety of colors. By experimenting and exploring with the primary colors, the groups should be able to make other colors. This is the exploration phase of the learning cycle;

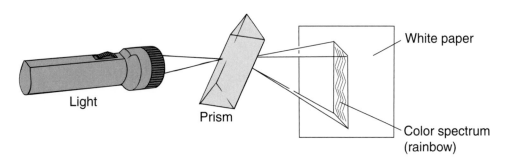

**Figure 5–2.** Spectrum

simply move around the room and facilitate safe and creative discovery. Students should keep records of their experiments, so that, after having sufficient time to discover, each group can report to the class about their experiences. In this conceptual invention phase of the learning cycle, concepts are "attached" to the students' discovery-based experiences, thus expanding their conceptual understanding. What did they learn from their exploration? As they report their results, gently guide the discussion into the realm of specific concepts, which may include *primary colors* (red, yellow, blue), *secondary colors* (green, orange, purple), the *color wheel* (the primary and secondary colors in a circular formation; see Figure 5–3), *value* (the relative lightness or darkness of a color), and *hue* (gradation of color). In the conceptual expansion phase, the final step of the learning cycle, students are asked to apply what they have learned in the first two phases. In this case you might attempt one or more of the following, depending on the students' age and ability: (a) create and name a new color, making sure to develop a "recipe" of drops used, and making sure to make it several times so that the recipe is clearly replicable, (b) try to match a teacher-created "unknown" color, again keeping a record of unsuccessful and successful experiments, (c) mix specific ratios of the primary colors, such as 2:1 red to yellow versus 3:1 red to yellow, recording the results and looking for patterns in the data, (d) similarly, mixing specific percentages of primary colors, such as 50% blue and 50% red versus 30% blue and 70% red, again making sure to record results and watch for patterns. Hold a class discussion to find out what the groups learned, and display particularly attractive, interesting, and/or innovative mixtures.

2. Now that students are familiar with color mixing, you can mix colors "magically." Using tempera paints, have each group of students paint one side of a cardboard disk one primary color and the other side another. Make holes on opposite sides of the disk, attach strings, and spin the disk by winding it up and gently pulling on the strings (as in Figure 5–4). For variety, have each student group work on a different color combination. Make sure that all students predict what colors will appear when the disks are spun and that they compare the predicted colors with the actual colors observed. What's happening is this: The eye and brain mix the two colors because the disk spins too rapidly for the eye to distinguish between them. The eye continues to see each color, briefly, even as it spins out of sight. Thus, the eye sends a message to the brain of a color mixture.

3. To expand on this activity, have student groups paint the disks with different color ratios, proportions, or percentages and record their results. For example, paint one side of a disk with a 1:1 ratio of red to blue and the other side with a 1:1 ratio of blue to purple. Or paint one side of the disk 60% red and 40% orange and the other side 30% blue and 70% green. Be sure that students record the colors used and their predictions. Obviously there are an infinite number of combina-

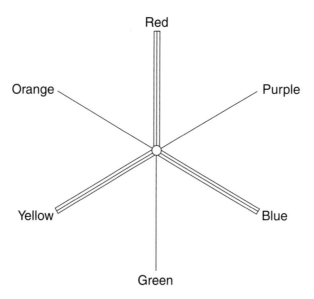

**Figure 5–3.**    Color wheel

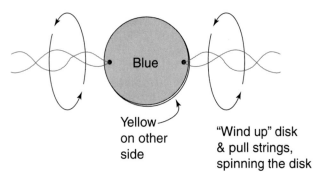

**Figure 5–4.**   Spinning disk

tions. Assist students in noticing patterns in the data. What happens when primary colors are mixed? When secondary colors are mixed? When primary colors are mixed with secondary colors? Do any particular hues predominate? Were any surprises noted? How does math help us design our color experiments?

A slightly different type of spinning color disk can be made by painting a piece of cardboard in alternating colors and threading a string through two holes near the center (see Figure 5–5). By winding up and spinning the disk, the colors will mix. Again, students can vary the ratio, proportion, or percentage of the colors on the disk and note the perceived results. Which sort of disk mixed the colors best? How do you know?

## Follow-up Activity

The human eye, or any vertebrate eye for that matter, is a very complex and amazing organ. During the lesson on colors, we began to explore the function of the eye. How is it constructed and how does it work?

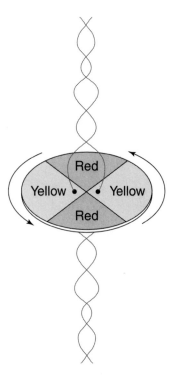

**Figure 5–5.**   Another spinning disk

We already discovered some answers to these questions, but let's look at the eye itself as an anatomical structure (see Figure 5–6). Light enters the eye through a hole called the *pupil,* which is protected by the clear *cornea.* The pupil is surrounded by the colored part of the eye, the *iris,* which adjusts the size of the pupil by growing larger or smaller. (You can demonstrate this by observing the eye of a partner as you flash a light into his/her eye. The pupil shrinks, which means the iris expands, in bright light in order to control the amount of light entering the eye. The opposite effect can be noted in dim light. Enlargement of the pupils is called *dilation,* and shrinkage is called *contraction.*) The image passes through the *lens* and is focused by *muscles* that attach to the margins of the lens and control its shape. The image then falls onto the back surface of the eye, called the *retina,* producing a chemical message that transmits the image as a nerve impulse to the visual part of the brain via the *optic nerve.* The eyes, therefore, are really extensions of the brain and as such are considered part of the nervous system.

To find out how the image forms on the retina, have each group of students create a model of the eye by first cutting a 2 cm diameter hole in the center of a 15 × 60 cm piece of white construction paper (the hole acts as the pupil of the eye). Tape a plastic hand lens over the hole, and attach the two loose ends of the paper strip together using paper clips. In a darkened room, leave one window or door open and aim the "eye" at the lighted area. An inverted image should form on what would be the retina, i.e., the back of the inside of the eye model (see Figure 5–7). To get a focused image, students may need to adjust the circumference of the "eye," securing it again with the paper clips. This model is not unlike the camera obscura from Activity 3. Students will see that the retinal image is in fact upside down (the brain automatically reinverts the image, making it appear right side up) and that the shape of the eye affects one's ability to focus (accounting for far- and near-sightedness). Have students measure the optimal focal length (distance between the lens and the retina) of the eye model using a meter stick. Compare class data. How would this compare with the focal length of an actual human eye?

## Questions for Discussion

1. What did you enjoy about mixing colors (either with colored water or with painted disks)? What surprised you about the composition of colors? What else do you want to know about colors and their composition? How could you find out?

2. What does mathematics have to do with the study of light and color? That is, how can mathematics help us understand those subjects?

3. Can you think of any art projects that would include the "magical" mixing of colors using either the spinning disks or the spinning top?

4. What sorts of variables can affect color perception? How do you know?

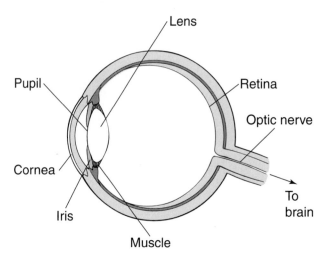

**Figure 5–6.**   The human eye (cross section)

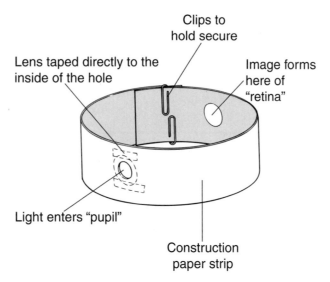

Clips to
hold secure

Lens taped directly to the
inside of the hole

Image forms
here of
"retina"

Light enters "pupil"

Construction
paper strip

**Figure 5–7.** Eye model

## Assessment

1. Did students recognize the primary and secondary colors, and the organization of those hues on the color wheel? Did they create new colors, and were they able to explain how they did so? [embedded, performance, journal entries]

2. Could students successfully mix colors "magically" by spinning a multicolored disk? Could they explain how the colors "magically" blended? [embedded, performance]

3. Were students able to successfully predict which colors would be produced after painting the disks with different color ratios, proportions, or percentages? [embedded]

## Connecting Activity

Artists must consider many variables when producing and displaying their work, because color perception will vary based on the environment and the viewer.

For instance, an individual's color perception can depend on the ambient light available. Have the students look at a painted surface (one side of one of the disks painted in the main activity will do) under three different lighting sources: incandescent light (a typical light bulb), fluorescent light, and sunlight. In each case, have them write a brief description of the color as they perceive it. This would be an opportune time to introduce several terms related to color: *hue* (the distinct colors on the color wheel, such as blue, green, violet), *intensity* (brightness and purity of color; the colors of the spectrum are high-intensity hues, and dull, neutral hues are of low intensity), and *value* (the relative lightness or darkness of a color, i.e., luminosity, which may be described as light, medium, or dark). Students may find these terms useful as they describe their color observations. How do their perceptions of the colors vary in different types of light? Do they notice any patterns in their results? For instance, how do intensity and value vary in the three types of light, if they vary at all?

Another way that color perception can vary is in contrast to other colors. You can demonstrate this by placing various hues of painted surfaces next to each other. Compare the way a blue surface looks next to a yellow surface with the way it looks next to orange or green or red. For example, the boundary between blue and yellow tends to look washed out. Students can explore a variety of color combinations (again, the painted disks will be fine, or you might paint index cards in varying hues), making sure to keep a written record of their observations. Color contrast is used by painters to evoke certain reactions in the viewer. Compare the muted and balanced *Mona Lisa* by Da Vinci to any of the brightly colored Fauvist works, such as those of Matisse or Derain.

Finally, color perception varies with the viewer's mental context, expectations, and assumptions. Paint a simple illustration of an apple and a tree, both of the same shade of gray paint. Mount them separately on pieces of white paper. Survey the class to find if they believe that the two paintings are the same color. Many viewers will find the apple to be more reddish and the tree to be more greenish. Students may conduct their own surveys by making their own apples and trees and taking them home to ask family members what they see.

## Other Options and Extensions

1. Students might be interested to know that different cultures break the continuous color spectrum up into different colors, that is, different cultures see the "natural" breaks between colors in different places, perhaps grouping what we might call red and orange into a single color category. See if you can find more information on this cultural phenomenon.

2. Dissect a vertebrate eye (obtain a cow, sheep, or pig eye from a butcher or from a science supply catalog), noting the important anatomical features and tracing the path of light as it moves through the eye to become an image in the brain.

3. Have each student paint a picture, and then reproduce the same composition again, this time using entirely different colors. Encourage the use of "unnatural" colors (e.g., red trees and green skies) in the second painting. Then compare the two paintings for impact, meaning, and aesthetics. Hold a class discussion about the importance of color in paintings, using the student art as evidence (perhaps also referring to reproductions of famous works by Impressionists, Fauvists, and so forth), and attempt to notice regularities and patterns in color perception and interpretation.

## Resources and Further Information

Dalby, D. K. (1991). Fine tune your sense of color. *Science and Children, 29* (3), 24–26.

Engels, C. J. (1985). Chasing rainbows. *Science and Children, 22* (6), 13–14.

Mandell, M. (1959). *Physics experiments for children.* New York: Dover.

McIntyre, M. (1981). Color awareness. *Science and Children, 18* (7), 40–41.

Ostwald, T. (1995). An eye for learning. *Science and Children, 33* (2), 25–26.

Sands, N. L. (1991). A splash of color. *Science and Children, 28* (6), 38–39.

Williams, S. (1991). Colorful chemicals. *Science and Children, 28* (4), 20–21.

# Determining the Size and Shape of the Blind Spot

## Overview

What exactly is the blind spot? It is the place where the optic nerve meets the back of the retina (see Activity 5 for details of the eye's anatomy). Because no sensory cells are present in the retina at the meeting point, a "hole" is created in the field of view of each eye. The brain "fills in" the hole with what "ought" to be there, so we usually don't notice the blind spots. In this activity, students will determine several characteristics of the visual blind spot, including its approximate size and shape, as well as its impact on daily life. This lesson will tie nicely with Activities 2, 5, or 7. This can be a challenging activity, however, in terms of method and mathematics. Not all students, especially younger students, are able to actually locate their blind spot, and they often become frustrated with the procedure. For this reason, the lesson is recommended for the higher grades only.

## Concepts

Students investigate the size, shape, and nature of the eye's blind spot, using active exploration, ratio, metric measurement, and transformation of units of length.

## Processes/Skills

- Observing
- Comparing
- Describing
- Making conclusions
- Experimenting
- Identifying shapes and patterns
- Predicting
- Estimating
- Measuring
- Calculating
- Applying

- Communicating
- Problem solving
- Developing spatial reasoning
- Inquiring
- Cooperating

## Recommended for

| | |
|---|---|
| K–2 | Individual |
| 3–5 ✔ | Small Group ✔ |
| 6–8 ✔ | Whole Class |

## Time Required

2–3 hours

## Materials Required

- Paper
- Pencils or fine-point marking pens
- Metric rulers
- The classroom chalkboard
- Chalk
- Calculators (optional)

## Standards

**SCIENCE**

- Abilities Necessary to Do Scientific Inquiry
- Understanding About Scientific Inquiry
- Characteristics of Organisms
- Structure and Function in Living Systems
- Diversity and Adaptation of Organisms

**MATH**

- Problem Solving
- Communication
- Connections
- Numbers and Operations
- Geometry
- Measurement

## ◐ *Objectives*

- Students will successfully locate blind spots in both eyes.
- Students will determine the approximate percentage of the entire field of view and the approximate shape of the blind spot.
- Students will be able to explain the everyday implications, including the potential hazards, of having blind spots.

## *Main Activity, Step-by-step*

1. Have pairs of students try the following procedure. On a piece of paper, with a marking pen, make a small X (about 1 cm long), then make a dot (about 0.5 cm in diameter) about 5 cm to the right of the X. Closing your left eye, and holding the paper close to your face, focus on the X. Then slowly move paper away from your face, still focused on the X, until the dot disappears from your peripheral vision. The X should disappear at a distance of about 30 cm. Try this procedure a number of times so that you are very comfortable with locating your blind spot. Be sure that your partner can find his/her blind spot, too. If not, offer helpful suggestions. Can you find the blind spot in the left eye? How did you have to change the experimental set up? (You must flip the X to the left of the dot, as opposed to the right.)

2. Just how much of the field of view is taken up by the two blind spots? To estimate, first we will determine the approximate field of view, then subtract the approximate size of the two blind spots from it. To determine the approximate field of view, stand approximately 30 cm (or whatever distance you used above to make the entire X disappear) from a chalkboard, and *look straight ahead*. With a partner assisting you, find out how much of the chalkboard you can see at this distance (with eyes straight ahead) by marking the outer limits of what you can see. Move a pencil to determine the points above, below, to the right, and to the left at which the pencil just moves into view. That is, mark the outer limits of your entire field of view at approximately 30 cm (or at whatever distance the entire X disappeared above). These four points describe a rectangle, whose area you can now determine. Using the approximate size of the blind spot, you can now calculate the approximate percentage of your entire field of view that is taken up by your two blind spots (remember, there is a blind spot in each eye). Why is this an approximation and not an absolutely accurate measurement?

3. What is the approximate shape of the blind spot? Modify the "dot and X" method a bit. Use the same sort of dot, but instead of an X try different shapes and see which ones are the easiest to make disappear. Try a square, a triangle, a rectangle, an oval, and a circle. You can try any other shapes you can think of, too. Which do you predict will be closest to the shape of the blind spot? Hint, think of the cause of the blind spot: It occurs where the optic nerve meets the retina (see Activity 5), resulting in a small area with no optical sensory cells. What shape is the optic nerve? How might its shape affect the shape of the blind spot?

4. How might the blind spot affect our everyday life? Could we miss seeing things because of the blind spot? Is it possible that something as big as a person could fall within the blind spot so that we would be unable to see them? Using the "dot and X" method, determine how large an X you can "lose" at about 30 cm distance from your eye (start with a small X and continue making the X larger until it will no longer entirely fit in the blind spot, keeping the distance of the paper with the dot and X constant throughout the process). Use ratio to determine how far away a person would have to be to be able to be completely "lost" in your blind spot. That is, X size divided by distance equals human size divided by distance. Consider human size to be 1.5 m tall. X cm/30cm = 1.5m/unknown meters, where X cm is determined via the "dot and X" technique as noted above,

then transformed into m, as is the 30 cm distance (so that all distances in the problem are in the same units).

5. Who should be concerned about the presence of their blind spots? (Drivers, meat cutters, baseball players, etc.). How can a driver, for instance, surmount the problem of the blind spot? (Remember, the blind spot is only a problem if the eyes are focused on a single point, so if you keep your eyes moving, you get a good view of the entire area in front of you. Drivers should remember this and keep their eyes moving around, looking here and there ahead of them, rather than just at a single part of the road ahead.)

## Questions For Discussion

1. How much of your field of view is taken up the blind spot? How do you know?

2. What shape is the blind spot? How do you know?

3. How might this blind spot be a problem for drivers? How else might it affect a person's life? How could the blind spot affect *your* life?

## Assessment

1. Were students able to successfully locate blind spots in each eye? [embedded, performance]

2. Were they able to determine the approximate percentage of the field of view that is taken up by the two blind spots? [embedded, performance]

3. Were they able to come to a conclusion about the approximate shape of the blind spot? [embedded, performance]

4. Could students calculate how far away a person would have to be to be able to become completely "lost" in one's blind spot? [embedded, performance]

5. Were students aware of the implications of the blind spot for everyday life? [embedded, journal entries]

## Other Options and Extensions

1. Do all vertebrates have blind spots, and if so, are they affected in any way? How can you find out?

2. Dissect a vertebrate eye and observe the region of the blind spot. Does it look different from the surrounding retinal surface? If so, how?

3. Make a survey of adult drivers and find out how many of them are aware of the potential hazards associated with their blind spots. Share your findings with the class. Keep class records and discuss the implications of the survey.

## Resources and Further Information

Ostwald, T. (1995). An eye for learning. *Science and Children, 33* (2), 25–26.

Walpole, B. (1988). *175 science experiments.* New York: Random House.

# Investigating Perception and Illusion

 ## Overview:

For a motivating and baffling experience, try this investigation of perceptual illusions and their causes. Designed for grades 3 through 8, this exploration allows students to observe, analyze, and compare a variety of optical illusions. They will also create their own optical illusions with pencil, paint, and paper. Their results will lead them to make conclusions about visual perception and to generalize about broader aspects of sensory perception. In the process students will discover that shapes play a major role in illusions, and that it can be difficult for one individual to simultaneously maintain two different perspectives.

## Concepts

Students will discover some causes of optical illusions and will find that arithmetic and geometric patterns are often associated with such phenomena.

 ## Processes/Skills

- Observing
- Measuring
- Predicting
- Describing
- Inferring
- Recognizing mathematical relationships
- Communicating
- Reflecting
- Recognizing patterns
- Problem solving
- Analyzing
- Inquiring
- Creating
- Cooperating

## Recommended for

| | |
|---|---|
| K–2 | Individual |
| 3–5 ✔ | Small Group ✔ |
| 6–8 ✔ | Whole Class |

## Time Required

1–2 hours

## Materials Required

**MAIN ACTIVITY**

- Illustrations of optical illusions
- General art supplies (paper, pens, pencils, paints)
- Drawing tools (erasers, protractors, drawing compasses)
- Transparency of Figure 7–7 ("old lady/young lady")

**CONNECTING ACTIVITY**

- Transparency of Figure 7–8 ("vase/face")
- General art supplies (paper, pens, pencils, paints)

## Standards

**SCIENCE**

- Abilities Necessary to Do Scientific Inquiry
- Understanding About Scientific Inquiry
- Characteristics of Organisms
- Structure and Function in Living Systems
- Regulation and Behavior in Living Systems

**MATH**

- Reasoning and Proof
- Geometry
- Representation

## ● *Objectives*

- Students will successfully explain the causes of some optical illusions and variances in visual perception.

- Students will make and describe their own optical illusions.

- Students will identify arithmetic and geometric patterns associated with optical illusions.

## *Main Activity, Step-by-Step*

1. Ask the students what they know about optical illusions. You can record their responses in a brainstormed list on the chalkboard or overhead transparency for all to see. Where have they seen optical illusions? What is it that they think creates an optical illusion?

   Ask the students, working in cooperative groups of two to four individuals, to observe the optical illusions illustrated in Figures 7–1 through 7–6. Analyze them, one by one, considering the following:

   a. What is the illusion, as you see it? (It will help to describe the illusion in words, recording the description in writing.)

   b. Measure different aspects of each illustration, keeping written records of each measurement.

   c. How does what you perceive differ from what is actually there in each illusion?

   d. Look for patterns in each illusion and for similarities between the various illusions (describe and record ideas in writing). Pay special attention to arithmetic and geometric patterns and relationships. For example, will Figure 7–2 still fool you if segments A and B are very long or very short? Will Figure 7–5 still fool you if each long segment has only one cross-hatched line instead of many?

   e. Consider the "context" or "setting" of each illusion. That is, how would you describe the foreground or the background. If you change the background or the foreground, will it alter your perception of the figure?

      Lead a class discussion of the groups' findings. Ask, "Can you make any general statements about these optical illusions and how we perceive them?" Consider all possibilities, and encourage divergent responses. These particular illusions are all the results of context or setting. For example, in Figure 7–1, circle A *contains* a square, whereas circle B is *set into* a square. This appears to "draw in" circle A and makes it appear smaller than circle B.

2. Next, the students can create their own optical illusions. They may use Figures 7–1 through 7–6 as models, but if they do, encourage them to change some aspect(s) of the drawing to look for varying effects in perception. Can they alter the illustration so that the illusion is even more pronounced? Or they may want to design an entirely novel illusion. Either way, be sure that they have access to drawing tools: pencils, erasers, protractors, compasses, and so on. Encourage innovation, exploration, and "play."

**Figure 7–1.** Which circle, A or B, is larger?

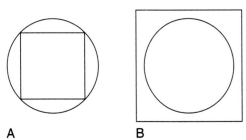

A          B

**Figure 7–2.**   Which line segment, A or B, is longest?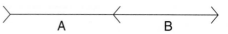

They can also add color to their illusions. How does color affect perception in their illusions? An interesting experiment might be to design an illusion using only pencil and paper, and then to make an exact copy, except with color added. Does the addition of color change how they perceive the illusion?

Discuss with your students what they now know and/or believe about optical illusions. What creates such illusions? Can they recall seeing any optical illusions in real life? Consider the apparent convergence of parallel railroad tracks, the apparently larger size of the full moon when it's near the horizon as opposed to being high in the sky, and desert mirages. How are these real-life illusions explained? Here is an excellent opportunity for some student research.

3.   Show an overhead transparency of Figure 7–7 (the "old lady/young lady"), and ask students to silently write down what they see. Have them each explain what they saw to a partner. Was there any disagreement about what was portrayed in the figure? Could anyone see both images? Did anyone have any difficulty seeing the second image? Could anyone see both images simultaneously? Were students surprised by this illusion? What surprised them about the experience? If any students can't see both the old and young lady, have them work with a partner who can point out both images.

The phenomenon being explored here is known as *perspective,* which means point of view. Whenever you observe anything, you observe it only from a single point of view, or perspective. An image of the old lady/young lady, for instance, strikes the retina and is sent via the optic nerve to the brain where it is interpreted (see Activity 5 for more information about how the eye works). The brain can only interpret it one way at a time, however. That "one way" is called perspective. If you see the old lady, you can't simultaneously see the young lady, and vice versa. Your perspective can change from one to the other, though. How did you manage the change your perspective? That is, if you first saw the old lady, how did you change perspectives to see the young lady? Did anyone have any trouble seeing the second perspective? This is not uncommon. Often, when people see things one way they have a hard time seeing any other way. This also seems to be true of ideas. Once we interpret things one way, it may be difficult to see it any

**Figure 7–3.**   Which is larger center circle, A or B?

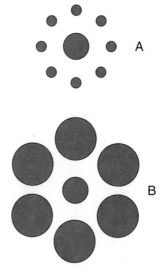

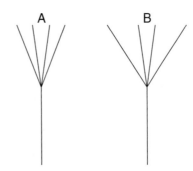

**Figure 7–4.** Which inner angle is larger, A or B?

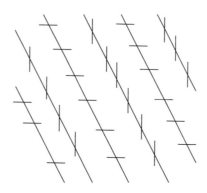

**Figure 7–5.** Are any of the long lines parallel? If so, which ones?

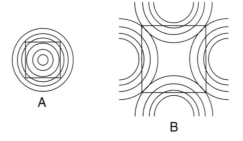

**Figure 7–6.** Are either of the shapes perfect squares? If so, which one(s)?

**Figure 7–7.**   What do you see?

other way. Can you think of any examples of this in your life? How can we improve at seeing things from different perspectives?

## Questions for Discussion

1.  Which of the illusions you've seen were most effective in fooling you? How do you explain their effectiveness? Did your classmates agree on the most effective illusions, or did different people have different perceptions of the various illusions?

2.  Were you able to illustrate your own optical illusion? Was it an effective illusion? What would you do differently next time?

3.  What arithmetic or geometric patterns were you able to identify in the various optical illusions?

4.  Which did you see first: the old lady or the young lady? Were you able to see the other perspective? Was it difficult to see the other perspective, and, if so, how did you figure it out?

## Assessment

1.  Were students able to explain the causes of some optical illusions and variances in visual perception? [embedded, performance, journal entries]

2.  Did they successfully make their own optical illusions for display? [embedded, performance]

3.  Were they able to identify arithmetic and geometric patterns associated with optical illusions? [embedded, journal entries]

## *Connecting Activity*

For an art connection, show the class an overhead transparency of Figure 7-8 (the "vase/face"). Try to see both perspectives at once. Can it be done? Using paints, or other media, have students create their own vase/face figures. Have them try out the illusions on each other. Are there two perspectives in each figure?

Students can use their vase/faces for a homework survey. Instruct students to conduct a survey of at least ten people (not students in your class), showing them the vase/face figure and recording their first impression. Before conducting the survey, ask, "Which perspective (vase or face) do you predict will be more frequently seen first, or will it be even split between vase and face? Why do you predict that? Which perspective did *you* see first? Did you predict the same perspective that you saw first? Why or why not?" The next day compare student data, discussing the results and looking for patterns in the responses.

Finally, consider how perspective affects paintings. Show students a variety of representational paintings (e.g., still lifes, landscapes, and/or portraits). How would the paintings differ if portrayed from a different perspective? What other perspectives were available to the artist? Why do you think that he/she chose this particular perspective? Students can paint or draw a particular scene (perhaps a still life scene that you set up in class) several times, each time from a different perspective. How do they feel about the resulting products? How did perspective affect the portrayals? Which do they like best? Why? Which least? Why?

## *Other Options and Extensions*

1.  Investigate stereograms, such as those from *Magic Eye.* In a sense, they are similar to the "old lady/young lady" illustration because a viewer can't see both perspectives simultaneously. Look into the production of stereograms: how are they made? Have students practice seeing the stereoscopic, three-dimensional images. Are all students able to do so? If not, can they be "taught" to see? What sorts of directions work best for those who had been unable to see the 3-D image? Record all observations.

2.  Investigate 1960s style *op art* by such artists as Vasarely, Bridget Riley, and Richard Anuszkiewicz. When viewing op art pieces, the eye searches for a comfortable point of focus, and the retina becomes fatigued when it is unable to find one. After-images then occur following retinal fatigue. The repetitive and high contrast appearance of op art adds to the viewer's perceptual confusion. Students can verbalize and document their visual sensations as they observe pieces of op art. Have students create op art of their own.

**Figure 7–8.** What do you see?

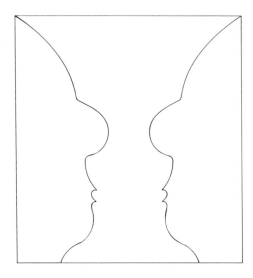

## Resources and Further Information

Churchill, E. R. (1990). *Paper science toys.* New York: Sterling.

Filliman, P. (1999). Patterns all around. *Teaching Children Mathematics, 5,* 390–394.

N. E. Thing Enterprises. (1993). *Magic Eye.* Kansas City: Andrews & McMeel.

Ritter, D. (1995). *Math art.* Cypress, CA: Creative Teaching Press.

Thompson, K. B., & Loftus, D. S. (1995). *Art connections.* Glenview, IL: Good Year Books.

# Science and Math on Television

## Overview

Students certainly enjoy watching television, and they traditionally favor shows about science, mathematics, and technology. Consider the popularity of *Bill Nye the Science Guy, Beakman's World, Newton's Apple, National Geographic Explorer, The Crocodile Hunter,* and, of course, *Mr. Wizard.* Why not combine schoolwork with that interest in watching television? In this activity, students will view a show that they select, and not only examine the scientific, mathematical, and/or technological content being broadcast, but also reflect on their experience of viewing the show. The value of this activity lies in the development of media awareness and the cultivation of critical-thinking skills.

## Concepts

Students analyze a math/science television show for content and impact.

## Processes/Skills

- Describing
- Analyzing
- Concluding
- Inferring
- Inquiring
- Communicating

## Recommended for

| | |
|---|---|
| K–2 | Individual ✔ |
| 3–5 ✔ | Small Group ✔ |
| 6–8 ✔ | Whole Class ✔ |

## Time Required

1 hour

## Materials Required

- Activity Sheets for all class members

## Standards

**SCIENCE**

- Abilities Necessary to Do Scientific Inquiry
- Science and Technology in Society

**MATH**

- Communication
- Connections

## Objectives

- Students will choose, view, and reflect on an appropriate science, math, or technology related television show.
- Students will effectively discuss the content and personal impact of the show.

## Main Activity, Step-by-step

1.  Ask, "Who has seen a television show that has to do with science or math? Which show was it? Tell a partner what you liked about the show." You're bound to get a big response. Explain that the class will do an assignment that has them watch a television show of their choice and report back to the class on what they saw and thought about the show.

2.  Instruct students to watch a television show whose topic is science, math, technology, or a combination of those topics. For the sake of choice and variety, it is a good idea to allow several days, even up to a week, for students to complete this assignment. During and after the show they need to complete Activity Sheet 8 and be prepared to discuss their observations and analysis in class.

3.  Students can initially share their findings in small, classroom discussion groups. Next, build on the individual analyses by examining the assignment with the entire class. Expand the discussion by posing a variety of open-ended questions. Ask, "What science was involved? What math was involved? Was technology involved, and if so, how? What would you change about the show? What did it make you wonder about? What did you learn by watching this show?"

    With older students you can explore more reflective lines of questioning. Ask, "Did you agree with everything the show presented? If not, what did you disagree with and why? Who sponsored the show? Was the sponsor's product in any way related to the content of the show itself? Why do you suppose that particular sponsor decided to support this particular show (think of as many possible reasons as you can)?"

## Questions for Discussion

1.  How were scientists and/or mathematicians portrayed in the show?

2.  Did the show make math or science look to you like an attractive career possibility? Explain your answer.

## Assessment

1.  Did students choose, view, and reflect on an appropriate science, math, or technology related television show? [embedded]

2.  Were they able to explain the content of the show, as well as discuss the show's impact on them? [embedded]

## Other Options and Extensions

The teacher videotapes a television show or movie about science, math, or technology, and then undertakes the following explorations with the class, using that videotape:

● *Freeze Frame*—Freeze the picture in random spots to observe in greater detail that particular "slice" of the show. What images are portrayed? What feelings are being encouraged in viewers? How does the frozen image promote the show's message?

● *Get Up Close*—View the screen with a hand lens. Describe the experience in words or make a drawing, painting, or mosaic representation.

● *Get Far Back*—Stand back at least 5 m from the screen and describe your impressions. How does long-distance viewing change the experience of viewing?

● *No audio*—Watch with the sound off for several minutes. Describe your impressions.

● *No video*—Cover the screen with a sheet of heavy paper. Listen only. Describe your impressions.

## *Resources and Further Information*

Dubeck, L. W., Moshier, S. E., & Boss, J. E. (1988). *Science in Cinema.* New York: Teachers College Press.

McLaren, P. (1995). *Critical pedagogy and predatory culture.* New York: Routledge.

### Activity Sheet 8. Science and Math on Television

Choose a television show that is based on some aspect of science, math, technology, or some combination of those subjects. Watch the show and complete the analysis below.

1.  Name of show:
    Date and time of broadcast:
    Channel:
    Sponsors/Products:

2.  Summarize the show in 30 to 50 words. List any new words that you don't understand.

3.  Why did you choose this particular show?

    _____

    _____

4.  What science and math did you learn?

    _____

    _____

5.  What did you like about the show?

    _____

    _____

6.  What didn't you like about the show?

    _____

    _____

7.  Rate the show on a scale of 1 to 10 (where 1 is low). Would you recommend the show to a friend? Explain.

    _____

    _____

# Learning Cycle Studies in Symmetry

 ## Overview

Here is an engaging lesson that simultaneously involves animals, flowers, mathematical patterns, and art. Students will learn to discern between radial symmetry, bilateral symmetry, and asymmetry by observing and classifying objects, shapes, and photos, and by determining their own rules for classifying according to symmetry. The lesson utilizes a very effective instructional technique known as the Learning Cycle. Options for creating several art projects demonstrating symmetry are also provided.

## Concepts

Students explore the concept of symmetry through a series of science and mathematics Learning Cycle activities.

 ## Processes/Skills

- Observing
- Comparing
- Classifying
- Measuring
- Describing
- Identifying patterns
- Problem solving
- Developing spatial reasoning
- Reflecting

## Recommended for

| | |
|---|---|
| K–2 | Individual |
| 3–5 ✔ | Small Group ✔ |
| 6–8 ✔ | Whole Class ✔ |

 ## Time required

2–3 hours

## Materials Required

**FOR MAIN ACTIVITY**

- An assortment of photos, shapes, and objects representing radial symmetry, bilateral symmetry, and asymmetry
- Several hand mirrors
- Plain and colored paper
- Scissors
- Metric rulers

**FOR CONNECTING ACTIVITY**

- Tempera paint
- Small plastic bowls to hold paint
- String
- Basic art supplies

 ## Standards

**SCIENCE**

- Abilities Necessary to Do Scientific Inquiry
- Understanding About Scientific Inquiry
- Characteristics of Organisms
- Structure and Function in Living Systems

**MATH**

- Problem Solving
- Connections
- Geometry
- Representation

## 🔵 *Objectives*

- Students will classify objects and shapes according to their symmetry.

- Students will develop specific rules that allow them to sort shapes based on symmetry.

- Students will apply their understanding of symmetry by constructing symmetrical objects of their own design, including snowflakes and flowers.

## 🔵 *Background Information*

1. Symmetry refers to the shape of an object and is defined as the state of having balanced proportions. In this activity we will be concerned with *bilateral symmetry*, in which a median plane divides the object into two sides, and *radial symmetry*, in which there is a balance of parts around a central point. We could say that a bilaterally symmetrical object has right and left, upper and lower, or back and front halves, and that the halves are mirror images of each other. We could say that a radially symmetrical object radiates out, for 360°, around a central point. Orchids, insects, and humans exhibit bilateral symmetry, whereas daisies, sea urchins, and sea stars (a.k.a., starfish) exhibit radial symmetry. Objects that are not balanced are said to be *asymmetrical*.

2. This activity includes a learning cycle lesson, a constuctivist technique based largely on Piagetian theory. The learning cycle is composed of three phases: *exploration* (in which student explorations with concrete materials and problems allow them to make new connections with past experiences), *conceptual invention* (in which meaningful terms and concepts related to the students' exploratory experiences are introduced), and *conceptual expansion* (in which students apply the experiences and concepts to a new, but related activity allowing them to grow in their understandings of the subject). The learning cycle is particularly useful in providing students with opportunities to tie their prior experience to new and unfamiliar concepts and terminology.

## *Main Activity, Step-by-Step*

1. Begin the *exploration phase* of the learning cycle by showing the students a wide variety of objects/photos (rocks, shells, nuts and bolts, flowers, plastic bottle, garlic clove, bones, photos of jellyfish, mammals, apple, insects, etc.), and ask, "When we consider shape, how is a jelly fish like a daisy? How is a butterfly like an orchid?" There are two ways to proceed at this point, depending on time constraints and the number of objects/photos available. One option is to divide the class into cooperative groups and have each group sort the objects/photos into different piles based on the shapes of the objects. The other option would be for you to categorize the objects/photos into piles, and to challenge the students to decide what your criteria were for the sorting process. The first option is hands-on, the second more of a minds-on demonstration, but both should encourage divergent thinking and analysis of the shapes presented.

2. Proceed with the *conceptual invention phase* of the learning cycle by introducing the terms *symmetry, bilateral symmetry, radial symmetry,* and *asymmetry*. Be sure that the students understand which of the objects demonstrate these concepts. Conceptual invention is particularly meaningful to the students if you help them connect the concepts and terms from this phase with their efforts and experiences in the exploration phase. That is, you might say something like, "I notice that Group 3 separated several objects (jellyfish, daisy, pie) into a pile. Do you see that all of these objects, in addition to being round, are radially symmetrical because they all radiate from a central point, unlike the bilaterally symmetrical or asymmetrical objects?" Or, "Did any groups classify objects into an 'unusual shape' pile, an 'unbalanced' pile? Well, those objects were unbalanced, or asymmetrical."

   Now, to carry out the *conceptual expansion* phase of the cycle, let the groups (or the entire class, if you're doing this as a demonstration) reclassify the objects/photos into radially symmetrical, bilaterally symmetrical, and asymmetrical piles, visiting each group and checking for comprehension as they proceed. Finally, in groups or as a class, direct the students to make three lists of objects other than those included in the objects/photos that are radially symmetrical, bilaterally symmetrical, or asymmetrical (see Activity Sheet). Discuss the lists as a class, noticing which list was difficult, which was easy, and why.

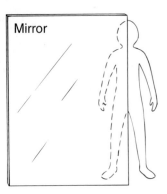

**Figure 9–1.** Bilateral symmetry

3. Next, ask the class to name some geometric shapes and to determine which of the three categories each shape belongs in. You can facilitate this by making cardboard cutout shapes ahead of time and presenting a set to each cooperative group of students. Include various triangles, circles, ovals, parallelograms, trapezoids, etc. You could also include numerical relationships, such as equations, or graphic portrayals, such as a parabola on a graph, as an extra challenge.

4. Some objects may appear to be both bilaterally and radially symmetrical. A 2-liter plastic bottle, for example, is bilaterally symmetrical if viewed from the side, and radially symmetrical if viewed from the end (either end). Give each student group several objects/photos from each of the three categories, and challenge them to develop specific rules that will allow them to determine radial symmetry versus bilateral symmetry versus asymmetry. Encourage a diversity of solutions to the challenge. As a class, consider each group's rules, and decide if those rules will work for any object presented. Discuss the advantages and disadvantages of the various rules presented. To add an extra dimension to the search for symmetry rules, you could give each group a small hand mirror along with their objects. Can the instrument (i.e., the mirror) be an aid in developing rules for symmetry? By placing an object partially behind the mirror, and using the mirror's edge as a plane to "split" the object, the object's form of symmetry may be determined: (a) it is *bilaterally symmetrical* if it can only be split into two halves along only one central plane (see Figure 9–1), (b) it is *radially symmetrical* if it can be split in any plane that goes through its center or its long axis (see Figure 9–2), and (c) it is *asymmetrical* if there is no plane along which it may be evenly split (see Figure 9–3).

5. Next, you can include an art-related mathematical application of the symmetry concept. Instruct students to fold a piece of paper in half, then draw half of a snowflake, flower, or sun shape along the edge with the fold (see Figure 9–4). First ask, "If you cut along the line through both halves of the paper, will the resulting image be radially symmetrical, bilaterally symmetrical, or asymmetri-

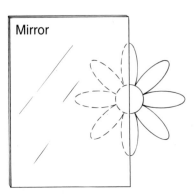

**Figure 9–2.** Radial symmetry

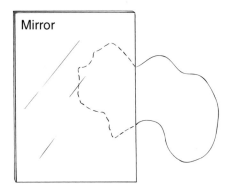

**Figure 9–3.**   Asymmetry

cal? How do you know? If the drawing you made is 10 cm from the fold to its widest point, how wide will the cutout, unfolded figure be? How do you know?" Have them measure the width of the folded drawing before cutting, and have them predict the final, unfolded width of their snowflake/sun/flower. Let them proceed to cut and measure. Check their results and the reactions to their predictions. Because these cutouts were folded into right and left halves, they should demonstrate bilateral symmetry.

You can repeat the same basic activity, this time folding the paper in half *twice* instead of just once, and drawing a quarter of a snowflake, flower, or sun shape along the edge with the fold. Repeat again making three folds in half and drawing an eighth of a snowflake, flower, or sun along the edge with the fold. Do students see the relationship between the number of folds in the paper and the fraction of the object represented? That is, one fold—one-half of the object, two folds—one-fourth of the object, three folds—one-eighth of the object. Based on this evidence, what fraction of the object would be drawn after making four folds? Five folds?
One fold,

$$\frac{1}{2^1} = \frac{1}{2}$$

Two folds,

$$\frac{1}{2^2} = \frac{1}{4}$$

And so on for any number of folds. Can your students discover this relationship on their own? How did they discover it and how did they express it?

6.   Now for an open-ended problem (i.e., one that has more than one feasible solution). Ask students, in small groups, to design and construct a paper cutout or a collage/mosaic of a radially

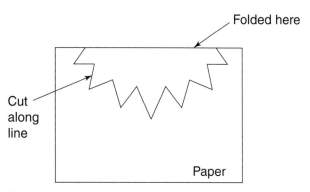

**Figure 9–4.**   Folded figure

symmetrical flower that is adapted to a specific environment (e.g., rainforest, desert, mountain, prairie). Have them keep a written record of their method of construction. When all groups have finished, ask each to display its flower, tell where and how it might grow, and explain the method of construction to the class.

## Questions for Discussion

1. Why is symmetry important in the study of animals and plants?

2. How is symmetry related to mathematics?

3. How would your life be different if nothing was symmetrical? If everything was symmetrical?

4. How would you complete this sentence: Of all the symmetrical objects or living things that I know, the most beautiful is the _____ because _____.

## Assessment

1. Were the students able to classify the objects and photos into piles according to their symmetry? [embedded, performance tasks]

2. Were they able to classify the geometric shapes into piles according to their symmetry? [embedded, performance tasks]

3. Were students able to develop specific rules that allowed them to differentiate between radial symmetry, bilateral symmetry, and asymmetry? [embedded, performance tasks, journal entries]

4. Did students successfully make folded-over snowflakes? Were they able to predict the symmetry and width of the snowflake image? [embedded, portfolio]

5. Were student groups able to construct a cutout or a collage/mosaic of a radially symmetrical flower? Could they explain their rationale and method of construction? [embedded, portfolio, journal entries]

6. Did they come up with any explorations, questions, and/or extensions of their own? [embedded, journal entries]

7. If students worked in groups, were they able to do so cooperatively? [embedded]

## Connecting Activity

Here is a project involving symmetry and painting. Explain to the students that they are going to fold over a piece of paper (colored paper if available), place a piece of paint-saturated string (which was dipped into wet tempera paint) inside the folded-over paper, press on the paper while the string is inside, and then pull out the string while still pressing lightly on the paper. Ask them to predict whether the resulting painting, when unfolded, will be radially symmetrical, bilaterally symmetrical, or asymmetrical?

The paper can be trimmed in interesting ways along the edge (before or after folding, or while folded), and the string can either be pulled out from the edge of the paper, or through a small slit cut along the fold (see Figure 9-5). Various cords with interesting texture work well in this project. Several different strings, with different color paints can be used on each painting. Students may also want to add dots, lines, new patterns and so on after unfolding.

When these projects are completed, ask each student to write about what the resulting pattern reminds them of and why. How would the results differ if their symmetry differed? Display work, with the permission of the artist(s).

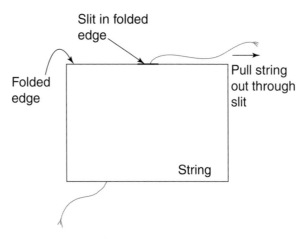

**Figure 9–5.** String and paper painting

## Other Options and Extensions

1. Homework: Challenge the students to make drawings and/or descriptions of radially symmetrical, bilaterally symmetrical, and asymmetrical objects found in or near the home. Bring the observations to class and compare them with those found by the other students.

2. Make a butterfly mosaic using colored paper, tile, colored macaroni (soaked for a time in food coloring diluted with water and then allowed to redry). Is the butterfly symmetrical? Bilateral or radial? Explain how a butterfly's life might be different if it was radially symmetrical, or asymmetrical.

## Resources and Further Information

Bidwell, J. K. (1987). Using reflections to find symmetric and asymmetric patterns. *The Arithmetic Teacher, 34,* 10–15.

Gabel, D. L. (Ed.). (1994). *Handbook of research on science teaching and learning.* New York: Macmillan.

Jenkins, P. D. (1980). *Art for the fun of it.* New York: Fireside.

Kohl, M. A., & Potter, J. (1993). *Science arts.* Bellingham, WA: Bright Ring.

Morris, J. P. (1977). Investigating symmetry in the primary grades. *The Arithmetic Teacher, 24,* 181–186.

Ritter, D. (1995). *Math art.* Cypress, CA: Creative Teaching Press.

Seidel, J. D. (1998). Symmetry in season. *Teaching Children Mathematics, 4,* 244–249.

Silverman, H. (1979). Geometry in the primary grades. *The Arithmetic Teacher, 26,* 15–16.

Williams, D. (1995). *Teaching mathematics through children's art.* Portsmouth, NH: Heineman.

## Activity Sheet 9. Learning Cycle Studies in Symmetry

Make a list of objects or living things that demonstrate the following.

| Radial Symmetry | Bilateral Symmetry | Asymmetry |
|---|---|---|
| | | |

# Applying Simple Chromatography

## ⦿ Overview

This activity involves chemistry, mystery, colors, and measurement. Students observe the composition of various inks by separating them using water-based chromatography. They use what they learn about chromatography to solve a mystery involving a suspicious note and five different marking pens. Working together, they devise a plan to find out who wrote the note. The activity can easily be adapted for grades K–8 and requires only simple and inexpensive materials. This lesson is a great introduction to color mixing.

## ⦿ Concepts

Students find that color perception sometimes differs from what is expected as they separate inks via simple water-based chromatographic technique, using math to help analyze their results.

## ⦿ Processes/Skills

- Observing
- Measuring
- Predicting
- Describing
- Inferring
- Experimenting
- Communicating
- Estimating
- Comparing
- Reflecting
- Recognizing patterns
- Problem solving
- Analyzing
- Creating
- Inquiring
- Cooperating

## ⦿ Recommended for

| | |
|---|---|
| K–2 ✔ | Individual |
| 3–5 ✔ | Small Group ✔ |
| 6–8 ✔ | Whole Class |

## ⦿ Time Required

1–2 hours

## ⦿ Materials Required

**MAIN ACTIVITY**

- Paper towels
- A variety of water-soluble markers, inks, and/or paints
- Shallow plastic plates or saucers
- Empty 2-liter soft drink bottles

**CONNECTING ACTIVITY**

- A variety of inks, paints, and/or dyes
- An assortment of types of paper
- Various drawing and painting materials

## ⦿ Standards

**SCIENCE**

- Abilities Necessary to Do Scientific Inquiry
- Understanding About Scientific Inquiry
- Properties of Objects and Materials
- Properties and Changes of Properties in Matter

**MATH**

- Problem Solving
- Measurement

53

## ◐ *Objectives*

- Students will successfully carry out several chromatographies.

- Students will recognize and be able to explain that some colors are actually mixtures of constituent colors.

- Students will use chromatographic techniques to solve the "mystery pen" problem.

- Students will estimate and measure the ink's "rate of climb" during the chromatography process.

## ◐ *Background Information*

Chromatography is a technique used by scientists to separate mixtures of pigments or other substances. It usually involves filter paper and solvents such as acetone, ether, or ethanol—chemicals that are unsuitable for elementary-level activities. In these explorations, however, we will use water, rather than potentially hazardous chemicals, to demonstrate the fundamentals of chromatography. The term *chromatography* is derived from

the Greek: *chroma* means "color" and *graphien* means "written or visual representation."

In these activities your students will perform simple chromatography with various types and colors of water-soluble inks. The inks should separate as they rise through the filter paper (i.e., paper towel), allowing the students to observe their constituent colors. Why does the water rise (against the force of gravity) into the paper towel, and why does the ink sometimes separate into other colors? The attraction of the water molecules to the fibers of the towel is stronger than the force of gravity acting on the water. The water is therefore absorbed by the towel (the same force that creates surface tension; see Activity 11). When the water reaches the ink spot, the ink pigment dissolves. The water and pigment molecules continue to rise together. Many colors of ink or paint are actually combinations of more than one color (as you will see when you perform the chromatography). As the water and dissolved pigments rise, the heavier weight pigments settle out first (lower in the towel), and the lighter weight pigments continue to rise, leaving a colorful pattern on the towel. Different black inks are composed of different color combinations, so each brand of ink can be identified by its distinguishing chromatography color pattern.

## *Main Activity, Step-by-Step*

1. The first phase of this lesson is taught as a guided discovery experience. Begin by asking students what they know about colors. Can they identify colors just by looking (you might hold up a few different colored pens or other objects to make the point)? Can colors be combined into other colors? Can colors be separated into other colors? Provide each student group (3 to 5 students per group) with a paper towel and several colors of water-soluble markers. Have them make a 0.5 cm dot with each marker along the long edge of the towel (about 1 cm from the edge), marking in pencil the pen type and color used along the opposite long edge (see Figure 10–1). Tape the paper towel around a 2-liter plastic bottle with the ink spots at the base of the bottle. Place the bottle and towel into a shallow plate or saucer of water (less than 1 cm deep) so that the paper towel just makes contact with the water, as in Figure 10–2. What do the students observe? One of the group members should record their observations. The water begins to "climb up" the towel, taking with it the ink from the spots. Wait a while, timing the ink's climb up the towel and recording observations. Observe intermittently for an hour or so. Remove the towel from the bottle (let it dry overnight if your schedule allows), and study the chromatogram that has been produced. Are the colors that climb the same colors as the original ink spots? It depends on the ink and the color used. Some will separate into a variety of colors, indicating their composition. Which colors separated? Which colors did not separate? Which colors are actually made up of other colors? Were you surprised by any of your results? Measure the length of the various shades generated from each spot. Compare the patterns produced. How do the chromatography patterns from the various colors, or the various brands or types of pens, compare? How do your students explain their results? Have each group report its results and explanations. Ask each group what they learned from this exploration.

2. Present the student groups with a problem to solve. Explain that, in this hypothetical situation, five different people wrote notes in black ink on paper towels, but you don't know who wrote

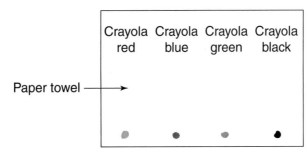

Figure 10–1.    Initial set up

which note. You do know that each of the five people is known to write with a particular type of pen. Here are the pens that they use:

Person 1: Pentech Washable Fine-Line Marker

Person 2: Avery Outer Limits Washable Marker

Person 3: Crayola Washable Classic Colors Marker

Person 4: Sanford Calligraphic Waterbase Ink Pen

Person 5: Paper Mate Washable Fine Point Marking Pen

(Each of these pens has a different type of black ink; you can certainly use others but check first to see that the ink separates and that each chromatogram is readily distinguishable). The challenge here is to identify the writer of each note. Each student group has access to the five types of pens, and each receives a towel with the brief note written along the lower edge. You prepare the notes ahead of time, each written in a single type of ink. Be sure to keep track of which note has which ink by numbering the towels and keeping a hidden list of which ink was used on which towel (see Figure 10–3). Recommend that the groups discuss their plan of investigation before setting out. You can coach and/or gently guide their experimental design, as necessary. By performing two chromatographies (one on the five known inks, and one on the paper towel with the unknown ink), it should be a simple matter for students to determine the chromatographic pattern of each ink type, and of the ink from the note. They can then compare the patterns of the known and unknown inks to identify the writer.

3.   Ask students to estimate how long it takes for the ink colors to separate on the chromatography towel. Ask them how they know. Then ask how they could actually measure the time needed for the water and ink to rise in the paper. Will the different inks vary in terms of time needed to separate? One possible method to time the ink separation is to prepare a paper towel with pencil marks at each centimeter along the short side (see Figure 10–4). Then have each group perform a chro-

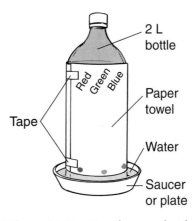

Figure 10–2.    Towel tape to bottle

Paper towel

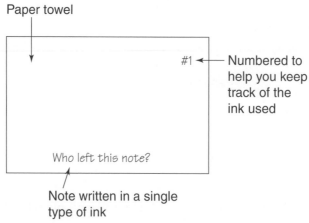

**Figure 10–3.**   Mystery set up

matography on a particular ink and time the rise of the ink and water in the towel in cm/minute, resulting in a measurement of "rate of climb." What do students predict will happen? Will the inks rise at different rates?

## Questions for Discussion

1. What did you think would happen to the ink/paint spot on the towel? What did you think would happen to the water in the saucer?

2. What happened to the ink/paint spots on the paper towel? Can you explain how and why the colors separated?

3. Why do you suppose that some colors separated and others did not?

4. Was it easy to tell the various pens apart, based on the way their colors separated during chromatography? Can you think of any ways that chromatography could be helpful to people in various jobs?

5. Was "rate of climb" an effective way to compare types of pens/inks/paints? Why or why not? What procedure did you use to measure rate of climb? How accurate was your estimate of the time it took for the colors to separate?

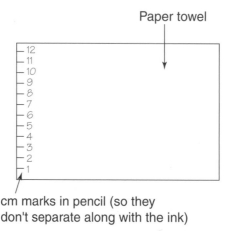

**Figure 10–4.**   Rate set up

## Assessment

1. Were students able to successfully perform the chromatographies? [embedded, performance]

2. Did they recognize that some colors are actually made up of other, constituent colors? [embedded, journal entries]

3. Were students able to solve the "mystery pen" problem by comparing chromatography results? Were they able to explain their method of investigation? [embedded, journal entries, portfolio]

4. Were they able to estimate the time it would take for the colors to separate, and to accurately measure the ink's rate of climb in the towel? [embedded, performance]

## Connecting Activity

Working in groups or on their own, have students create pictures using chromatography. Use a variety of inks, paints, and/or dyes on different types of paper. Once the paper dries, they can add lines or drawings as they wish. Encourage experimentation and innovation. Display the finished products, with the artist's approval, and encourage a supportive and respectful discussion of the results.

## Other Options and Extensions

1. Brainstorm as a group: What variables might affect the quality of the chromatogram, or the time needed to separate? Water temperature? Sort of paper used? Sort of liquid used (e.g., what if we substituted vegetable oil or milk for the water?)? Allow student groups to explore ways to vary the quality and/or time. Be sure that they have plenty of materials at their disposal. Have each group share its findings in classwide presentations. What did they learn about chromatography? What did they learn about colors and the mixing of colors?

2. Look into methods of coloring fabric using batik or tie dye. Using those methods, create colorful shirts, puppets, greeting cards, or other fabric projects.

## Resources and Further Information

Barber, J. (1985). *Crime lab chemistry—Teachers' guide.* Berkeley, CA: Great Explorations in Math and Science (GEMS).

Beals, J. (1994). See Spot run: Elementary lessons on chromatography. *Science and Children, 31* (4), 28–30.

Coleman, D., & Hounshell, P. B. (1982). Fun with paper chromatography. *Science and Children, 20* (2), 28–29.

Jenkins, C. L. (1986). Kool-aid chromatography. *Science and Children, 23* (7), 25–27.

Olshansky, B. (1990). *Portfolio of illustrated step-by-step art projects for young children.* West Nyack, NY: Center for Applied Research in Education.

Paulson, D. R. (1995). *Identification of water soluble marking pen ink.* Unpublished manuscript.

Scharmann, L. C. (1984). Autumn leaf chromatography. *Science and Children, 22* (1), 11–13.

Van Cleave, J. (1989). *Chemistry for every kid.* New York: Wiley.

# Investigating Surface Tension and Soap

## Overview

Your students encounter soap and water every day, but when they do this activity they will learn something new about both substances. They will find out why water can actually *overfill* a cup without spilling, and why soap makes dust or dirt particles seem to "run away." The key to both phenomena is *surface tension,* which is easily investigated by all grade levels using simple materials. In the process, students can collect data, compute averages, graph results, and reach conclusions.

## Concepts

Students collect and analyze data regarding surface tension and the interaction among soap, dust or dirt, and water.

## Processes/Skills

- Observing
- Predicting
- Creating
- Describing
- Analyzing
- Counting
- Calculating
- Graphing
- Communicating
- Reasoning
- Applying
- Cooperating

## Recommended for

K–2 ✔          Individual

3–5 ✔          Small Group ✔

6–8 ✔          Whole Class ✔

## Time Required

1–2 hours

## Materials Required

- Water
- Cups
- Pennies (or other small, standardized masses)
- Liquid soap or detergent
- Graph paper
- Pepper
- Graphite or other colored dustlike substance
- Paper towels

## Standards

**SCIENCE**
- Properties of Objects and Materials
- Properties and Changes of Properties in Matter

**MATH**
- Reasoning and Proof
- Communication
- Numbers and Operations

## Objectives

- Students will carry out their own investigations of surface tension and will successfully draw conclusions from their data.
- Students will understand how soap affects surface tension.

## Background Information

The molecules within the bulk of a liquid are attracted to each other in all directions, resulting in a neutral overall force on any single molecule of that liquid. At the surface of the liquid, however, the molecules are attracted only inward and sideways, causing the surface to exhibit a tension or a skinlike quality, which is known as *surface tension.* Surface tension causes a liquid surface to act as if a membrane was stretched over it, allowing us to gently float a needle or a paper clip on water. Surface tension also causes the molecules in dripping water to pull together and form drops. It also causes wet paintbrush bristles to cling together (they won't cling when dry). *Soap* reduces water's surface tension and reduces water's cling on small particles, such as dust or dirt, by getting in between the water molecules and the dirt molecules. This enables the dirt molecules to become suspended in the water, where they can easily be washed away.

## Main Activity, Step-by-Step

1. This activity begins with a demonstration by the teacher. Show the class a full cup of water (best to use a clear cup or glass, and be sure that it's filled right up to the rim). Ask, "How many pennies do you predict that I can place in the water before it overflows?" Record student predictions. Gently drop pennies into the water (edgewise works best here) until the water actually overflows the rim of the cup. You will probably use more pennies than either you or the students expect, so be sure to have plenty on hand. The water will actually rise above the rim of the cup, forming a domelike bulge. When the water finally spills and the demonstration is complete, give student groups a few minutes to discuss what they've seen, and ask them to explain what happened. The water in the cup was able to rise above the rim and to accommodate so many pennies due to the water's *surface tension* (explained above in Background Information).

2. Next try the same process, but first add a single drop of liquid soap or detergent to the surface of the water in the cup. Ask for student predictions regarding the number of pennies it will take for the water to spill out, and then carry out the demonstration. You should find that you need far fewer pennies this time. Graph the number of pennies used in each case (bar graph), and ask students to try to explain why the soap lowered the number of pennies needed.

3. Give student groups time and materials to try the penny demonstrations (with and without soap) on their own. They should make predictions, collect data (number of pennies), and graph their results using Activity Sheet 11. The students can then compare class results (averages) and try to answer these questions: What effect did the soap have on the water, and how do you know?

4. Now for a final demonstration for the whole class to observe. Float some dust (any sort of colored dust will do: graphite, pepper, etc.) on water. Add a single drop of soap to the water. What happens? (The dust particles will move quickly away from the drop of soap.) When students consider the effects caused by soap in this and the previous demonstrations, can they offer any explanations about why soap is used as a cleaning agent?

## Questions for Discussion

1. What allows the water to rise above the rim of the cup/glass as pennies are added?

2. What effect did the drop of soap have on the number of pennies added to the water? How do you explain this?

3. Based on what you've observed about soap, water, and dust particles, why is soap able to get us clean?

## Assessment

1. Did students successfully carry out their own investigations of surface tension? [embedded, performance]

2. Were students able to successfully graph, analyze, and draw conclusions from their data? [embedded, journal entries]

3. Were students able to understand how soap affects surface tension? [embedded, journal entries]

## Other Options and Extensions

1. Research "soap." What is it made of and just exactly how does it work?

2. Design and carry out some experiments involving various soaps. How effective is a particular type of soap at cleaning out different sorts of dirt? Compare several different soaps in terms of how effective they are in removing a particular type of dirt or stain.

3. Think of other ways we encounter or use surface tension (e.g., it allows a sponge to soak up water).

## Resources and Further Information

Barnes, G. (1978). Drops, sieves, and paintbrushes: Teaching about surface tension. *Science and Children, 15* (4), 28–29.

Blume, S. C., & Beisenherz, P. C. (1907). Turning your class on to cohesion. *Science and Children, 24* (7), 20–21.

Craig, A., & Rosney, C. (1988). *The Usborne science encyclopedia.* Tulsa, OK: EDC.

Donalson-Sams, M. (1987). Surface tension: The ways of water. *Science and Children, 25* (3), 26–28.

MacKinnon, G. R. (1998). Soap and science. *Science and Children, 35* (5), 28–31.

Russell, S. J., & Mokros, J. (1996). What do children understand about average? *Teaching Children Mathematics, 2,* 360–365.

Tolley, K. (1994). *The art and science connection.* Menlo Park, CA: Addison-Wesley.

## Activity Sheet 11. Investigating Surface Tension and Soap

1. How many pennies will it take to make the water overflow the container?

| Prediction | Actual |
|---|---|
|  |  |

2. How many pennies will it take to make the water overflow the container if a drop of soap is added to the water?

| Prediction | Actual |
|---|---|
|  |  |

Make a bar graph of the results above.

3. Group work: Count the number of pennies it takes to make the water overflow.

|  | Prediction | Actual | Your Average | Class Average |
|---|---|---|---|---|
| Water only (3trials) |  |  |  |  |
| Water and a single drop of soap (3 trials) |  |  |  |  |

What effect did the soap have on the water, and how do you know?

4. What happened to the dust floating on the water when the drop of soap was added?

Considering the effects caused by soap in these demonstrations, can you offer any explanations about why soap is used as a cleaning agent?

# Exploring the Dynamics of Temperature

 **Overview**

Would your students like to take care of a penguin? To be a penguin-sitter, they would have to know what conditions that bird needs to survive. One important factor would be temperature. In this activity, you will challenge student groups to prove that they could care for a penguin by demonstrating that they can maintain the temperature of a glass of water at 10° Celsius (using ice and/or body heat from their hands) for 15 minutes, recording the temperature every 30 seconds, and graphing their data. By reflecting on the procedure, they will learn about the dynamics of a closed system, the nature of water, and the value of adjusting to fluctuating environmental conditions.

 **Concepts**

Students investigate dynamic equilibrium, temperature dynamics, the physics of water, graphing, and data analysis via this attempt to maintain water at a constant temperature.

**Processes/Skills**

- Reading a thermometer
- Graphing
- Data analysis
- Observation
- Prediction
- Measuring
- Describing
- Inferring
- Experimenting
- Communicating
- Comparing
- Reflecting
- Inquiring
- Recognizing patterns
- Problem solving
- Cooperating

**Recommended for**

| K–2 | Individual |
| 3–5 ✔ | Small Group ✔ |
| 6–8 ✔ | Whole Class |

**Time Required**

1–2 hours

**Materials Required**

**PRELIMINARY ACTIVITY**

- Three 250 ml cups
- Ice
- Heat source
- Water

**MAIN ACTIVITY**

- Large (at least 250 ml) plastic drinking cups
- Water at room temperature
- Ice (cubes—enough for each group to have a cupful)
- 500 ml beakers
- Graph paper
- Alcohol-filled thermometers

**Standards**

**SCIENCE**

- Properties of Objects and Materials
- Transfer of Engery
- Organisms and Environments
- Regulation and Behavior in Living Systems
- Diversity and Adaptation of Organisms

**MATH**

- Reasoning and Proof
- Communication
- Measurement

## Objectives

- Students will maintain a cup of water in a state of dynamic thermal equilibrium and will be able to explain how they did so.

- Students will graph, explain, and compare their data.

- Students will identify examples of dynamic equilibria in everyday life.

## Preliminary Activity

Show the class three cups: one containing water at room temperature, one containing water that you have warmed slightly over a heat source, and one containing ice water. Ask student volunteers to touch each cup and describe how it feels. Then, have student volunteers measure the temperature of the water in each cup using thermometers. Be sure that all students understand how to read and use the thermometer. Ask the class where in the world we might find warm water, cold water, and room temperature water. It will be helpful here to refer to a map or globe. On the chalkboard, make a chart with columns headed "Warm Water," "Room Temperature Water," and "Cold Water." As a class, brainstorm locations on the map that students think would fall under one of the headings and list them on the chart. Also brainstorm and list the sorts of animals that students think might live in each of those three water temperature categories.

## Main Activity, Step-by-Step

1. Ask your students to use their imaginations as you describe the following scenario. "A friend recently returned from Antarctica and brought with her a young penguin for the local zoo. She has asked you to penguin-sit for 15 minutes, but she wants to be sure that you can keep the penguin comfortable. This particular bird likes to be kept at a constant temperature of 10° Celsius. Working with your group, you will start with a cup of water at room temperature. Your challenge is to alter the water temperature to 10° as quickly as possible using ice, and then to keep it there for the remainder of the 15 minutes. You must record your progress at 30-second intervals, graph your results, and present your observations and conclusions to the class."

2. Working in groups of four, students prepare for the activity. To ensure that duties are shared, members assume specific tasks: materials specialist, thermometer specialist, data specialist, and graph specialist. Using a 500 ml beaker, the materials specialist must measure out 200 ml of tap water into the cup. The thermometer specialist places the thermometer into the water and waits several minutes, until it has adjusted to the initial water temperature, reading out that temperature. The data specialist records that initial temperature on Activity Sheet 12 and keeps track of timing for the duration of the 15-minute activity (if you have a limited number of watches, you may prefer to be the timekeeper for the entire class, calling out the 30 intervals for all). The graph specialist is responsible for troubleshooting during the activity, and creating a graph of the temperature data once the observations are completed (plotting time on the x axis and temperature on the y axis).

3. Before beginning the activity itself, discuss how to raise and lower the water temperature. Students may suggest such methods as adding and/or removing ice, wrapping their hands around the cup, or inserting their fingers into the water. *They may not, however, remove any liquid water from the cup.* Allow them several minutes to determine their thermal strategies. Ask students also to predict what will happen during the activity and to write their predictions at the top of Activity Sheet 12.

4. Once the initial room temperature thermometer reading has been made and recorded, the materials specialist adds ice to the cup of water to drop the temperature as quickly as possible. Every 30 seconds for the next 15 minutes the data specialist records the temperature reported by the thermometer specialist. When the temperature drops below 10° C, the cup must have ice removed and/or be warmed. When it rises above 10° C, it must be cooled with more ice. When all the data

are recorded, the graph specialist makes the graph of time versus temperature and the group members make conclusions about their findings. How did their predictions differ from their results?

5. As a class, compare the groups' graphs, looking for similarities, differences, and patterns. Usually, graphs will indicate a radical decrease to below 10°, followed by an increase to above 10°, then by minor fluctuation around the 10° mark for the remainder of the 15 minutes. Also, discuss the methods used by the various groups to try to maintain the temperature. Students are commonly surprised to find that, at least initially, it is difficult to maintain a stable 10° C temperature. They realize that they need to make ongoing thermal adjustments to keep the water temperature relatively stable. Introduce the concept of *dynamic equilibrium*, explaining that the term refers to the way a system, such as our cup of water, is constantly affected by cooling and warming influences, yet seems to remain at a fairly constant temperature. *Dynamic* because it is always changing, and *equilibrium* because nonetheless it tends to remain in balance. The apparent lack of overall temperature change is caused by a balance of the heating and cooling influences, creating a state of dynamic equilibrium. Dynamic equilibria are found in many places (not all of which involve heat), including trying to drive a car in a straight line, thermal regulation of the human body, the human appetite, the temperature of a room when it is maintained by a thermostat, or the complementary processes of evaporation and condensation of water in a closed container (such as a terrarium).

## Questions for Discussion

1. How can penguins adapt to constant changes in environmental temperature? How do they adjust to colder or warmer water?

2. What sorts of problems did you run into when trying to maintain the water temperature?

3. Can you think of other examples of dynamic equilibria in the real world?

4. How effectively did you work as a group? Did any problems arise among group members? How did you solve those problems?

## Assessment

1. Were the students able to maintain the cup of water in a state of dynamic thermal equilibrium? Were they able to describe the technique(s) used to do so? [embedded, performance]

2. Were they able to graph and explain their data? [embedded, journal entries]

3. Were they able to identify similarities and differences between the classes' graphs? Could they explain what was represented by the graphs? [embedded, performance, journal entries]

4. Could they identify other examples of dynamic equilibria? That is, can you think of any other systems that seem to be constant but are actually constantly fluctuating? [embedded, journal entries]

## Other Options and Extensions

1. Find out more about how penguins and other aquatic animals or plants adapt to their thermal environments.

2. How does the role played by your blood (a fluid) in regulating your body's thermal equilibrium resemble the role played by the oceans (another fluid) in regulating global climates?

3. Research polar exploration, human living conditions in polar regions, and ethical questions regarding the use of arctic and antarctic resources.

4. Find out more about the physiology of warm-blooded and cold-blooded animals.

## *Resources and Further Information*

Arnold, C. (1988). *Penguin.* New York: Morrow Junior Books.

Biological Sciences Curriculum Study. (1994). *Middle school science and technology: Investigating systems and change.* Dubuque, IA: Kendall/Hunt.

Cowcher, H. (1990). *Antarctica.* New York: Farrar, Straus and Giroux.

Curtis, P. (1992). *Aquatic animals in the wild and in captivity.* New York: Lodestar.

Eichinger, J. (1996). Science is constantly cool. *Science and Children, 33* (7), 25–27, 43.

Lucas, S. B. (1976). Crystals, snowflakes, and frost. *Science and Children, 14* (2), 16–17.

Moore, D. A. (1999). Some like it hot. *Teaching Children Mathematics, 5,* 538–543.

Roth, W. (1989). Experimenting with temperature probes. *Science and Children, 27* (3), 52–54.

*(continued)*

## Activity Sheet 12. Exploring the Dynamics of Temperature

*Prediction:* What do you think will happen to the water temperature over the 15-minute period?

_____

_____

_____

Record your data in the table below.
(*Starting time:* _____:_____)

| | Time | Temperature (°C) |
|---|---|---|
| 1 | 0 min.    0 sec. | |
| 2 | 0 min.    30 sec. | |
| 3 | 1 min.    0 sec. | |
| 4 | 1 min.    30 sec. | |
| 5 | 2 min.    0 sec. | |
| 6 | 2 min.    30 sec. | |
| 7 | 3 min.    0 sec. | |
| 8 | 3 min.    30 sec. | |
| 9 | 4 min.    0 sec. | |
| 10 | 4 min.    30 sec. | |
| 11 | 5 min.    0 sec. | |
| 12 | 5 min.    30 sec. | |
| 13 | 6 min.    0 sec. | |
| 14 | 6 min. 30 sec. | |
| 15 | 7 min. 0 sec. | |
| 16 | 7 min. 30 sec. | |
| 17 | 8 min. 0 sec. | |
| 18 | 8 min. 30 sec | |
| 19 | 9 min. 0 sec. | |
| 20 | 9 min. 30 sec. | |
| 21 | 10 min. 0 sec | |
| 22 | 10 min. 30 sec. | |
| 23 | 11 min. 0 sec. | |
| 24 | 11 min. 30 sec. | |
| 25 | 12 min. 0 sec. | |
| 26 | 12 min. 30 sec. | |
| 27 | 13 min. 0 sec. | |
| 28 | 13 min. 30 sec. | |
| 29 | 14 min. 0 sec. | |
| 30 | 14 min. 30 sec. | |
| 31 | 15 min. 0 sec. | |

What techniques did your group use to maintain a stable 10° C temperature for the 15-minute period?

Graph your data (time on the x axis and temperature on the y axis).

What can you conclude about keeping a cup of water at a stable temperature, based on your data?

How did your predictions differ from your actual results? How do you know?

# 13  Learning About Acids and Bases

## Overview

The chemistry of acids and bases is a fundamental area of study in the physical sciences. This activity is really two exercises in one. First, students will learn to discern between acids and bases using various color-changing indicator solutions. Second, students will use their new knowledge of indicators to determine the relative acidity of several everyday foods. The lessons involve data collection, problem solving, and quantitative reasoning as your class learns how chemists work with acids and bases. The lessons are very dynamic and motivating, and may be adapted for students from grades 3 to 8.

## Concepts

Students study the basics of acid/base chemistry, including the use of indicator solutions and the process of titration.

## Processes/Skills

- Ordering
- Predicting
- Measuring/counting
- Comparing
- Investigating
- Describing
- Explaining
- Cooperating
- Asking questions
- Recognizing patterns
- Communicating

## Recommended for

| | | |
|---|---|---|
| K–2 | | Individual |
| 3–5 ✔ | | Small Group ✔ |
| 6–8 ✔ | | Whole Class ✔ |

## Time Required

2–3 hours

## Materials Required

**MAIN ACTIVITY**

- Safety goggles
- Vinegar
- Water
- Orange juice
- Baking soda
- Ammonia
- Measuring instruments (e.g., beaker, graduated cylinder, spoons, and/or balance)
- Droppers or drinking straws
- Clear plastic cups
- Cookie sheets or aluminum foil
- Red (purple) cabbage
- Turmeric powder
- Grape juice
- Ex Lax pills (sugar coated, not chocolate)
- Rubbing alcohol
- Plastic spoons
- A variety of fruits and vegetables (e.g., corn, peas, carrots, tomatoes, peaches, pineapples, apples, cherries, oranges, and lemons)

**FOLLOW-UP ACTIVITY**

- Safety goggles
- Turmeric solution
- White paper
- Paint brushes
- Ammonia solution in spray bottle

## Standards

**SCIENCE**

- Abilities Necessary to Do Scientific Inquiry
- Understanding About Scientific Inquiry
- Properties of Objects and Materials
- Properties and Changes of Properties in Matter

**MATH**

- Reasoning and Proof
- Connections
- Numbers and Operations
- Data Analysis and Probability

 ## Objectives

- Students will differentiate between acids and bases, based on color changes in indicator solutions.

- Students will titrate and rank order the food juices in terms of their acidity.

 ## Background Information

*Acids* and *bases* are important compounds that are chemical opposites of one another in many ways and that *neutralize* each other when mixed. Acids are often thought of as chemicals that can harm us by burning the skin, and bases are often thought of as chemicals that are bitter and have a slippery feel. Chemists often use various *indicators* (such as litmus paper) to determine whether substances are *alkaline* (i.e., basic) or *acidic*. When aqueous solutions of acids and bases are mixed in the proper proportions, the resulting solution (composed of water and a salt) is *neutral.* That is, it does not demonstrate the characteristics of either acid *or* base. Students should wear safety goggles throughout these exercises.

## Main Activity, Step-by-step

1. Ask students what they know about acids and bases. What do you want to know about acids and bases?

   Offer a basic definition for the terms *acid* and *base* (see Background Information above). Note some examples (common acids: vinegar, orange juice; common bases: baking soda, ammonia). Encourage student questions as you check for comprehension.

2. In this portion of the lesson, students will test the four common acids/bases listed above. Have students prepare the following solutions: *vinegar*—mixed 50:50 with water; *orange juice*—straight; *baking soda*—about 30 g, which is about 15 ml or one tablespoon, mixed into 250 ml, or a cup, of water; *ammonia*—mixed 10:90 with water) with various indicators, detailed below, to determine what color changes occur. Students, working in small groups, should add a small amount (using a dropper, or a drinking straw with one finger held over the open end to transfer liquid) of each acid and base to small amounts (a few ml) of each of four indicators, and record their findings on Activity Sheet 13-1. Students should get a feel for the indicators and how the acids/bases react in their presence. All the tests can be performed in clear plastic cups (to observe color changes more easily), on top of a cookie sheet or sheet of aluminum foil to keep desks clean. *Safety first:* Be sure that students know not to ingest any chemicals found in the lab, or even to touch their hands to their mouths after handling chemicals (which, of course, includes the acids, bases, and indicator solutions).

   The teacher should prepare the following indicator solutions ahead of time:

   a. Cabbage juice—Quarter and grate a red cabbage (half a cabbage will be sufficient for an entire class). Place it into a saucepan, cover with water, and boil for about 5 minutes. Strain out the water/juice mixture into another container and keep it in the refrigerator. This cabbage solution will be blue, but will turn red when mixed with an acid and green when mixed with a base. If you add acid, then base, the cabbage juice will go from blue to red and back to blue.

   b. Turmeric—Mix 5 ml turmeric powder (this spice is available in most grocery stores) into 120 mL of water. The spice won't dissolve completely, but that's okay. The turmeric solution will change from yellow to reddish brown when a base is added. The original solution won't change color when a base is added, however. To test for the presence of an acid, you must first add a base to the tumeric solution, turning it reddish-brown. The addition of an acid then will return the liquid to its original color.

c.  Grape Juice—Grape juice is naturally acidic and will turn green when a base is added. To test for an acid, first add a base to turn the solution green, then add the acid to return it to its original color.

d.  Laxative—Dissolve several Ex-Lax pills (sugar coated, not chocolate) into a jar full of rubbing alcohol and let it sit overnight. Stir to dissolve the pills completely, making a tan indicator solution. The laxative contains *phenolphthalein,* which is an indicator that turns pink in the presence of an acid. When a base is added to the pink liquid, it will return to its original color.

When student groups complete their investigations, ask them what they learned about acids and bases and indicators so far. Check for comprehension and clarify concepts if they are confused about some points.

3.  Although most foods are acidic, they are not all equally so. In this portion of the lesson student groups will rank order several fruits and vegetables based on their levels of acidity, by using a method called *titration.* That is, they will count the number of teaspoons of food juice needed to generate an acidic color change in an indicator (in this case, cabbage juice). *The fewer teaspoons added, the more acidic the food.* Remember that the rank order for acidity is also the opposite of the rank order of alkalinity, because by definition, high acidity equals low alkalinity.

First, students should predict the order of acidity, recording their responses on Activity Sheet 13-2. Prepare four or five of the food juices ahead of time (using a blender and adding water for the solid specimens such as corn and carrots). Suggested options include corn, peas, carrots, tomatoes, peaches, pineapples, apples, cherries, oranges, and lemons. Student groups then place 5 teaspoons of cabbage juice indicator into a clear plastic cup, and add and stir each of the specimen food juices with a plastic spoon, a spoonful at a time, until the cabbage indicator turns red. They should then record that number of spoonfuls for each specimen juice. Again, perform all activities on a cookie sheet or sheet of aluminum foil, and be sure that students understand that they must not ingest any of the liquids.

Finally, let each group present their results to the class by asking what they learned about acids and bases in this lesson.

## Follow-up Activity

In a well-ventilated room, have students "paint" a "secret picture" on white paper with the laxative indicator. When the pictures are thoroughly dry, they should be invisible. Simply spray them with an ammonia solution (e.g., glass cleaner with ammonia) to have the "secret paintings" emerge again.

## Questions for Discussion

1.  How does an acid differ from a base? How can you tell the difference between the two?

2.  Why shouldn't you touch your hands to your mouth after handling chemicals?

3.  How were you able to tell which food juices were most acidic?

## Assessment

1.  Were students able to successfully record the color changes that occurred when the vinegar, orange juice, baking soda, and ammonia were added to the four indicator solutions? [embedded, performance]

2. Could students differentiate between acids and bases, based on color changes in indicator solutions? [embedded, journal entries]

3. Were students able to titrate and rank order the food juices in terms of their acidity? [embedded, journal entries]

## Other Options and Extensions

1. Test baking powder with an indicator solution for acid/base (e.g., cabbage juice). Baking powder is actually a combination of sodium bicarbonate and a powdered acid; when moistened the two combine and release carbon dioxide gas to make the food rise. What happens when the liquid is added to the dry baking powder?

2. Titrate various soaps and cleansers using cabbage juice; rank order the results.

3. Bring in an example of your favorite food to test for acid/base.

## Resources and Further Information

Cobb, V. (1979). *More science experiments you can eat.* New York: Harper & Row.

McBride, J. W. (1995). Acid tests and basic fun. *Science and Children, 33* (4), 26–27.

Sullivan, A. (1989). Acid basics. *Science and Children, 27* (2), 22–24.

Tolley, K. (1994). *The art and science connection.* Menlo Park, CA: Addison-Wesley.

Van Cleave, J. (1989). *Chemistry for every kid.* New York: Wiley.

## Activity Sheet 13–1. Learning About Acids and Bases

1. In each box, record any color changes that occurred when the acid or base were added to the indicator solutions.

| Acids/Bases | Indicators | | | |
|---|---|---|---|---|
| | Cabbage juice | Turmeric | Grape juice | Laxative |
| Vinegar (acid) | | | | |
| Orange juice (acid) | | | | |
| Ammonia (base) | | | | |
| Baking soda (base) | | | | |

2. Conclusions: What did you learn about acid/base indicators? Which was most effective? How do you know?

## Activity Sheet 13–2. Learning About Acids and Bases

1. Rank order the juices in terms of their acidity. First, make your predictions, then carry out the experiments and list the actual order based on your data.

| | Predicted |
|---|---|
| Most acidic: | 1. |
| | 2. |
| | 3. |
| | 4. |
| Least acidic: | 5. |

| Juices Tested | Teaspoons Used |
|---|---|
| | |
| | |
| | |
| | |
| | |

| | Actual |
|---|---|
| Most acidic: | 1. |
| | 2. |
| | 3. |
| | 4. |
| Least acidic: | 5. |

2. Conclusions:

# Observing the Effects of Acids and Bases on Eggs

##  Overview

Combining acid/base chemistry, cell biology, and quantitative research methods, this "egg-ceptional" activity promotes a truly interdisciplinary perspective. First, students find out what effect acids and bases have on calcium-based substances such as egg shell and bone. Second, they discover what changes occur when decalcified eggs are placed in solutions of water and corn syrup. Throughout the two exercises, student groups will be measuring, analyzing, and using data to reach valid conclusions.

## Concepts

Students will use quantitative and qualitative methods to observe the effects of acids and bases on eggs, which will include the concepts of decalcification, membranes, permeability, and osmosis.

## Processes/Skills

- Observing
- Predicting
- Measuring
- Calculating
- Graphing
- Analyzing
- Questioning
- Comparing
- Describing
- Cooperating
- Communicating
- Making conclusions based on data

## Recommended for

| | |
|---|---|
| K–2 | Individual |
| 3–5 | Small Group ✔ |
| 6–8 ✔ | Whole Class ✔ |

## Time Required

2–3 hours

## Materials Required

- Safety goggles
- Chicken eggs
- Chicken bones
- Meter sticks
- String
- Balances
- Beakers/measuring cups
- Graduated cylinders/measuring spoons
- Vinegar
- Water
- Baking soda
- Large plastic cups
- Paper towels
- Corn syrup
- Calculators
- Graph paper

## ◉ Standards

**SCIENCE**

- Properties of Objects and Materials
- Properties and Changes of Properties in Matter
- Characteristics of Organisms
- Structure and Function in Living Systems
- Regulation and Behavior in Living Systems

**MATH**

- Reasoning and Proof
- Measurement
- Data Analysis and Probability

## ◉ Objectives

- Students will effectively describe the changes in eggs and bones caused by acids and bases and explain why those changes took place.

- Students will be able to discern and explain the differences between decalcified eggs in water and in corn syrup based on their measurements and data analyses.

## Main Activity, Step-by-Step

1. Begin by asking students what effect they think a weak acid or a weak base will have on an egg or a chicken bone if the egg or bone is soaked in either solution for three days. Encourage diverse responses and ask for their rationale. Give each student group two fresh eggs and a chicken bone (leg bones work best here), and direct them to measure the eggs (length and width using a meter stick; circumference using a string and meter stick; mass using a balance) and the bone (length and mass only), recording their data on Activity Sheet 14-1. Students should then predict and record what they think will happen to each of the objects in each of the solutions over the next three days.

2. Wearing safety goggles (which should be worn throughout these exercises), students should then prepare the two solutions needed. The first is acid, using vinegar (acetic acid): mixed 50:50, vinegar to water. The second is base, using baking soda: 30 g, which is about 15 ml or one tablespoon, mixed into 250 ml, or a cup, of water. The same container of vinegar solution can accommodate both an egg and the chicken bone. Place the eggs and bones into the solutions, and wait 3 days (students can look at the progress over the 3- day period, but they shouldn't touch the specimens).

3. After the 72-hour wait, student groups should remove all three objects from the solutions, gently blotting each dry with a paper towel. Using Activity Sheet 14-1 to record data, students should describe and remeasure each object. How have the eggs changed? Which solution (the acid or the base) caused the greatest change? How did the bone change? Can you explain your observations? Explain to the class that the acid caused *decalcification,* that is, it removed the calcium from the egg shell and from the bone. It is calcium that makes bones, shells, and teeth hard (here is a wonderful opportunity to discuss calcium in the diet, the importance of dental hygiene, and so on). The base does not cause decalcification, as the second egg should demonstrate. The bone, when decalcified, can even be tied in a knot!

4. Explain that the hard, calcified shell protects the fragile egg inside. Just inside the shell, however, is a thin membrane containing the egg. When the shell has been leached away by the acid, this membrane becomes evident. It holds the egg together. It also controls the flow of materials into and out of the egg. The membrane, as well as the shell, have tiny pores that allow materials to pass in and out. A membrane that allows materials to pass through it is known as a *permeable* membrane.

   Student groups now will take their decalcified egg and place it into a container of either water or corn syrup, as directed by the teacher (half of the eggs in one liquid and half in the other). Be sure that the eggs are gently blotted, weighed, and measured before placing them into the assigned liquids (using Activity Sheet 14-2). The eggs will be soaked for 30 minutes. At 10-minute intervals students must remove the egg from the liquid, gently blot it dry, and record its mass, length, width, and circumference. As a means of comparison (i.e., a control), each group should also undertake the same procedure with a normal egg, complete with shell.

When all student groups have completed the 30-minute task, student groups can compare their data for the decalcified eggs. They should also graph the class averages of the egg mass data (on the y axis) versus time (the 10-minute intervals, on the x axis). Plot the egg-in-water and egg-in-syrup data on the same graph for easier comparison. Were the eggs affected differently by the two liquids? Can the students offer explanations for their results? Explain that *osmosis* occurred in the decalcified eggs; that is, water moved through the membrane either into or out of the egg. The water moves through the membrane from higher to lower concentration. That is, in the syrup, the water moved out of the egg, causing it to lose mass (because there was a higher concentration of water inside the egg, when compared with the outer syrup—the water coming out of the egg attempted to "dilute" the corn syrup to create a balance of molecules on either side of the membrane). The egg in water enlarged, however, because water moved into it (because the inside of the egg had a lower concentration of water when compared with the water bath in which it soaked—again attempting to create a balance by "diluting" the liquid inside the egg). Were any changes observed in the normal egg? How can this be explained? (The shell protects the egg from osmosis.)

You might add that most living tissues have membranes and undergo osmosis. In fact, when we bathe for a long time our skin cells swell with water (as the water tries to "dilute" us by osmotically passing through our skin cell membranes). When we get out of the bath, we begin to lose the water we gained, and our stretched and previously swollen skin wrinkles. This shriveling is particularly apparent on our hands and fingers.

Find out if the students have any questions of their own about the effect of acids and bases, decalcification, or osmosis. Offer research ideas so that they might find their answers.

## Questions for Discussion

1. How do acids and bases affect such materials as eggs and bones?

2. If you wanted to make a decalcified egg grow larger, what sort of liquid could you put it in? How do you know?

3. Why is osmosis important to a chicken egg? Why is osmosis important to living cells?

4. Why is a shell important to an egg? How do you know?

## Assessment

1. Were students able to effectively describe the changes in eggs and bones, and to explain why the changes took place? [embedded, journal entries]

2. Were students able to discern and explain the differences between decalcified eggs in water and in corn syrup based on their measurements and data analyses? [embedded, journal entries]

## Other Options and Extensions

1. Try to decalcify eggs in other weak acids (e.g., orange juice).

2. Put a water-soluble dye (e.g., methylene blue, methyl green, or safranine O—all available through biological supply catalogs) into water with a decalcified egg. The egg will take on the color of the dye. Why? Food coloring will not pass through the egg's membrane however. Why not?

3. Do all egg-laying animals have shelled eggs? Find out how an amphibian's eggs differ from bird or reptile eggs, and how those differences affect how amphibians live.

## Resources and Further Information

Chambless, M. S., Blackwell, S., Redding, C., & Oswalt, A. (1998). A data "eggs"ploration. *Teaching Children Mathematics, 4,* 448–451.

Cocanour, B., & Bruce, A. S. (1986). The case of the soft-shelled egg. *Science and Children, 23* (6), 13–14.

Cooper, G., & Lonsdale, S. M. (1986). Eggs and science in Katmandu. *Science and Children, 24* (6), 18–19.

MacKinnon, G. R. (1998). Soap and science. *Science and Children, 35* (5), 28–31.

Sullivan, A. (1989). Acid basics. *Science and Children, 27* (2), 22–24.

Tolley, K. (1994). *The art and science connection.* Menlo Park, CA: Addison-Wesley.

## Activity Sheet 14–1. Observing the Effects of Acids and Bases on Eggs

| | Predicted Changes | Measurements Before | Measurements After | Description of Any Changes |
|---|---|---|---|---|
| Egg in Vinegar (Acid) | | Length -   mm<br>Width -   mm<br>Circumf. -   mm<br>Mass -   g | Length -   mm<br>Width -   mm<br>Circumf. -   mm<br>Mass -   g | |
| Egg in Baking Soda (Base) | | Length -   mm<br>Width -   mm<br>Circumf. -   mm<br>Mass -   g | Length -   mm<br>Width -   mm<br>Circumf. -   mm<br>Mass -   g | |
| Bone in Vinegar (Acid) | | Length -   mm<br>Width-   mm<br>Circumf. -   mm<br>Mass -   g | Length -   mm<br>Width-   mm<br>Circumf. -   mm<br>Mass -   g | |

How do you explain the changes in the eggs and/or bone?

## Activity Sheet 14–2. Observing the Effects of Acids and Bases on Eggs

| | Predicted Changes | Starting Measurements | 10 Minutes | 20 Minutes | 30 Minutes |
|---|---|---|---|---|---|
| Decalcified Egg in Water | | Length - mm<br>Width - mm<br>Circumf. - mm<br>Mass - g | Length - mm<br>Width - mm<br>Circumf. - mm<br>Mass - g | Length - mm<br>Width - mm<br>Circumf. - mm<br>Mass - g | Length - mm<br>Width - mm<br>Circumf. - mm<br>Mass - g |
| Decalcified Egg in Corn Syrup | | Length - mm<br>Width - mm<br>Circumf. - mm<br>Mass - g | Length - mm<br>Width - mm<br>Circumf. - mm<br>Mass - g | Length - mm<br>Width - mm<br>Circumf. - mm<br>Mass - g | Length - mm<br>Width - mm<br>Circumf. - mm<br>Mass - g |
| Normal Egg with Shell | | Length- mm<br>Width - mm<br>Circumf. - mm<br>Mass - g | Length - mm<br>Width - mm<br>Circumf. - mm<br>Mass - g | Length - mm<br>Width - mm<br>Circumf. - mm<br>Mass - g | Length - mm<br>Width - mm<br>Circumf. - mm<br>Mass - g |

How do you explain the changes in the eggs?

# Surveying Science and Mathematics on the Internet

## 🔘 Overview

Students explore the Internet for interesting science and mathematics Web sites. They will be guided by an activity sheet as they identify, summarize, analyze, reflect on, and compare sites on the Internet. After reviewing their sites, students will have an opportunity to present their findings to the class, providing the teacher with a chance to lead the class toward a deeper understanding of the Internet and what it can do for us. This is a valuable lesson for students whose very livelihoods may someday depend on their ability to navigate on-line information resources. Although the activity is geared toward grades 5 through 8, interested students in lower grades could readily undertake this Internet survey.

## 🔘 Concepts

Students practice their Internet search skills as they identify sites in science and mathematics.

## 🔘 Processes/Skills

- Describing
- Analyzing
- Concluding
- Inferring
- Inquiring
- Communicating

## 🔘 Recommended for

| | |
|---|---|
| K–2 | Individual ✔ |
| 3–5 ✔ | Small Group ✔ |
| 6–8 ✔ | Whole Class ✔ |

## 🔘 Time Required

1–2 hours

## 🔘 Materials Required

- Computer(s) with Internet connection

## 🔘 Standards

**SCIENCE**
- Abilities Necessary to Do Scientific Inquiry
- Science and Technology in Society

**MATH**
- Communication
- Connections

## 🔘 Objectives

- Students will successfully identify, summarize, analyze, and compare science-related and/or math-related Web sites on the Internet.

## 🔘 Background Information

Certainly, the key component in this activity is student access to the Internet. Students may gain access through computers in your classroom, the school computer lab, the school library, a public library, at home, or at the home of a friend, neighbor, or family member. The point is that an Internet connection must be made available to all class members. If computer access is limited, let students work on the project in groups, and/or carry out this activity on a contractual basis. That is, all students or groups won't be working on this activity at the same time; you can spread the assignment over a week, a month, or the entire semester. The activity also presupposes that your students have some experience in finding and using Web sites on the Internet.

Examples of appropriate Web sites for this activity include

- Whyville—www.whyville.net
- Escher Tessellations—www.WORLDOFEscher.com
- The Yuckiest Site in the Internet—www.nj.com/yucky/
- San Francisco Exploratorium—www.exploratorium.edu
- Dave's Math Tables—www.sisweb.com/math/tables.htm
- Dragonfly—www.muohio.edu/Dragonfly
- Egyptian Mummy—www.uke.uni-hamburg.de/virtualmummy
- Bamdad's Math Comics—www.csun.edu/~hcmth014/comics.html
- Bird Paintings—rmc.library.cornell.edu/ornithology/frames/exhibit.htm
- Satellite Images—fermi.jhuapl.edu/avhrr/gallery

## Main Activity, Step-by-Step

1. Ask the students what they know about the Internet. Has anyone ever used a math or science site? What was their purpose in locating the site? What did they find there?

   Explain to the class that this activity involves the Internet. Challenge students to identify, explore, analyze, and report on an Internet Web site that meets the following criteria:

   - It is related to science, mathematics, an integration of science and mathematics, an integration of science and some other school subject, or an integration of mathematics and some other school subject.
   - It is interesting to you.

2. Provide students or small student groups with sufficient time and computer access (see Background Information) to complete Activity Sheet 15. If students can undertake this activity on school computers, so much the better, because it provides you with an opportunity to observe, facilitate, and assess.

3. Once students have explored their Web sites and have completed their written reports, provide them with an opportunity to share their findings with the class. You can expand their analyses by asking, "Would you add anything to this site? Subtract anything? What questions do you have about the site you visited?" Allow students to share their excerpts and graphics in small groups, then lead them in a comparison of the various sites explored. How did the excerpts compare? How did the graphics compare? Which sites would students revisit? For older or more advanced students, you can ask more reflective questions, such as, "Who authored this site and how might their position bias their site's perspective?"

## Questions for Discussion

1. How did the various Web sites compare? How were they similar? How did they differ?
2. If you could reorganize the site that you visited, what would you change?
3. If you were going to start your own science/math Web site, what would you call it, what sort of information would it contain, and how would it look?

## Assessment

1. Were students able to successfully identify, summarize, analyze, and compare science-related and/or math-related Web sites? [embedded, performance, journal entries, portfolio]

## *Other Options and Extensions*

Try an Internet scavenger hunt. Students, working in teams or as individuals, are challenged to find as many of the following sites as possible. For each site, they must write a brief description and list the address. Sites to find (add more of your own ideas, too):

- site with information about butterflies
- site dealing with geometry
- site of your state's weather
- site with pictures of the moon
- site that tells you something about the abacus
- site with Uruguay's weather
- site dealing with mathematics in Africa
- site with information about bridges
- site containing data about rainforest research

## *Resources and Further Information*

Ebeneezer, J. V., & Lau, E. (1999). *Science on the Internet.* Upper Saddle River, NJ: Merrill.

O'Brien, G. E., & Lewis, S. P. (1999). Connecting to resources on the Internet. *Science and Children, 36* (8), 42–45.

## Activity Sheet 15. Surveying Science and Mathematics on the Internet

Name of Web site:
Site Internet Address:

Respond to the following:

1. What information is available at this site?

2. Why is the site important? Or, to whom might it be important?

3. Why did you choose this site? What interested you?

4. Is the site basically science, math, or a combination? Explain your answer.

5. Is there anything that you would change about this Web site, and if so, what?

6. Do you have any questions about the information presented in the site, or about the site itself? If so, list those questions here.

7. Choose an excerpt from the site that you find particularly interesting. Print it and attach it to this report. Why did you choose this particular excerpt?

8. Print out a graphic, graph, or table from the site that you find particularly interesting. Attach it to this report. Why did you choose this particular graphic?

9. Would you recommend this site to a friend? Why or why not?

# A One-Sided Paper Loop: The Möbius Band

## Overview

What can you make from a sheet of paper that has only one side, where inside equals outside? The answer is a Möbius band, of course, the one-sided paper loop. In this activity students in grades 3 through 8 will explore a mathematical conundrum: how do we determine the number of sides an object has, and how can it be that this object has only one side? Through guided discovery, your students will find their own answers, making this a great lesson to encourage the development of inquiry skills.

## Concepts

Students explore the design and properties of a Möbius band.

## Processes/Skills

- Observing
- Comparing
- Describing
- Predicting
- Sketching
- Communicating
- Constructing
- Recognizing shapes
- Analyzing
- Developing spatial reasoning
- Inquiring
- Creating
- Cooperating

## Recommended for

| K–2 | Individual |
| 3–5 ✔ | Small Group ✔ |
| 6–8 ✔ | Whole Class |

## Time Required

1–2 hours

## Materials Required

**MAIN ACTIVITY**

- Strips of newspaper
- Glue sticks
- Scissors
- Marking pens

**CONNECTING ACTIVITY**

- Butcher paper
- Art (painting and/or drawing) supplies
- Marking pens

## Standards

**SCIENCE**

- Abilities Necessary to Do Scientific Inquiry
- Understanding About Scientific Inquiry

**MATH**

- Problem Solving
- Reasoning and Proof
- Communication
- Geometry

## Objectives

- Students will decide how to determine whether a paper loop has one or two sides.
- Students will construct and explore the properties of a Möbius band.

## O  Background Information

It is true; the Möbius band, named after its inventor, German mathematician August Ferdinand Möbius, has only one side. It also has only one edge, and is known as a "nonorientable surface" in mathematical terminology. B. F. Goodrich patented conveyor belts in the shape of Möbius bands long ago because the belts will last twice as long. Such belts are still commonly used in industry. The Möbius band has also served as a model for high performance, nonreactive electronic resistors. Interestingly, the chemical compound tetrahydroxymethylethylene, discovered in 1983, naturally takes the shape of a Möbius band.

## Main Activity, Step-by-Step

1. Show the students a typical sheet of newspaper. Ask, "How many sides does this piece of paper have?" Two, of course, is the expected answer. Next, cut a strip (about 5 cm wide) from the sheet of newspaper. Ask again, "How many sides does this piece of paper have?" Two, again. Cut another strip and glue the ends together, making a simple loop. Ask, "How many sides does the loop have?" Then ask, "*How do you know* how many sides the loop has?" Give each student group a loop to observe and handle, and allow them time to discuss and respond. Record student responses. Ask, "If a paper has two sides, and I want to make a continuous line with my marker on both, what do I have to do with the marker?" Help them see that you must *pick up the marker* at some point. Have them try this in their groups, first with a flat sheet of paper, and then with the loop. Do they agree that the "lift the marker" test works to determine two sides?

2. At this point the students will really begin to wonder what you're up to, so what better time to throw in a little twist? In sight of the students, cut another strip from the newspaper and make a loop, but turn one end so that the top faces down before gluing. That is, put a twist into the loop. Ask once again, "How many sides does the loop have?" Students are likely to respond, "two." Ask, "How can we test for number of sides? Let's try the pick-up-the-marker test. What do you think will happen?" Record their responses. Now demonstrate the pick-up-the-marker test (an extra pair of hands will be helpful here). Students will be surprised when you never have to lift the marker to make a continuous line on what appear to be two sides of the loop. Ask students for their reactions to this demonstration. Explain that this special loop is called a Möbius band, after its inventor, August Möbius, a 19th-century German astronomer and mathematician.

3. Let each group make several Möbius bands of their own. The activity will proceed more smoothly if you have the strips (newspaper or butcher paper) precut. For younger students, you should construct the Möbius bands for them ahead of time, or at least assist them in the construction of the bands. Encourage students to "explore" the band and to try the pick-up the-marker (or pencil) test themselves. Is this what they would have expected? How do they explain this phenomenon?

4. Now return to your original Möbius band with the continuous line down the middle, used in step 2 above. Ask, "What do you think will happen if I take my scissors and cut along the line that I drew on this band?" Record student responses, then try it out. What happens? A loop with a double twist in it! Ask, "How many sides does this loop have? How can we find out?" Hopefully, students will suggest the pick-up-the-marker test, which you can try. Oops, two sides. Let the students try this, too, with their own Möbius bands.

5. Referring to your double-twist loop constructed in procedure 4, you can ask about the possible outcomes, facilitating a range of options: "What will happen if I cut along the line I drew on this loop? What are some possibilities? One simple loop? A simple loop with a double twist? With a triple twist? A Möbius band? Two Möbius bands? A double loop? Any other possibilities that you can think of?" Record their responses and try it. Interlocking, twisted loops! Is either of these loops a Möbius band? *How do you know?*

## Questions for Discussion

1. How can you explain the fact that the Möbius band has only one side? Can you think of any other objects or shapes that have only one side?

2. How might a belt shaped like a Möbius band be more practical than a simple loop in a belt-driven machine? (Both sides wear out evenly, as opposed to one side only, thus lengthening the life of the belt and saving money.)

3. How is a cycle (such as the yearly seasons or a plant's life cycle) like a Möbius band? How do they differ?

## Assessment

1. Could students determine that, while a simple loop has two sides, the Möbius band has only one? [embedded, performance]

2. Were students able to test and explore their own Möbius bands? [embedded, performance]

3. Did they enjoy the activity?

## Connecting Activity

For an art and science connection, you can construct larger Möbius bands using strips of white butcher paper, approximately 25 cm wide and 1.5 m long. This activity can be undertaken by students working in groups, in pairs, or individually. Ask the students to name some things that occur in time "loops," such as the seasons, the water cycle, the carbon cycle, or a plant or animal's life cycle. Ask them to choose one such cycle, and illustrate it with a series of drawings or paintings on their large Möbius band. They'll have to consider the number and width of their illustrations in order to have a good fit on the continuous loop. This project can be done in pastels, watercolor, or any other available, colorful materials. The completed cycle illustrations can be displayed by hanging them from the ceiling or by attaching them to a bulletin board.

## Other Options and Extensions

1. Ask students to go home and demonstrate the amazing properties of the Möbius band to their families. Then ask them to brainstorm, again with family members, some more practical applications of the band. They may want to interview other adults to come up with ideas. Share the ideas in class and determine which are most useful, most practical, most innovative, and most artistic. Which applications have the most to do with math? With science? With art? With some combination of math, science, and/or art?

2. Encourage students to research the life and work of August Möbius. What sort of man was he? How did he feel about his discovery/invention?

## Resources and Further Information

Curran-Everett, D. (1997). The Möbius band: An unusual vehicle for science exploration. *Science and Children, 34*(4), 22–25.

Fleron, J. (1999). The Möbius metaphor. *Humanistic Mathematics Network Journal, 19,* 38.

Richardson, L. I. (1976). The Möbius strip: An elementary exercise providing hypotheses formation and perceptual proof. *The Arithmetic Teacher, 23,* 127–129.

# Learning About Levers

 ## Overview

We see, use, and enjoy levers daily: in the operation of pliers, the action of a seesaw, or the beauty of an Alexander Calder mobile. In fact, parts of us are levers—think of the knee, elbow, and other joints as fulcrums and the long bones as levers. In this activity, student groups will expand their understanding of levers and balance by discovering how weight and fulcrum placement affect lever performance. As a connecting activity, the students will apply what they learn about levers into the creation of dynamic science- or mathematics-related mobiles.

 ## Concepts

Students discover the basic properties of levers, including the notion that their operation is predictable and measurable. Investigators will also find that dynamic balance, or equilibrium, may be achieved in many ways.

## Processes/Skills

- Observing
- Measuring
- Describing
- Comparing
- Designing investigations
- Communicating
- Inferring
- Analyzing
- Collecting data
- Drawing conclusions from data
- Problem solving
- Recognizing patterns
- Appreciating
- Cooperating

- Applying
- Creating
- Reflecting
- Enjoying

 ## Recommended for

| K–2 | | Individual | |
|---|---|---|---|
| 3–5 | ✔ | Small Group | ✔ |
| 6–8 | ✔ | Whole Class | |

## Time Required

1–3 hours

## Materials Required

**MAIN ACTIVITY**

- Meter sticks
- Cardboard fulcrums (see Figure 17–1)
- Any sort of small, uniformly shaped weights (coins, gram weights, fishing weights, etc.)
- Masking tape
- Cord/string

**CONNECTING ACTIVITY**

- Cord, string, and/or fishing line
- Lightweight levers for the mobile (drinking straws, bamboo shish kabob skewers, dowels, sticks or branches, or sturdy wire such as cut up clothes hangers, etc.)
- Tape
- A variety of materials to act as weights (cardboard cutout, shells, leaves, feathers, aluminum foil shapes, old electronic components, etc.)
- Various art materials (paint, paste or glue, etc.)

## ◐ *Standards*

**SCIENCE**

- Abilities Necessary to Do Scientific Inquiry
- Understanding About Scientific Inquiry
- Position and Motion of Objects
- Motions and Forces

**MATH**

- Problem Solving
- Reasoning and Proof
- Connections
- Measurement
- Algebra

## ◐ *Objectives*

- Students will balance their levers in different ways, and will be able to explain their techniques.

- Students will deepen their understanding of levers and balance, including identification of the fulcrum, and will be able to identify levers in the classroom and in their lives.

- Students will determine the mathematical relationship between the location of the fulcrum and the distance the weight must be placed from the fulcrum to make the lever balance.

- Students will use the lever concept to build creative science/math mobiles.

## *Main Activity, Step-by-Step*

1. Demonstrate the following for the class: balance a meter stick on your horizontally held index finger. In this case, your finger (acting as the *fulcrum,* or balance point) will be at the 50-cm mark. You could also use a cardboard fulcrum: a piece of sturdy cardboard bent and taped into a "tent" or wedge shape (see Figure 17–1) and set on a desk or table. Ask, "What will happen to this 'system' if I move my finger (or the cardboard fulcrum) to the 40-cm mark?" Entertain hypotheses, then demonstrate the result. Ask students, working in small groups, to explain why the stick didn't fall when the fulcrum was at 50 cm, but it did when the fulcrum was shifted to the 40-cm mark. The responses will probably include the notions that in the first case, the stick was balanced, but it was unbalanced in the second case. Ask, "What do you mean by 'balanced'?" Students should clarify their thinking on this point. Point out that a balanced system can be said to be at *equilibrium.* Inform students that the meter stick is acting as a *lever.* Where else do we find levers? (Seesaw, pry bar, catapult, long bones of the body, scales, etc.)

2. Next, give each student group a set of weights, a meter stick, and a cardboard fulcrum. Ask them to balance the stick on the fulcrum. Now, *without changing the balance point* of the stick (that is, keeping the 50-cm mark at the fulcrum) ask them to tape a small weight (e.g., five pennies, five grams, one fishing weight) on top of one end of the meter stick (see Figure 17–2). Does the stick balance? (No.) Ask, "What can you do to make the stick balance again, *without moving the weight?*" Let the student groups puzzle over this and come up with their own solutions to the problem. You might mention that although they can't move or remove the weights, they can move the stick and they can add weights to the stick. Challenge them to devise as many solutions as they

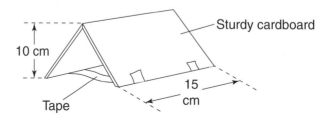

**Figure 17–1.**   Fulcrum

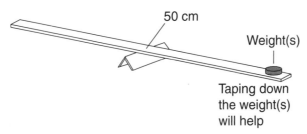

**Figure 17–2.** Unbalanced lever

can, try them out, and record (in words, drawings, and numbers) their ideas under question 1 on Activity Sheet 17. As a class, discuss their explorations: What worked and what didn't? What did they think would work that didn't and why didn't it? What patterns do they see in the successful solutions? (The obvious solution may be to simply place an equal weight at the other end of the lever. But how was balance maintained if the balance point was changed, or if more weight was added to the original end of the lever?) What did students discover about levers and balance?

3. Remove all weights from the lever, and move the fulcrum to the 45-cm mark. Does the lever balance? (No.) Challenge the student groups to find as many ways as possible to make the lever balance, *without moving the fulcrum* from the 45-cm mark. Try using only one weight. Two weights. Three weights. Again, they must keep a written record of their attempts (Activity Sheet 17, question 2), whether successful or not. After allowing sufficient time for exploration, discuss and analyze the results as a group. What worked? What didn't? Why or why not? What combinations of weights did you try? Do you notice any patterns? What have you learned about levers? What more do you want to know about levers?

4. The next step in this investigation is to collect numerical data about how the lever operates. Using the Figure 17–3 as a guide, have student groups determine the relationship between the location of the fulcrum and the distance the weight must be placed from the fulcrum to make the lever balance. Using the meter sticks and a single weight (the weight will vary depending on the sort of meter stick and the type of weights being used; experiment here, then use the same weight throughout the procedure), start with the fulcrum at the 45-cm point on the meter stick, and determine the distance from the fulcrum to the weight to make the lever balance. Record that distance in the table, question 3, on Activity Sheet 17. Next, move the fulcrum to the 40-cm mark, and again determine and record the distance from fulcrum to weight when balanced. Repeat, moving the fulcrum to the 35-, 30-, 25-, and 20-cm marks, each time recording the weight's distance from the fulcrum when balanced. What do the results tell you about levers? Based on your research, please complete the following statement: "To balance the lever as the fulcrum is moved farther from the center, the weight must _____."

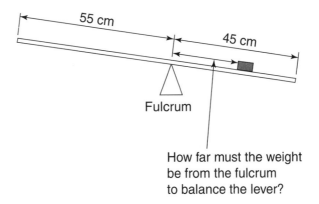

**Figure 17–3.** Distance from fulcrum

5. For the next portion of this lesson each student group will need to have access to a dangling piece of cord. This can be accomplished by running several horizontal "clotheslines" for support at a 5- or 6-foot height across the classroom and hanging the cords from those—or use whatever means available (e.g., taped or tied to top of doorway or ceiling). Direct the groups to then tie that string to the middle of a lightweight horizontal beam (e.g., drinking straw, sturdy wire, bamboo shish kabob skewer, etc.) so that it hangs evenly. Ask the students if this balancing horizontal beam reminds them of anything. That horizontal piece is actually a lever, although it is "upside down" compared to our earlier levers. The string by which it hangs is the fulcrum. Next, have them tie or tape a short string to each of two small but unequal weights (e.g., a penny and a nickel), and tie the other end of each string to either end of the horizontal lever. By sliding the weights on the lever, they can try to balance it again. How is this lever like the levers used earlier? How is it different? How were you able to make it balance?

## Questions for Discussion

1. What is meant by "balance"? How were you able to make your lever balance?
2. What have you discovered about levers?
3. What does a mobile have to do with levers?
4. Why do you think it's called a "mobile"?

## Assessment

1. Were students able to balance their levers in different ways and explain their techniques? [embedded, performance, journal entries]
2. Could they identify the fulcrum in each case? [embedded]
3. Did students deepen their understanding of levers and balance? Were they able to identify levers in the classroom and other areas of their lives? [embedded, journal entries]
4. Were students able to determine the mathematical relationship between the location of the fulcrum and the distance the weight must be placed from the fulcrum to make the lever balance (procedure #4)? [performance, embedded]
5. Did they use the lever concept to build creative science/math mobiles? [performance]

## Connecting Activity

Have students use the "upside down" lever idea (see procedure #5) to construct their own mobiles. Pick a science or mathematics theme (geometry, repeating number patterns, found objects from nature, planets, atomic structure, rain, organs of the body, electronics, endangered species, plant anatomy, etc.). Get some sticks, wires, driftwood, or other "lever" crosspiece and some string or fishing line. Also, students can help to compile objects related to their topic, such as shapes cut out of cardboard, photos pasted onto cardboard or other substances, shells, feathers, leaves, yarn bubbles (saturate yarn with paste, wrap it around a small balloon, allow yarn to dry, pop and remove balloon), crumpled aluminum foil, toothpick sculptures, papier-mâché shapes, or electronic components taken from that broken phone answering machine you've been meaning to throw away. The sky is the limit. Tie the objects onto each end of the levers, balancing each lever by moving the "weights" closer to or farther from the fulcrum (i.e., the supporting string). For older students with well-developed motor skills, try to make at least a three- or four-layer mobile (see Figure 17–4). For younger students, two or three layers will suffice. Encourage imagination. Consider making the levers of different lengths, or of tying another lever onto one end of a lever, or tying more than two objects onto a single lever. In fact,

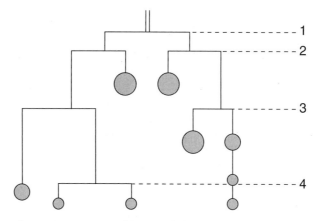

**Figure 17–4.**    Four-layer mobile

does the mobile lever have to be perfectly straight or could it be a curved wire? What other shapes would work? Does the lever have to be perfectly horizontal? How else could it be oriented? Allow each student or student group to explain their mobile to the class.

## Other Options and Extensions

1.  Find levers in use at school, at home, around the neighborhood, or on television. Make a list of levers that you find. Compare them. Categorize them by their operation, their size, their shape. Compare your findings with those of other students.

2.  Find an adult who uses levers in her or his work. What kind of levers do they use? How are the levers used? How would their job be different without levers?

3.  Investigate the art of Alexander Calder.

## Resources and Further Information

Cross, B. (1992). a balancing feat. *Science and Children, 29* (7), 16–17.

Kirkwood, J. J. (1994). Simple machines simply put. *Science and Children, 31* (7), 15–17, 40–41.

Streitberger, H. E. (1978). Levers have we got levers. *Science and Children, 16* (3), 9–12.

Williams, D. (1995). *Teaching mathematics through children's art.* Portsmouth, NH: Heineman.

## Activity Sheet 17. Learning About Levers

1. Find and list as many ways as possible to make the lever balance *without moving or removing the taped weight.*

2. Find and list as many ways as possible to make the lever balance *without moving the fulcrum* from the 45-cm mark.

3. Determine the mathematical relationship between the location of the fulcrum and distance the weight must be placed from the fulcrum to make the lever balance by collecting data.

| *Location of Fulcrum* | *Distance From Weight to Fulcrum* |
|---|---|
| 45 cm | cm |
| 40 cm | cm |
| 35 cm | cm |
| 30 cm | cm |
| 25 cm | cm |
| 20 cm | cm |

To balance the lever as the fulcrum moved father from the center, the weight must

_____

_____

_____ .

# Experimenting With Force and Motion Using Origami Frogs

##  Overview

Objects in motion and the forces that move them are the subjects of this lesson. This is a practical series of activities that will offer your students a dynamic understanding of Newton's three laws of motion. In particular, the third law is investigated as students measure and analyze the jumping abilities of origami frogs. The activities are designed for older grades, but would be appropriate for younger students by simplifying the terminology and the mathematical analysis.

##  Concepts

Students focus on Newton's laws of motion, especially the third law, as they collect, compare, and analyze origami jumping frog data. The concept of experimental "variables" is also examined.

## Processes/Skills

- Observing
- Comparing
- Describing
- Making conclusions
- Experimenting
- Identifying patterns
- Predicting
- Constructing
- Measuring
- Applying
- Communicating
- Problem solving
- Developing spatial reasoning
- Inquiring
- Reflecting

- Creating
- Cooperating

## Recommended for

| | |
|---|---|
| K–2 | Individual ✔ |
| 3–5 ✔ | Small Group ✔ |
| 6–8 ✔ | Whole Class |

## Time Required

2–3 hours

## Materials Required

**PRELIMINARY ACTIVITY**

- Rubber ball
- Index card
- Cup or glass
- Quarter
- Spring

**MAIN ACTIVITY**

- Paper (various sizes and weights, including plenty of standard 8.5" × 11" photocopy paper
- Scissors
- Meter sticks
- Calculators
- Graph paper

**CONNECTING ACTIVITY**

- Various art supplies for decorating frogs

## ◉ Standards

**SCIENCE**

- Abilities Necessary to Do Scientific Inquiry
- Understanding About Scientific Inquiry
- Position and Motion of Objects
- Motions and Forces

**MATH**

- Reasoning and Proof
- Communication
- Numbers and Operations
- Measurement

## ◉ Objectives

- Students will construct, test, and graphically compare the jumps made by the three sizes of frogs.
- Students will be able to successfully predict how far a fourth frog would be expected to jump.

- Students will identify and test variables that affect frog jumping ability.

## ◉ Background Information

Newton's three laws of motion may be stated in the following way:

- Law 1—Every object continues in its state of rest or of uniform motion, unless acted on by a force applied from the outside.
- Law 2—Change of motion is proportional to the applied force and takes place in the direction in which the force acts.
- Law 3—Whenever one object exerts a force on a second object, the second exerts an equal and opposite force on the first.

It will be helpful to have the three laws of motion written out on the chalkboard or on an overhead transparency as you proceed with this lesson.

## *Preliminary Activity*

1. Set a rubber ball on a desk. Ask, "What forces are acting on the ball?" If students respond, "None," point out that, surely, gravity acts on the ball because it isn't floating away. "Yes," they must agree. Yet, if gravity is acting on the ball, why doesn't it fall to the ground? (The desk stops it.) Is the desk providing an upward force that counteracts the downward force of gravity? Yes. Express this relationship on the chalkboard as a simple diagram (Figure 18–1). Explain that the ball is not moving because the forces are in balance. We could say that the ball is at rest or is in a state of *equilibrium*. Why does the ball stay at rest? (Because the forces acting on it are in balance.) Which of Newton's laws of motion do we see demonstrated here? Allow students time to work in groups to try to determine a response. (Law 1, because the ball remains at rest.)

2. Next, place an index card over an empty glass. Place a quarter on top of the card (see Figure 18–2). Ask students to predict what will happen to the quarter when you flick the card (in a direction parallel to the table top) away from the cup. Ask, "What could the quarter *possibly* do when I flick the card?" (It could go flying along with the card, it could fall into the cup, etc.; encourage divergent answers). Now flick the card. The quarter will fall straight down into to cup. Ask students to explain why this happened, giving them a few minutes in groups to work out an explanation. What forces had been acting on the quarter? (Gravity pushes down and the card pushes up.) When the card was removed, though, only gravity was acting on the quarter, and it was forced to drop straight down. You can let students try this themselves in their groups with a cup, an index card, and a quarter. Which of Newton's laws of motion do we see demonstrated in this activity? Again, allow students time to work in groups to try to determine a response. (Laws 1 and 2, because the coin remained at rest until the card was quickly removed, allowing the force of gravity to act on it, pulling it down.)

3. Hold the rubber ball in your hand at about shoulder height. Which law(s) of motion are being demonstrated? (Law 1, because the ball continues in its state of rest.) Then ask, "What will happen

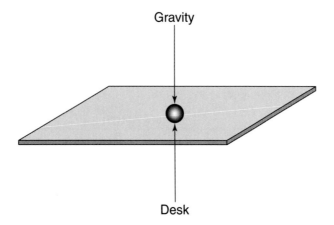

**Figure 18–1.** Gravity pushes down. Desk pushes up.

to the ball if I let it go?" Likely response: it will fall. Will anything else happen to the ball? Wait for responses. Demonstrate by letting the ball go. Which law(s) of motion does the falling ball demonstrate? (Law 2, because by releasing the ball we allowed gravity to act on it.) Are students getting the idea? Are you waiting a few seconds after asking your questions to allow more students to consider the information and to come up with answers? Now bounce the rubber ball on the floor. What forces are acting on the ball? (The force of your throw and the force of gravity.) Why does it bounce back? (The falling ball exerts a force on the floor, but the floor also exerts a force back on the ball.) Which of Newton's laws of motion do we see demonstrated in this activity? Again, allow students time to work in groups to try to determine a response. (In the bouncing ball, we see a demonstration of all of the laws of motion. The first, because the motionless ball is placed in motion by the forces acting on it—by the force of the throw and the force of gravity. The second, because the ball's motion is in the direction in which the forces—throwing and gravity—act, and is in proportion to the strength of those forces, i.e., the harder you throw, the more significant the change of motion of the ball. Newton's third law is also demonstrated, because the first object, the ball, exerts a force on a second object, the floor, which exerts an equal and opposite force on the first, shown by the ball bouncing back away from the floor.)

You can also demonstrate the third law by standing on a skateboard or on roller skates and pushing against a wall. You push into the wall, but you roll back away from the wall. You can even show this by just standing still and pushing on the wall, but it's more dramatic with the wheels underneath you. Another way that the third law is sometimes stated is that "for every action there is an equal and opposite reaction."

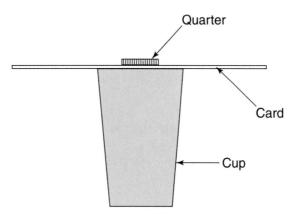

**Figure 18–2.** Quarter and index card on empty cup.

4.  Compress a spring against a desk or other flat surface and then release it, after asking students to predict what will happen. What did happen? How can the spring's motion be explained? Are any of Newton's laws of motion at work here? What forces are acting on the spring? (The spring demonstrates all laws, but especially Newton's third law of motion: as it pushes into the desk, the desk pushes back, sending it flying into the air, away from the desk.) This demonstration allows you to check for student comprehension before proceeding with the main activity.

## Main Activity, Step-by-Step

1.  Show students an origami frog that you've constructed (see Figure 18–3). Explain that origami is the Japanese art of paper folding. To make the frog hop, press down with your finger in the middle of its back at the edge, and let your finger slip off. This should provide the frog with a springing motion. Show them how it jumps, and they'll be anxious to build their own. Let them work in groups, but have each student build her/his own jumping frog according to the diagram (Figure 18-3), using standard-sized notebook or photocopy paper (8.5 × 11 inches—constructing the frog from a 217 mm, or 8.5 inch, square). With younger students, it might be easier to lead them through the folding process, step-by-step. Give students some time to just "play" with their frogs, trying to make them jump well (high and/or far). Ask what techniques seem to work to make the frogs jump well? Encourage divergent responses. Next, show the students a small and a medium-sized frog that you have constructed. Ask, "Which of these frogs do you think will jump the

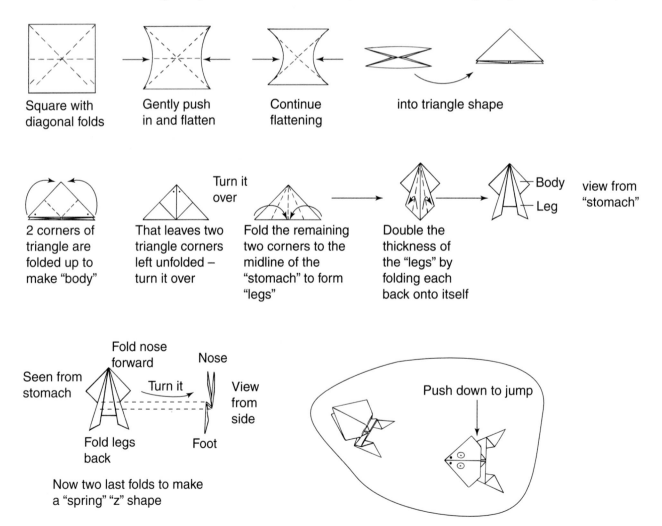

**Figure 18–3.**   Constructing the origami frog

farthest? How could we find out?" Pass out copies of Activity Sheet 18 and have students complete the "Predictions" portion. Allow the students to make two more frogs (from the same sort of paper as the first), one from a square that is 63 mm wide, and another from a square that is 140 mm wide.

2. At this point, all students should have a "frog family": a large frog, a middle-sized frog, and a small frog. They're now ready to test the frogs for their distance jumping abilities. Using meter sticks and working in groups, they should record three good jumps per frog on Activity Sheet 18. Students can then calculate the average jump distance for each of the three frogs. They can also plot a graph of the frog jumps using the three averages (frog size on the x axis in mm, and jump length on the y axis in cm). How did their predictions stack up? Did frog size have an effect on jumping distance? Why or why not? Were they surprised by the outcome? Would the winning frog actually win *every* contest (if the contest is based on a single jump) or would it *tend to win most* of the contests, i.e., are the jumps consistent in their distances? What did they learn from the frog-jumping activity? What does this activity have to do with Newton's laws of motion? (The folded frog acts like a compressed spring—when released it hops, demonstrating Newton's third law of motion.) Based on the graph of the three average jump lengths, how far can a fourth frog (built from another 180 mm wide square of the same paper) be expected to jump? Record predictions, ask for rationale for those predictions (written or oral), build the fourth frog and find out. Then ask for an explanation of the results.

3. Introduce the concept of *variables* by asking the students to name things that have an effect on the frog's jumping ability, such as paper used or origami design. Variables are aspects of the frog (such as its size), or characteristics of the frog's environment (such as the surface on which it is placed) that may be changed and that may have an effect on the frog's ability to jump. Ask the class to brainstorm all the variables they can think of that may have an effect on the frog's distance jumping ability. These may include the frog's design, it's size, the type of paper used, added weight such as a paper clip, the method of making it jump, and so on. Encourage divergent thinking here, even if you believe that the student's variable won't affect jumping ability (such as the color of the frog). Next, instruct each group to choose one variable and to explore its effect on the distance jumping ability of the origami frog. They should do this by varying that chosen variable and recording the results. For instance, one group could make several different frogs each out of a different kind of paper. They would then record several jumps from each frog and calculate the averages, which should indicate which paper worked best. Be sure that students understand that only one variable is varied at a time, or else the results will be inconclusive. That is, if they vary the paper *and* the size at the same time, they won't know whether it was the paper or the size change that was responsible for any differences in jump length. If paper is the variable to be tested, all other variables (size, design, etc.) must be held constant. Although this can be a slippery concept for elementary students, it is easiest for them to understand in relation to their own experiments. You can point out in a concrete way the need for changing only one variable at a time if you refer to the experiments and explorations that they are in the process of conducting. For example, as you circulate about the room and observe the group testing "paper type," ask "What would happen if you varied the size of the frog at the same time you varied the type of paper used?" Continue with this line of inquiry, as necessary, referring to their own frogs. When their research is complete, each group can report its findings to the class. How do they explain their findings? For example, if paper type seemed to matter, how can this finding be explained?

## Questions for Discussion

1. How is the paper frog similar to a real frog? How is it different?

2. Which of Newton's laws of motion do you think you encounter most often in everyday life? Explain.

3. Can you think of any forms of transportation that use or demonstrate Newton's laws of motion? Can you think of any that do not?

4. Why do real frogs jump? Why would a real frog who can jump far or accurately have a survival advantage over frogs who can't jump as well? Think of as many reasons as you can.

## Assessment

1. Were students able to construct, test, and graphically compare the jumps made by the three frogs in their "frog family"? [embedded, performance]

2. After test jumping their three frogs, were students able to predict how far a fourth frog (built from another 180 mm wide square of the same paper) would be expected to jump, based on their graph of the three average jump lengths? [performance]

3. Were students able to successfully identify and test variables that affected frog jumping ability?

## Connecting Activity

At any point in the frog activities students can decorate their origami frogs in any number of ways. Make a beautiful frog, a scary frog, a camouflaged frog (one that lives in a rainforest or one that lives in a desert pond), a happy frog, a confident frog, or a shy frog. Encourage divergent and creative thinking. Some frogs are poisonous (poison arrow frogs, genus *Dendrobates,* from tropical Central and South America); if they want predators to know that they are dangerous, should they be dull or brightly colored? (See if students can find a picture of a poison arrow frog to check their predictions—they are very brightly colored to alert potential predators.) Ask students to decorate a frog for life in a specific habitat (such as rainforest, desert pond, large lake, small pond, weedy pond, tree, mountain lake) and to explain in a journal writing assignment why it looks as it does. Students can show and tell about their decorated frogs. Encourage divergent and innovative thinking.

## Other Options and Extensions

1. Challenge the class to use what they know about distance jumping to produce the longest-jumping frog possible. Hold a class competition to see which group can build the longest-jumping frog. Have several different sorts of paper, paper clips, brads, and so forth on hand, as well as plenty of tools (rulers, meter sticks, paper punches, compasses, etc.). Was the winning frog the one they would have predicted as the best jumper? Why or why not?

   Hold other sorts of frog-jumping competitions: the frog that jumps highest, the most accurate jumper (from lily pad A to lily pad B), the biggest jumper, the smallest hopper, etc. If you opt to eschew classroom competition in favor of a cooperative effort, each student group could explore a different aspect of frog hopping, after which the class could demonstrate and discuss froggy abilities in a "frog-hopping exposition."

2. Read "The Notorious Jumping Frog of Calaveras County" by Mark Twain.

## Resources and Further Information

Dana, T. M., Perkins, R., Ledford, K., & St. Pierre, M. (1993). Fun-filled physics. *Science and Children, 30* (7), 28–31.

Meyer, K. J. (1993). Folding frogs. *Science and Children, 30* (5), 12–14.

Needham, K. (1992). *The Usborne book of origami.* London: Usborne.

## Activity Sheet 18. Experimenting With Force and Motion Using Origami Frogs

1. Prediction: Which frog will jump the farthest, on average? (Circle one)

   Large Frog        Medium Frog        Small Frog

   Why do you think so?

2. Prediction: Which frog will jump the shortest distance, on average? (Circle one)

   Large Frog        Medium Frog        Small Frog

   Why do you think so?

3. Data collection:

| Frog | Frog Width (mm) | Frog Length (mm) | Jump Distance #1 (cm) | Jump Distance #2 (cm) | Jump Distance #3 (cm) | Average Jump Distance (cm) |
|------|------|------|------|------|------|------|
| Large | | | | | | |
| Medium | | | | | | |
| Small | | | | | | |

4. Analysis: Were your predictions accurate? Why or why not?

5. Analysis: Was the frog with the largest average jump distance also the frog that had the single longest jump? How do you explain this?

6. Analysis: Graph your data, with frog length on the x axis and average jump length for each frog on the y axis.

7. Conclusions: Based on your experiment, data, and analysis, what have you learned about the jumping origami frogs? Does frog size have an effect on jumping ability? How do you know?

8. Further study: What other factors can you think of that will affect an origami frog's jumping ability?

9. Further study: Based on your graph, how far can a fourth frog (built from a 180 mm wide square of the same paper) be expected to jump? (Be sure to record your procedure, data, and results below.)

# What Makes a Boat Float?

## Overview

Whether or not a boat floats is determined by its shape and its density. In this activity, fashioned to be adaptable to all grades in the K–8 range, students discover how and why boats float by designing different hull shapes and finding which design can hold the most weight. They will record, calculate, and interpret data as they learn about buoyancy in this very hands-on activity.

## Concepts

Students investigate floating, displacement, density, mass, volume, graphing, calculating, areas, and averages by designing boat shapes.

## Processes/Skills

- Observing
- Problem solving
- Predicting
- Describing
- Analyzing
- Concluding
- Measuring
- Calculating
- Inquiring
- Communicating
- Recognizing shapes and patterns
- Developing spatial sense
- Cooperating

## Recommended for

K–2 ✔     Individual

3–5 ✔     Small Group ✔

6–8 ✔     Whole Class

## Time Required

1–3 hours

## Materials Required

**PRELIMINARY ACTIVITY**

- Aluminum foil
- Small tub of water

**MAIN ACTIVITY**

- Aluminum foil
- Small tubs of water
- Small weights (pennies, metric weights, metal washers, or any small, standardized objects)
- Metric rulers
- Calculators
- Graph paper

## Standards

**SCIENCE**

- Properties of Objects and Materials
- Properties and Changes in Matter

- Abilities of Technological Design

- Understanding About Science and Technology

**MATH**

- Problem Solving

- Connections

- Numbers and Operations

- Geometry

- Representation

## ⦿ *Objectives*

- Students will design and build boats to carry loads and will be able to explain why some designs worked better than others.

- Students will be able to explain why a boat floats, using their own data and the concepts of displacement, density, mass, and volume.

## ⦿ *Background Information*

What makes a boat float? Two factors, density and shape, determine whether an object will float or sink. The first factor, *density*, is the relative weight of an object, defined mathematically as the object's *mass* divided by *volume*. A more dense object or material has more tightly packed internal particles. A brick, for instance, is more dense (that is, has more tightly packed particles within it) than a piece of wood (whose particles are more loosely packed). A brick is more dense than water, and it will sink. Most wood, however, is less dense than water, allowing it to float. Therefore, it is not an object's weight alone that determines whether it will sink or float; it is the object's weight (really its mass) divided by its volume. Consider a really large piece of styrofoam (say, 500 kg): it will float in water despite its large mass because it is less dense than the water. That is, it has less mass per unit of volume than water, or put another way, if we have two equal volumes (say, 250 cm$^3$) of styrofoam and of water, the styrofoam will be lighter in weight (or contain less mass). The styrofoam is less dense than the water and therefore it will float. Density is related to *buoyancy*, which can be thought of as the tendency of an object to float in a liquid, or as the upthrust that the liquid exerts on an object floating within it. Dense materials are not very buoyant, and buoyant materials are not very dense.

The other factor that determines sinking or floating, is *shape*. The shape of an object, like a boat, allows it to push water out of the way, which is referred to as *displacement* of the water. If a boat, and the air contained in it, displace more water than the weight of the boat itself, it will float. Large boats and/or heavy boats, therefore, must displace a great deal of water. If the boat displaces less water than the weight of the boat itself, it will sink. The shape of the boat, then, is crucial in determining how much weight the boat can carry and whether the boat will float (as demonstrated in the following activity). You could say that a boat's shape strongly influences its buoyancy, or that a boat's buoyancy is determined by that boat's density and shape.

## *Preliminary Activity*

Begin by showing students a small, flat piece of foil. Bend it into a very roughly shaped boat. Ask, will it float? Then try it. It floats. Next, crumple it into a tight ball. Will the ball float (after all, it's the same foil)? Try it. It sinks. Ask students to conclude what they can about floating and sinking in this situation. Give them a moment in groups to discuss and then listen to their ideas. Obviously the shape matters. Does the boat's size matter? Demonstrate that we can double or triple the size of the foil and it still will float if boat-shaped, but will sink if in a ball shape. The boat's shape matters, apparently more than its size.

## *Main Activity, Step-by-Step*

1. Now try an exercise to challenge your students. Each student group receives three 15 × 15 cm pieces of aluminum foil, a pile of pennies, and a small tub of water (you can substitute metric weights, metal washers, or any small, standardized objects for the pennies). The challenge: Shaping boats any way that you choose, you must design a boat that can float as many pennies as possible. Each boat has to float with its load of pennies for at least 5 seconds for the trial to count. Brainstorm before beginning the activity: What boat shapes are possible? They must try at least

three different boat shapes, predicting how many pennies each will hold before loading it up. Then each group runs three trials with each of the three boats and records data in a table (see Activity Sheet 19, problem 1). In the table they briefly describe each of three boat shapes (younger students could draw a picture of each boat rather than describe in words) that they tried, list how many pennies each shape held in each trial, and average the trials for each boat. Finally, groups record and discuss their conclusions.

2. In the next exercise, student groups will discover whether the area of the base of the boat is related to the number of pennies that it will hold. Using three more 15 × 15 cm sheets of foil, groups perform three trials with each of three boat designs again (designs should include low, flat boats and tall, slim boats), this time recording the area of boat base (i.e., the bottom of the hull) versus the maximum number of pennies held in each trial. Hull area can be determined using metric rulers, calculators, and area formulas ($\pi r^2$ for generally circular hulls, and length × width for generally rectangular hulls). Predictions and data can be recorded on Activity Sheet 19, problem 2. Students can then graph the area of the base of each boat (x axis) versus the number of pennies that it held (y axis). They should look for patterns in the data and the graph, and document their conclusions. (Generally, the wider the hull, the more weight the boat can handle without sinking, because the load is spread over a wider area).

3. Finally, hold an open competition for the boat design that can hold the greatest number of pennies. Student groups design and construct their best boat, using what they've learned in the lesson so far. Test all boats in a classwide demonstration to determine the winner. Students can then write their observations, thoughts, reactions, conclusions, and questions in their science journals.

## Questions for Discussion

1. With your boat, did the height of the sides matter? Why? In a real boat, would the height of the sides matter? Why?

2. What kinds of boats have wide flat bottoms (or hulls)? What are they generally used for? (Barges; used for carrying heavy loads). What kind of boats have small, knifelike hulls? What are they generally used for? (speed boats, sail boats, etc.; used for speed and maneuverability).

3. Describe the sort of boat you'd want if you were hauling heavy loads of ore on a river. Describe the design you'd want it you were trying to race other boats.

4. Of the two factors determining floating/sinking (density and shape), which do you think is more important to boat design, and why?

## Assessment

1. Were students able to design and build boats that supported loads, and could they explain, based on their own data, why certain hull designs worked better than others? [embedded, performance, journal entries]

2. Could students explain why a wider hull generally holds more weight, and how they determined an answer to that question? [embedded, journal entries]

3. Were students able to explain how a boat floats, using their own data and the concepts of displacement, density, mass, and volume? [embedded, performance, journal entries]

## Other Options and Extensions

1. Research boat design using the library and/or the Internet. Do any of the boats you found look like boats that you designed? Explain.

2. What are some things that float, other than boats? What makes those objects float?

## *Resources and Further Information*

Bloom, S. J. (1994). Data buddies: Primary grade mathematicians explore. *Teaching Children Mathematics,* 1, 80–86.

Craig, A., & Rosney, C. (1988). The Usborne science encyclopedia. Tulsa, OK: EDC.

Halpin, M. J., & Swab, J. C. 1990). It's the real thing—The scientific method. *Science and Children,* 27 (7), 30–31.

Ostlund, K. L. (1992). *Science process skills.* Menlo Park, CA: Addison-Wesley.

Saltonstall, S. (1986). Ship shape. *Science and Children,* 24 (1), 48–49.

Scheckel, L. (1993). How to make density float. *Science and Children,* 31 (3), 30–33.

Walpole, B. (1988). *175 science experiments.* New York: Random House.

## Activity Sheet 19. What Makes a Boat Float?

1. Prediction (Which boat shape will hold the most pennies?):

|  | Boat 1 | Boat 2 | Boat 3 |
|---|---|---|---|
| Describe the boat's shape |  |  |  |
| Prediction of number of pennies it will hold |  |  |  |
| Pennies held, Trial 1 |  |  |  |
| Pennies held, Trial 2 |  |  |  |
| Pennies held, Trial 3 |  |  |  |
| Average number of pennies held |  |  |  |

Conclusions:

2. Prediction (Which boat shape will hold the most pennies?):

|  | Boat 1 | Boat 2 | Boat 3 |
|---|---|---|---|
| Area of hull base ($cm^2$) |  |  |  |
| Prediction of number of pennies it will hold |  |  |  |
| Pennies held, Trial 1 |  |  |  |
| Pennies held, Trial 2 |  |  |  |
| Pennies held, Trial 3 |  |  |  |
| Average number pennies held |  |  |  |

Graph the average for each boat versus the area of that boat's hull.

Conclusions:

# Layered Liquids

 ## Overview

This activity involves another exploration of density. Why does oil float on water? How does drain cleaner sink down into the clogged pipe right through standing water? These questions will be answered as students make a layered "parfait" of colored liquids based on the varying densities of those liquids. They will calculate densities of the liquid samples as they investigate, describe, and explain the "layered liquids" phenomenon. The activity is adaptable to grades K–4 by cutting down on the mathematics and terminology involved.

## Concepts

Students find out about density and its impact on floating and sinking.

## Processes/Skills

- Observing
- Problem solving
- Predicting
- Describing
- Analyzing
- Concluding
- Measuring
- Calculating
- Inquiring
- Communicating
- Cooperating

## Recommended for

K–2 ✔                Individual

3–5 ✔                Small Group ✔

6–8 ✔                Whole Class

## Time Required

1–2 hours

## Materials Required

**PRELIMINARY ACTIVITY**

- Water
- Food coloring
- Corn syrup

**MAIN ACTIVITY**

- Tall, clear containers
- Beakers or graduated cylinders for measuring liquids
- Paper cups
- Balances
- Calculators
- Water
- Maple syrup
- Vegetable oil
- Dishwashing detergent
- Mineral oil

## Standards

**SCIENCE**

- Abilities Necessary to Do Scientific Inquiry
- Understanding About Scientific Inquiry
- Properties of Objects and Materials
- Properties and Changes of Properties in Matter

**MATH**

- Reasoning and Proof
- Communication
- Numbers and Operations
- Measurement

 ## Objectives

- Students will successfully layer the four liquid samples and will be able to explain their results.

- Students will successfully determine the layered position of a fifth, unknown liquid, based on its density, which they will calculate.

## Background Information (from Activity 19, What Makes a Boat Float?)

*Density* is the relative weight of an object, defined mathematically as the object's *mass* divided by *volume*. A more dense object or material has more tightly packed internal particles. A brick, for instance, is more dense (that is, has more tightly packed particles within it) than a piece of wood (whose particles are more loosely packed). A brick is more dense than water, and it will sink. Most wood, however, is less dense than water, allowing it to float. Therefore, it is not an object's weight alone that determines whether it will sink or float; it is the object's weight (really its mass) divided by its volume. Consider a really large piece of Styrofoam (say, 500 kg): it will float in water despite its large size because it is less dense than the water. That is, it has less mass per unit of volume than water; or put another way, if we have two equal volumes (say, 250 cm$^3$) of Styrofoam and of water, the Styrofoam will be lighter in weight (or contain less mass). The Styrofoam is less dense than the water and it will therefore float.

## Preliminary Activity

Begin by showing the class a two-layered liquid "parfait": water (the effect is more dramatic if you first mix a little food coloring into the water, and if you let them see you pour the two liquids carefully together) "floating" on corn syrup. Ask, "Why do you suppose these liquids form into two layers?" Accept divergent answers, but help them see that density is the reason.

## Main Activity, Step-by-Step

1. Working together in small, cooperative groups, students begin by measuring out 100 ml each (students measure out the samples) of four different liquids: water, maple syrup, vegetable oil, and dishwashing detergent. Each sample must be poured into the same sort of container (because their masses will be compared); paper cups work well. List the substances by sample number in Activity Sheet 20, Table 20–1.

2. Next, students predict the order of the layers that the four samples will form when poured carefully into the same jar. Which will be on top, and so on? They should record their predictions in Table 20–2.

3. Using a balance, students measure the mass of each of the samples (this is why they need to be in identical containers; subtract the mass of the cup, weighed when empty, from the mass of each cup when filled with the liquid sample). Record all data in Table 20–3.

4. Calculate the density of each liquid (mass divided by volume: 100 ml each). Record the densities, and again predict the order of the layers that will form when the four samples are poured into the same container (using Table 20–4). Did your prediction change? Why or why not?

5.  Carefully pour the liquids into a single, tall, clear container, one at a time over a spoon so that they don't mix. Record the results of the layering effect (in Table 20–5). Explain your results, particularly in the light of your predictions.

6.  Before having students pour out their samples, try this method of Performance Assessment and/or application of the concepts. Each group receives a fifth liquid sample (for instance, mineral oil; again 100 ml in an identical paper cup). They must determine where in the layered column it will come to rest by measuring its mass, calculating its density, and using the density to predict correctly (in Table 20–6). Then they can pour the fifth liquid into the column to check their calculation, analysis, and prediction. Students can write science journal entries about how density affects floating and sinking.

## Questions for Discussion

1.  What does density have to do with sinking and floating?

2.  If you tried the layering activity aboard the Space Shuttle in outer space, would the results differ, and if so, how? (Weightless, so no layers form.) What about if you tried it on the surface of the moon? (Same layers as on earth, despite lower gravitational pull.)

3.  Can you think of any jobs that might involve the concepts of density, sinking, and/or floating? Explain your answer for each job example that you can name.

## Assessment

1.  Were students able to successfully layer the liquid samples? [embedded, performance]

2.  Were student predictions correct? If so, could they explain why? If not, could they explain why not? [embedded, performance, journal entries]

3.  Could students successfully determine the layered position of the fifth liquid, and did they explain how they arrived at their answer? [performance, journal entries]

## Other Options and Extensions

1.  Groups can place some small objects (pieces of wood, cork, rock, eraser, wax, fruit, plastic, metal, etc.) into the layered column (from Procedure 5, above), predicting where each will come to rest. Students will see that density applies to solid as well as liquid matter.

2.  Try the basic activity using water and any sort of fruit juice, soda, or other water-based mixture. The distinct layers will not form quickly, if at all (you may need to let the final product settle for several hours before any layering is evident). Ask students to explain why the results differ so significantly from the basic activity. [The fruit juice or soda is composed almost solely of water, hence it is neither more nor less dense than the pure water sample. The two samples will mix and clear layering based on density is not evident.]

## Resources and Further Information

Halpin, M. J., & Swab, J. C. (1990). It's the real thing—The scientific method. *Science and Children, 27* (7), 30–31.

Nesin, G., & Barrow, L. (1984). Density in liquids. *Science and Children, 21* (7), 28–30.

Ostlund, K. L. (1992). *Science process skills.* Menlo Park, CA: Addison-Wesley.

Pearlman, S., & Pericak-Spector, K. (1994). A series of seriation activities. *Science and Children, 31* (4), 37–39.

Scheckel, L. (1993). How to make density float. *Science and Children, 31* (3), 30–33.

United Nations Educational, Scientific, and Cultural Organization. (1962). *700 Science Experiments for Everyone.* New York: Doubleday.

Walpole, B. (1988). *175 Science Experiments.* New York: Random House.

## Activity Sheet 20. Layered Liquids

Table 20–1

| Sample # | Which Substance? |
|---|---|
| 1 | |
| 2 | |
| 3 | |
| 4 | |

Prediction: In what order will the sample layers end up?

Table 20–2

| Layer Order | Sample # | Substance |
|---|---|---|
| Top Layer | | |
| Second Layer | | |
| Third Layer | | |
| Bottom Layer | | |

Table 20–3

| Sample # | Substance | Mass (grams) | Volume | Mass/Volume | Density |
|---|---|---|---|---|---|
| 1 | | | 100 ml | /100ml | |
| 2 | | | 100 ml | /100ml | |
| 3 | | | 100 ml | /100ml | |
| 4 | | | 100 ml | /100ml | |

Prediction 2: After calculating the densities of the samples, what order do you think the final layers will take?

Table 20–4

| Layer Order | Sample # | Substance |
|---|---|---|
| Top Layer | | |
| Second Layer | | |
| Third Layer | | |
| Bottom Layer | | |

Results:

Table 20–5

| Layer Order | Sample # | Substance |
|---|---|---|
| Top Layer | | |
| Second Layer | | |
| Third Layer | | |
| Bottom Layer | | |

Explain your results:

Data for Sample 5:

Table 20–6

| Sample # | Substance | Mass (grams) | Volume | Mass/Volume | Density |
|---|---|---|---|---|---|
| 5 | | | 100 ml | /100ml | |

Prediction: Where will the Sample 5 layer be in relation to the other four samples, and how do you know?

Results, using Sample 5:

# Calculating the Speed of Sound

## ⦿ Overview

Who hasn't seen a dramatic flash of lightning, only to hear the dramatic "crack" of thunder several seconds later? But, why does the thunder reach our ears *after* we see the lightning? The sound and the sight of a distant, loud event are said to be out of phase, i.e., they aren't experienced simultaneously. Again, why? In this activity your students will collect data and determine the reason by calculating the speed of sound and comparing it to the speed of light. In the procedure, which can be undertaken with simple materials on any playground or large outdoor surface, they will measure, convert units, compare, and reach empirical conclusions based on their own investigation of the phenomenon.

## ⦿ Concepts

Students will calculate the speed of sound based on their own measurements, and in the follow-up portion of the activity, will compare it to the speed of light.

## ⦿ Processes/Skills

- Observing
- Describing
- Analyzing
- Concluding
- Measuring
- Calculating
- Inquiring
- Communicating
- Cooperating

## ⦿ Recommended For

| | |
|---|---|
| K–2 | Individual |
| 3–5 | Small Group ✔ |
| 6–8 ✔ | Whole Class |

## ⦿ Time Required

2–3 hours

## ⦿ Materials Required

**MAIN ACTIVITY**

- Calculators
- A hammer and another piece of heavy metal that will make a loud noise when struck with the hammer
- A clock with sweep second hand
- Meter sticks

**FOLLOW-UP ACTIVITY**

- Flashlight

## ⦿ Standards

**SCIENCE**

- Abilities Necessary to Do Scientific Inquiry
- Understanding About Scientific Inquiry
- Transfers of Energy

**MATH**

- Reasoning and Proof
- Communication
- Connections
- Numbers and Operations
- Measurement
- Algebra

## Objectives

- Students will successfully collect data regarding the speed of sound.
- Students will calculate and compare their figures for the speed of sound.
- Students will compare the speed of sound to the speed of light and will be able to explain why distant events like thunder and lightning appear to be out of phase.

## Preliminary Activity

Ask students what they know about the speed of sound. Discuss the "out of phase" experiences that the students might have had when they *saw* lightning before they *heard* the thunder or they *saw* a baseball being hit from far away before the actually *heard* the crack of the bat. What other such "out of phase" experiences have they had (any loud noise at a distance)? Expand on these experiences to get at the notion that sound travels at a particular speed, and its speed is less than that of light. Ask for ideas: How could we measure the speed of sound?

## Main Activity, Step-by-Step

1. In this activity, students should work in cooperative groups, but each should keep her or his own data. First, students must determine the length of their average steps in meters. Place three meter sticks on the floor, and each student measures the length of three of their steps, recording their data on Activity Sheet 21, Table 21–1. When they divide the distance by three (the number of steps), they'll arrive at a calculation of meters per step. They should make this measurement and calculation three times, and then divide by three to get an average figure for meters per step. (We run three trials of three steps here because our steps can vary a great deal from one to the next.)

2. The next step in the procedure will take you and the class outside to any large, open area on the school grounds. Before going out, of course, be sure that students know what is expected of them during this "field trip." Begin hitting any handy piece of metal (such as the blade of a short-handled shovel) with a hammer, making a loud "bang." You must make contact with the hammer once every second, using the sweep second hand of a wristwatch on your stationary arm to time your strikes. The trick here is to move your arm crisply and mechanically in an arclike motion, so that the hammer is clearly at one end of the arc every half second. One-half second, the hammer is clearly away from the shovel, and the next half second, it is contacting the shovel with a bang (see Figure 21–1). Once you find your rhythm, have the students walk away, moving backwards. When they are close, the sound and the sight of the hammer blow will be simultaneous, but as they move farther away from you the sound and sight will become increasingly out of phase. They must keep moving away until the sound and sight of the blow are one-half second out of phase, that is, until they hear the bang when the hammer is at the opposite end of the arc (i.e., in Figure 21–1, they hear the bang when the hammer is in Position B). Then they walk back to your position, *counting the number of steps that they take to return to you* (because you are the source of the sound). The number of steps should be recorded on the Activity Sheet, Table 21–2, and the procedure should be repeated three times.

3. When you have returned to the classroom, the students can begin their calculations for the speed of sound, again using the Activity Sheet, Table 21–3. The first step is to determine the distance, in meters, that they stepped off in Procedure 2. They need to multiply the number of steps (for each of the three trials from Procedure 2) times the average number of meters per step determined in

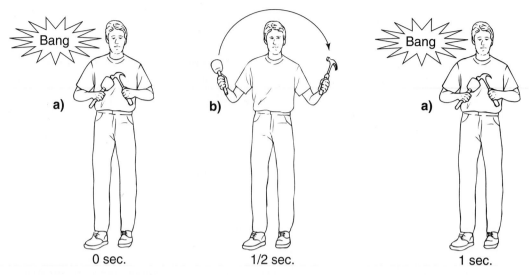

**Figure 21–1.** The speed of sound. Make contact, and loud noise, at 1-second intervals (Position A). Then crisply to Position B at the ½-second mark.

Procedure 1. This will give the speed that sound travels in one-half second (because the distance measured was based on the hammer's sound and sight being one-half second out of phase). To get the speed of sound *per second,* simply multiply by two.

To summarize the calculation: Distance in steps (from Procedure 2) times number of meters per step (from Procedure 1) times two = the speed of sound in meters per second.

Or put another way:

Distance (steps/0.5sec) × meters/step × 2 (0.5sec/sec) = speed of sound (m/sec)

After calculating the speed based on each of the three trials, find an average of the three for a final figure.

4. Students can easily convert the speed of sound from meters per second into feet per second, using Table 21–4. Because there are 39.37 inches in a meter, and 12 inches per foot, just multiply the speed of sound (that is, from Procedure 3 the average of the three trials; in meters per second) times 39.37 inches per meter, divided by 12 inches per foot. The result will be the speed of sound in feet per second.

To summarize the calculation:

speed of sound (meters/sec) × 39.37 in./meter ÷ 12 inches/foot = speed of sound (feet/sec)

5. At this point students can compare their results and discuss what they've learned about sound. How did the students' values for the speed of sound compare with the "official" value (343 meters per second or 1,125 feet per second)? What was the class average? How do they account for the differences between their values and the "official" value? What were the sources of error in their procedure? How could they obtain an even more accurate figure for the speed of sound? What problems did they have with the calculations? What did they learn about sound? What else would they like to know?

## *Follow-up Activity*

Shine a flashlight around the classroom, clicking it off and on repeatedly. Consider comparing the speed of sound to the speed of light (i.e., Why do we see something in the distance, such as lightning, before we hear it?) Light travels at 299,324 km/second or 186,000 miles/second. To convert these figures into the appropriate units for comparison with the calculated speed of sound (meters per second), multiply 299,324 km/sec times 1,000 meters/km to get the speed in meters/sec. Multiply 186,000 miles/sec times 5,280 feet/mile to get feet/second. Record all figures in the appropriate spaces on Activity Sheet 21. Once they compare the speed of sound with the speed of light, students should be able to explain why we see distant events (like lightning) before we hear them. (Because the light from an event travels MUCH faster than the sound.)

## Questions for Discussion

1. How accurate was your calculation of the speed of sound? Can you think of any sources of error that led to inaccuracies? If you were going to determine the speed of sound again, what, if anything, would you do differently?

2. Why is it that you see a distant event, like lightning, before you hear it?

3. What else would you like to know about sound and how it travels?

## Assessment

1. Were students able to successfully collect step data during their "field trip"? [embedded]

2. Could students calculate and compare their figures for the speed of sound? [embedded, performance, portfolio]

3. Were they able to compare the speed of sound to the speed of light and explain why distant events like thunder and lightning appear to be out of phase? [embedded, journal entries]

## Other Options and Extensions

1. Find out about the history of the speed of sound and how scientists originally calculated it.

2. Find out whether people can travel at or beyond the speed of sound.

3. Find out what causes a sonic boom.

4. Find out how the speed of light is determined.

5. Find out whether people can travel at or beyond the speed of light.

## Resources and Further Information

Macrorie, K. (1984). *20 Teachers.* New York: Oxford University Press.

Rezba, R. J., Sprague, C., Fiel, R. L., & Funk, H. J. (1995). *Learning and assessing science process skills.* Dubuque, IA: Kendall/Hunt.

Schaffer, L., Pinson, H., & Kokoski, T. (1998). Listening to rain sticks. *Science and Children, 35* (5), 22–27.

## Activity Sheet 21. Calculating the Speed of Sound

1.   Table 21–1. Calculate the average number of meters per step.

| Trials | Distance (in meters) | | Meters per Step |
|---|---|---|---|
| 1 - Three Steps | | ÷ 3 | |
| 2 - Three Steps | | ÷ 3 | |
| 3 - Three Steps | | ÷ 3 | |
| | | Average: | |

2.   Table 21–2. Record the distance from 0.5 seconds out of phase to the sound source (from "field trip").

| Trial # | Distance (in Steps) |
|---|---|
| 1 | Steps |
| 2 | Steps |
| 3 | Steps |

3.   Table 21–3. Calculate the *speed of sound* in meters per second.

| Distances in Steps (from Procedure 2) | Average Meters per Step (from Procedure 1) | | Speed of Sound in Meters per Second |
|---|---|---|---|
| Steps | ×    m/step | × 2 | |
| Steps | ×    m/step | × 2 | |
| Steps | ×    m/step | × 2 | |
| | | Average: | |

4.   Table 21–4. Convert speed of sound from meters per second to feet per second.

| Speed of Sound in Meters per Second (from Procedure 3) | 39.37 inches per meter | 12 inches per foot | Speed of Sound in Feet per Second |
|---|---|---|---|
| | × 39.37 | ÷ 12 | |
| | × 39.37 | ÷ 12 | |
| | × 39.37 | ÷ 12 | |
| | | Average: | |

5.   What have you learned about the speed of sound?

Follow-Up Activity. Compare the speed of sound to the speed of light.

| Speed of Light (km per second) | | Speed of Light (meters per second) |
| --- | --- | --- |
| 299,324 | × 1,000 meters per km | |

| Speed of Light (miles per second) | | Speed of Light (feet per second) |
| --- | --- | --- |
| 186,000 | × 5,280 feet per mile | |

| | |
| --- | --- |
| Speed of Light (meters per second) | |
| Speed of Sound (meters per second) | |

| | |
| --- | --- |
| Speed of Light (feet per second) | |
| Speed of Sound (feet per second) | |

Why is it that you *see* a distant event, like lightning, before you *hear* the thunder?

# Investigating the Properties of Magnets

## ◯ Overview

In this activity, younger students encounter, discuss, and apply the basic characteristics of magnets and magnetism within a learning cycle format. Student groups will implement some of the terminology and concepts appropriate to the study of magnets as they find out how far magnets can repel one another and how many paper clips a magnet can attract.

As introduced in Activity 9, the learning cycle format includes three phases: *exploration* (in which exploration with concrete materials and problems allows students to make new connections with past experience), *conceptual invention* (in which meaningful terms and concepts related to the exploration experience are introduced), and *conceptual expansion* (in which students use the experience and concepts to progress in their understanding of the subject).

## ◯ Concepts

Students explore properties of magnets and magnetism through simple quantitative experimentation.

## ◯ Processes/Skills

- Observing
- Connecting
- Describing
- Analyzing
- Concluding
- Measuring

- Calculating
- Inquiring
- Problem solving
- Applying terms and concepts
- Communicating
- Cooperating

## ◯ Recommended For

| | |
|---|---|
| K–2 ✔ | Individual |
| 3–5 ✔ | Small Group ✔ |
| 6–8 | Whole Class |

## ◯ Time Required

1–2 hours

## ◯ Materials Required

- An assortment of shapes and sizes of small magnets
- An assortment of miscellaneous objects and materials (such as paper clips, index cards, plastic pen caps)
- String
- Paper clips
- Meter sticks or metric rulers

## ◯ Standards

**SCIENCE**

- Abilities Necessary to Do Scientific Inquiry
- Understanding About Scientific Inquiry
- Light, Heat, Electricity, and Magnetism

**MATH**

- Problem Solving
- Reasoning and Proof
- Measurement
- Data Analysis and Probability

## ◯ Objectives

- Students will actively explore magnets and their interactions.
- Students will determine, via quantitative and/or qualitative inquiry, whether magnetism is cumulative.

## Main Activity, Step-by-Step

1.  The *exploration phase* of this lesson is very simple. Student groups are presented with some concrete materials (several magnets of varying shapes and sizes and a few miscellaneous objects such as paper clips, index cards, plastic pen caps), little or no introduction or direction by the teacher, and ample time to "play" with the materials. Simply give the groups time to experiment and explore with the materials, under the condition that when the agreed on time is up (15 minutes should be sufficient) each group will briefly report to the class regarding something that they learned about the materials and how they interact. During the exploration time, you can circulate among the groups, gently facilitating an inquiry of the materials' interaction, but not pressing students in any particular direction; encourage divergent and innovative thinking.

2.  When the exploration time is up, allow each group to choose a spokesperson who will report one aspect of what they learned to the class. This is the *conceptual invention phase* of the learning cycle. As students talk about their findings, reinforce or introduce appropriate terms and concepts through nurturing and inquisitive dialogue. Depending on the grade level, such terms might include, but would not be limited to, push, pull, attraction, repulsion, poles, attract, repel. Concepts and terms may be reinforced or introduced through comments and questions like: "I notice that you said the magnets 'stuck together'—in science we might say that they were *attracted* to each other." Or, "You mentioned that the magnets could push away from each other, even through the index card. That's a very good observation. We could say that the magnets push or *repel* each other. Can they do this no matter how they are arranged?" The point here is that through authentic dialogue, the students have an opportunity to connect science ideas to their own exploratory experiences.

3.  The *conceptual expansion phase* of the learning cycle can take the form of several quantitative investigations. Student groups can begin by measuring how far one magnet can push another magnet of similar size and shape (holding them together, let one "spring" away in repulsion from the first). After predicting the number, they can conduct five trials and record the data in Activity Sheet 22, Table 22–1 (for older students, average the trials). Next, measure and record how far can two magnets push a single magnet (Table 22–2). Then try it with three magnets pushing a single magnet (Table 22–3). Graph the class results (number of magnets pushing versus distance pushed). Compare results and reach conclusions. Is "magnet power" cumulative?

    Next, have each group tie a magnet to a string and tape the other end of the string to the edge of a desk so that the magnet hangs freely in the air. Students then predict how many paper clips the magnet can attract and hold (Table 22–4). Then they can try to find out just how many it can actually hold, running three trials. Record and average the data and reach conclusions. Try placing the paper clips end-to-end, just touching that is, not hooked together (see Figure 22–1). Ask, "How many can the magnet hold now? How do you explain the fact that the paper clips can attract other paper clips? Can they do this when they are not touching a magnet? You saw how many paper clips could be held up by a single magnet. Next, predict how many clips could be held by two magnets tied together? Try it out."

    Finally, find out what else the students want to know about magnets. Especially for older students, allow them to measure something else about magnets—something that they devise and want to know about. Each group should carry out and eventually report on its own investigation.

## Follow-Up Activity

As an additional aspect of the learning cycle's *conceptual expansion phase,* have each group discuss, invent, and report to the class on (though not necessarily build) an invention that uses magnets and/or magnetism.

**Figure 22–1.**  Magnet and paper clips (clips *just touching,* not hooked)

---

## Questions for Discussion

1. What have you learned about magnets and magnetism? What did you do to find out?

2. What do you still want to know about magnets and magnetism? How could you find out what you want to know?

3. How can magnets and magnetism be useful to us in everyday life?

4. When we measured how far one magnet would "spring away" from the other (Procedure 3), why did we conduct five trials and then calculate an average rather than just doing a single trial?

---

## Assessment

1. Did students actively explore magnets and their interactions? [embedded]

2. Were students successful in connecting meaningful science terms and concepts to their exploratory experiences, and in applying those concepts and terms to their expanded investigations? [embedded, journal entries]

3. Were students able, via quantitative and/or qualitative inquiry, to determine whether magnetism is cumulative? [embedded, journal entries]

---

## Other Options and Extensions

1. Find out how an electromagnet works. Try to make one from a battery and a length of insulated wire.

2. Find out how an electric motor works. What do magnets have to do with it? Can you build an electric motor of your own?

3. What does magnetism have to do with generating electricity? Can you find out how a generator works?

## *Resources and Further Information*

Barrow, L. (1990). Ceramic magnets pass the bar. *Science and Children, 27* (7), 14–16.

Burns, J. C., & Buzzelli, C. (1992). An active attraction. *Science and Children, 30* (1), 20–22.

Gabel, D. L. (Ed.). (1994). *Handbook of research on science teaching and learning.* New York: Macmillan.

Kohl, M. A., & Potter, J. (1993). *Science arts.* Bellingham, WA: Bright Ring.

Milson, J. L. (1990). Electromagnetic attraction. *Science and Children, 28* (1), 24–25.

Orozco, G. T., Alberu, P. S., & Haynes, E. R. (1994). The electromagnetic swing. *Science and Children, 31* (6), 20–21.

Ostlund, K. L. (1992). *Science process skills.* Menlo Park, CA: Addison-Wesley.

Sharp, J. (1996). Manipulatives for the metal chalkboard. *Teaching Children Mathematics, 2,* 280–281.

Teachworth, M. D. (1991). A memory for magnets. *Science and Children, 29* (2), 30–31.

### Activity Sheet 22. Investigating the Properties of Magnets

1. How far can *one* magnet "push" another (from Procedure 3)?
(Prediction: _____ cm)

Table 22–1

| Trial | Distance (cm) |
|---|---|
| 1 | |
| 2 | |
| 3 | |
| 4 | |
| 5 | |
| Average | |

2. How far can *two* magnets "push" another (from Procedure 3)?
   (Prediction: _____ cm)

Table 22–2

| Trial | Distance (cm) |
|---|---|
| 1 | |
| 2 | |
| 3 | |
| 4 | |
| 5 | |
| Average | |

3. How far can *three* magnets "push" another (from Procedure 3)?
   (Prediction: _____ cm)

Table 22–3

| Trial | Distance (cm) |
|---|---|
| 1 | |
| 2 | |
| 3 | |
| 4 | |
| 5 | |
| Average | |

Conclusions:
4. How many paper clips can the hanging magnet attract at one time (from Procedure 3)?
   (Prediction: _____ clips)

Table 22–4

| Trial | # Clips Held |
|---|---|
| 1 | |
| 2 | |
| 3 | |
| Average | |

Conclusions:

# Examining Current Events in Science, Mathematics, and Technology

## Overview

The national standards in science and mathematics call for these subjects to be taught from personal and social perspectives, thus strengthening students' decision-making skills. Preeminent science educator Paul DeHart Hurd called for "a curriculum that relates science to human affairs, the quality of life, and social progress" (1994, p. 109). In this activity, students will examine news articles not only from the perspective of science, math, and technology, but also based on the implications of the news story for its impact on real people, that is, based on human rights and social justice. Interdisciplinary connections are embedded in an engaging, accessible, and human context, as students read, analyze, and openly discuss a teacher-selected news article. By facilitating honest dialogue, the teacher helps students confidently face controversial topics and develop crucial critical-thinking skills.

## Concepts

Students analyze a current news event, considering not only the science, math, and/or technology involved, but also the human implications.

## Processes/Skills

- Describing
- Analyzing
- Concluding
- Inferring
- Inquiring
- Communicating

## Recommended for

| | |
|---|---|
| K–2 | Individual ✔ |
| 3–5 ✔ | Small Group ✔ |
| 6–8 ✔ | Whole Class ✔ |

## Time Required

1–2 hours

## Materials Required

- Enough photocopies of a news article for the entire class

## Standards

**SCIENCE**
- Abilities Necessary to Do Scientific Inquiry
- Science and Technology in Society

**MATH**
- Communication
- Connections

## Objectives

- Students will read and analyze a current event not only for its content in science, math, and/or technology, but also for its human rights and social justice implications.

# Main Activity, Step-By-Step

1. Begin by choosing a current event article from a newspaper or news magazine. The article should be directly relevant to some aspect of science, math, and/or technology. Because real-world issues seldom fall conveniently under a single subject heading, your article is likely to have indirect connections to other fields. Your choice of current events could raise issues and questions related to history, sociology, psychology, and politics. As you make your choice of articles, consider the human rights issues associated with the news event. Such issues are not beyond the scope of the elementary or middle school classroom, and are, in fact, highly motivating for students due to the relevance of the topics and the opportunities for authentic dialogue. Consider the human rights issues associated with news stories regarding immunization, cloning, colonization of other planets, organ transplants, environmental hazards, health care, and waste management. An integrated analysis of the news article, including consideration of human rights issues, is promoted by Activity Sheet 23.

2. Photocopy the article for all class members and read it together, clarifying new concepts and terms as necessary. Break into small groups for analysis of the article, with each individual student recording responses on Activity Sheet 23. The analysis should be facilitated by the teacher moving around the room, from group to group, listening, asking, and assessing.

3. Resume classwide instruction by discussing the groups' results and reactions to the article. Throughout the analysis and discussion, prompt students to notice and express their personal responses to the article. Encourage an awareness and use of authentic student voice, keeping in mind that this activity is designed to illuminate student perspectives via intellectual exploration, not simply to generate standardized, right/wrong responses. Aim for a balance between the affective and cognitive domains. Personalize the discussion, especially at elementary level (i.e., "How might a young person like you react to these conditions?"); consider the article's impact on various demographic groups.

   The basic approach to this analysis and discussion is as follows:

   a. Clarify the problem. What is going on? Broaden students' understanding of the situation.

   b. Define the basic pro and con reactions to the article, concentrating on science, math, and technology connections.

   c. Consider the human rights implications: violations, infringements, advancements. Who is affected by the situation, and how are they affected?

   d. Through open dialogue, determine workable solutions to the problem. Determine areas of impasse.

   e. What must be done to implement the solution(s)?

   f. What additional information is needed to help solve the problem?

   The teacher has a number of responsibilities in this activity: to help students understand that every problem may not have a simple answer, to learn to accept an element of uncertainty, to seek fairness in presenting and discussing the topic, to avoid proselytization and the tendency to oversimplify complex topics, and ultimately, to induce authentic, critical thought.

# Questions for Discussion

1. Do all situations in real life have simple solutions? Explain.

2. When faced with a complex problem, is it a good idea to consider more than one perspective before making any decisions? Explain.

3. What sorts of careers might involve solving complex problems?

## Assessment

1. Were students able to summarize the chosen article? [embedded]

2. Could they explain the importance of the article in terms of its science, math, and/or technology content? [embedded]

3. Were they able to discuss the human rights aspects of the current event? [embedded]

4. Did they, through open dialogue, arrive at solutions to the problem, or could they explain why a solution is not yet feasible? [embedded]

## Other Options and Extensions

1. Students, either individually or in groups, might wish to expand their knowledge about the news topic. They could present their research to the class in the form of a debate, a play, a poem, a video, or an art project.

2. Write letters related to the news report. Address them to parties in or related to the current event article, *and actually send them.* Be judicious about sharing your own perspective so that your students will more readily develop and record their own views. This exercise is especially empowering when the news issue is local and students can see the results of their correspondence.

3. Have students explore news sources for relevant articles of their own choosing. Let them present and discuss those articles in groups or in a classwide forum.

## Resources and Further Information

Hurd, P. D. (1994). New minds for a new age: Prologue to modernizing the science curriculum. *Science Education, 78,* 103–116.

Jennings, T. E., & Eichinger, J. (1999). Science education and human rights: Explorations into critical social consciousness and postmodern science instruction. *International Journal of Educational Reform, 8,* 37–44.

LeBeau, S. (1997). Newspaper mathematics. *Teaching Children Mathematics, 3,* 240–241.

McLaren, P. (1995). *Critical pedagogy and predatory culture.* New York: Routledge.

O'Connell, S. R. (1995). Newspapers: Connecting the mathematics classroom to the world. *Teaching Children Mathematics, 1,* 268–274.

Silbey, R. (1999). What is in the daily news? *Teaching Children Mathematics, 5,* 390–394.

## Activity Sheet 23. Examining Current Events in Science, Mathematics, and Technology

Respond to the following based on the news article from class.

1.  Summarize the article in 30 to 50 words. List any new words that you don't understand.

2.  What does this article have to do with science, math, or technology?

3.  Who might be affected by the situation or problem reported in the article? How might they be affected?

4.  Why is this article important (consider the viewpoints of several different people)?

5.  What additional information is needed to resolve the problem reported in the article?

# Alphabet Taxonomy

##  Overview

Your students constantly notice the world around them, and to make sense of it all, attempt to group and categorize those objects and experiences that they encounter. In science, the study of classification is referred to as taxonomy. To make this subject simple and relevant for younger learners, why not approach it from an interactive and relevant angle by allowing your students to classify objects with which they are already familiar? At the same time, they will be encouraged to employ many of the actual processes involved in scientific investigation, including observing, measuring, describing, questioning, and communicating.

##  Concepts

Students learn about the concept and process of taxonomy, the notion of a material's properties, as they search for patterns and relationships based on shape.

##  Processes/Skills

- Observing
- Classifying
- Creating
- Describing
- Analyzing
- Communicating
- Reasoning
- Recognizing shapes and patterns
- Cooperating

##  Recommended for

K–2 ✔        Individual ✔

3–5 ✔        Small Group ✔

6–8          Whole Class

##  Time Required

1 hour

##  Materials Required

**PRELIMINARY ACTIVITY**

- Assorted hardware (nails, screws, nuts, bolts, etc.)

**MAIN ACTIVITY**

- Paper
- Pens or pencils
- Scissors

##  Standards

**SCIENCE**

- Abilities Necessary to Do Scientific Inquiry
- Understanding About Scientific Inquiry
- Properties of Objects and Materials

**MATH**

- Reasoning and Proof
- Representation
- Algebra

## Objectives

- Students will group letters and numbers into categories based on their shapes and will be able to explain their rationale for doing so.

- Students will define taxonomy in their own words and will also be able to discuss the importance of classification to scientists and mathematicians.

## Background Information

*Taxonomy* is a subject worthy of consideration at the elementary school level. By comparing observable characteristics (known as *properties*) of a set of objects in question, scientists notice patterns, identify relationships, and differentiate between groups and individuals. In this way, meaning, context, and a sense of organization are constructed. Taxonomic principles are most often applied in science to the identification of plants and animals, but are also widely used in other areas, including the categorization of chemical substances, microorganisms, rocks, and various physical phenomena. Mathematicians, too, must use classification schemes to identify prime numbers, negative integers, acute triangles, and so on. Taxonomic methods, activities, and concepts can be used in the classroom to promote

logical, rigorous, and orderly thinking; to enhance the recognition of patterns and relationships; and to give students opportunities to effectively make more sense of the objects and experiences in their own lives.

Although many types of objects can be successfully grouped by young children, you can begin by using the alphabet as your population of objects to be classified. Your students already have experience with the letters and their shapes, thus minimizing any anxiety due to the introduction of novel stimuli. Perhaps more important, by focusing on familiar objects in this introductory activity the emphasis is placed on the process of taxonomy, rather than on the objects themselves. The observation and classification of the alphabetic shapes in this exercise can also encourage further literary and scientific proficiency.

## Preliminary Activity

Develop a context for the activity by clarifying and discussing with the students the need for identification and classification. You could begin by showing the students an assortment of hardware pieces (e.g., various nails, screws, nuts, bolts, hinges, etc.) and asking them how they manage to tell the difference between these objects. Who might use these objects? Why would those people need to differentiate between them? When holding up two different nails, for instance, ask, "What is similar about these objects? What is different?" Explain that their various responses (longer, shorter, thicker, darker, etc., that is, any observable aspects of the objects) are what we call "characteristics" of the nails (to simplify, you might substitute "things we notice" for "characteristics"; or for more advanced students, substitute "properties" or even "physical properties").

In what other situations do people need to tell the difference between one thing and another? What kinds of jobs involve this need? When do the students themselves need to differentiate between similar objects and how do they do so? Consider the perspectives of different people, such as a doctor, a recycler, an author, a carpenter, a pilot, a parent, and so on. Here is a great opportunity to weave in a book or story.

## Main Activity, Step-by-Step

1. Explain that scientists need to identify and classify things sometimes, just like everyone else, and that they use characteristics (or things they notice, or properties) of the objects to do so. What kinds of things might scientists need to classify or identify? Scientists even have a word for this.

   Write the word *taxonomy* on the chalkboard. Ask if anyone can define it, and explain that the activity they are about to do will help them understand what the term means. Of course, your emphasis on the actual terminology (e.g., taxonomy, classification, grouping, characteristics, properties) will depend on the readiness of your particular students. This activity is designed to promote process skills, and therefore is not dependent on vocabulary background.

2. Students, working individually or in small groups, must first prepare their materials by folding a standard piece of plain paper into a 6-by-6 box grid, that is, into 36 equal-sized boxes (about 47 mm × 36 mm each). For younger students, you may want to have the papers pre-lined or even make the letter and number cards ahead of time. Next, instruct the students to begin with the letter *A*, writing a single capital, block letter in each box, and continuing through *Z*. In each of

the 10 remaining boxes, they should write each of the digits 0 through 9. Finally, cut out the boxes along the creases, and make two stacks of boxes: letters and numbers.

3. Setting the number boxes aside, begin working with the letters alone. Ask the students to arrange the letters into two piles (they do not have to be equal-sized piles) *based on some characteristic (or property) that they notice about the shapes of the letters.* Tell the students, "Don't consider the sounds that the letters make—just pay attention to the shapes—and *be sure that you can explain why you placed the letters into the two piles.*" As they complete this task, circulate around the room, asking them why they placed the letters as they did. When all are finished, allow several volunteers to explain their classification schemes, enabling everyone to see that there are many plausible ways to separate the letters.

4. Students should combine the letters again into a single pile. Instruct them to separate the letters into three stacks this time, based again on some observable characteristic. Proceed as you did in Procedure 3, but leave the letters sitting in the three arranged piles. When all are finished, allow several volunteers to explain their classification schemes.

5. Next, each student or student group should retrieve the stack of numerical digits and place each one onto the appropriate stack of letters, using the same classification scheme invented in Procedure 4. Because they are looking at shape alone, the students should be able to classify each numeral based on its form alone, just as they did with the letters. The numbers act here as a set of unknowns that students must separate using a previously defined taxonomic scheme (a scheme that each student was allowed to create). When everyone is finished with this task, ask for volunteers to explain how their systems worked, again pointing out that although their individual taxonomic schemes may have been quite different, the various systems still worked. There are many ways to classify things; the system you use depends on what you observe and what you want to accomplish. Occasionally, however, a numeral won't fit easily into a particular scheme. If this occurs, explore the reason or reasons for its exclusion from the three letter stacks and discuss how the scheme might be modified to appropriately accommodate all of the digits (or if modification is not feasible, they may need to add another stack, just as scientists might have to do if they discover an entirely new species of animal or plant).

6. With older students you can now make a simple bar graph on the chalkboard of the frequencies of the general taxonomic schemes utilized by the students. For instance, count and graph the number of students who separated the shapes according to curves and straight lines, or into one or two stroke shapes. The graphic representation of students' classification schemes will visually reinforce the notion that there are many ways to classify the same objects. Now ask the students to explain, either orally or by writing in their science journals, their understanding of the term *taxonomy* and why it might be a useful idea.

## Questions for Discussion

1. Gold miners and geologists both must classify rocks, but because they have different needs and goals they might use different taxonomic schemes. Consider their needs and goals, then describe a rock classification scheme used by each and explain how the two schemes differ.

2. When you added the numerals to the three stacks of letters, were there any difficulties? That is, did all the numbers fit into your taxonomic scheme? If not, which one(s) didn't fit and why not?

3. What sorts of things do you classify in your own life and what properties do you use to classify them?

## Assessment

1. Were the students successful at grouping letters into two and three categories based on observable shape-related properties? Were they also able to successfully add the numerals to the three stack-scheme? [embedded, performance]

2. Were students able to describe what is meant by the term *taxonomy*? [embedded, journal entries]

3. Did students recognize the importance of taxonomic classification to scientists and mathematicians? [embedded, journal entries]

## Other Options and Extensions

1. Separate the letters based on the sounds that they make (which are observable auditory properties).

2. Extend the processes of taxonomy to piles of leaves from different trees or even from the same tree (discernible differences exist between leaves from the same tree), animal photos, shell collections, rock collections, books, foods, tools, miscellaneous household items, etc. As you do this, explore the idea that some systems of categorization are more appropriate and useful than others, depending on what one wishes to accomplish. For instance, a scientist studying volcanoes might want to arrange a rock collection into "volcanic" and "nonvolcanic" groups, whereas a miner might consider "rocks that contain ore" and "rocks that do not contain ore." The volcanologist's scheme is not appropriate and useful for the miner, and vice versa.

3. Promote the quantification of observable properties by introducing measuring instruments into the taxonomic process: metric rulers, scales or balances, thermometers, etc.

4. Encourage students to look individually, with friends, and with family members for ways that they currently categorize items in their own lives, and to discover new items and new, more useful means of classification.

## Resources and Further Information

Gaylen, N. (1998). Encouraging curiosity at home. *Science and Children, 35* (4), 24–25.

Gotsch, H., & Harris, S. (1990). Backyard taxonomy. *Science and Children, 27* (4), 25–27.

Ostlund, K. L. (1992). *Science process skills.* Menlo Park, CA: Addison-Wesley.

Williams, D. (1995). *Teaching mathematics through children's art.* Portsmouth, NH: Heineman.

# Exploring the Mysteries of Fingerprints

## ● Overview

This activity combines a variety of processes and skills into an investigation of something near and dear to your students, their fingers. Math and science will blend seamlessly as they observe, compare, and apply their ideas about fingerprints,

## ● Concepts

Students investigate the three basic fingerprint patterns: loops, arches, and whorls.

## ● Processes/Skills

- Observing
- Classifying
- Comparing
- Describing
- Recognizing shapes and patterns
- Predicting
- Collecting data
- Graphing
- Experimenting
- Communicating

## ● Recommended for

| | |
|---|---|
| K–2 | Individual |
| 3–5 ✔ | Small Group ✔ |
| 6–8 ✔ | Whole Class |

## ● Time Required

2–4 hours

## ● Materials Required

**PRELIMINARY ACTIVITY**

- Smooth latex gloves
- A coin

**MAIN ACTIVITY**

- Paper
- Soft lead pencils
- Transparent tape
- Hand lenses
- Loop, whorl, and arch transparencies for projector
- Graphite powder
- Clear packing tape
- Soft-bristled brushes

**FOLLOW-UP ACTIVITIES**

- Sponges
- Tempera paints
- Stamp pads
- Baby powder
- Flour
- Talcum powder
- Baking powder

## ● Standards

**SCIENCE**

- Abilities Necessary to Do Scientific Inquiry
- Understanding About Scientific Inquiry
- Characteristics of Organisms

- Structure and Function in Living Systems
- Diversity and Adaptation of Organisms

**MATH**

- Problem Solving
- Reasoning and Proof
- Connections
- Algebra

## Objectives

- Students will identify and classify their fingerprints based on shape.
- Students will count and graphically portray their findings.
- Students will collect fingerprints from around the classroom after predicting likely locations.

## Preliminary Activity

Ask students to look closely at the palm side of their fingers. What do they notice? Do they see the tiny ridges known as fingerprints? What do they know about fingerprints? What would they like to know? How could they find answers to their questions? How do fingerprints benefit us (for a quick answer, try picking up a dime while wearing smooth, latex gloves)?

## Main Activity, Step-By-Step

1.  Are your fingerprints all the same on all of your fingers? How could we get a better look at your prints? First, rub the lead of a soft pencil on a piece of scratch paper. Then rub your finger in the lead so that your finger tip picks up some of the coloring (like a rubber stamp on an ink pad). Next, take a small piece of transparent adhesive tape and stick it over the finger tip covered with pencil lead. If you gently press the tape on the finger, some of the lead will be transferred to the tape (see Figure 25–1). Stick the tape to a piece of white paper. You should be able to see your fingerprints, outlined in pencil lead, through the tape. You can make copies of all ten fingerprints this way, making sure to label each tape-print with the correct finger (for example, "right index finger"—see Activity Sheet). Now, are your prints the same on all fingers? How are they different? How are they similar? A hand lens may be useful here.

2.  Now, in small groups, students can compare their own print sets to those of other students. They should look for similarities and patterns. How many categories of prints do you see? How would you describe the categories that you see? Looking at the prints from the entire class, how many categories, based on shapes, can you identify? Count the number of students in each fingerprint category, and make a bar graph of the results.

3.  Introduce the notion of three basic fingerprint shapes: loop, whorl, and arch (see Figure 25–1). How do these categories compare with the categories named by the class? Count the number of people in class with loop, whorl, and arch prints, and make another bar graph of those results. In your class, which shape is most common? Least common? Are all loops the same? All whorls? All arches? Explain.

4.  Next, students can use what they've learned to identify unknown prints. Have each student make two tape-prints of the same finger (the index finger of the right hand, for instance). Have them keep one print and write their name on the back. They hand the other print to you as you come around the classroom. Secretly keep track of the actual "owners" of these tape-prints (you can use numbers from the roll sheet so that no names appear on the paper; this way only you will know who each print belongs to). These will be the fingerprint "unknowns." Ask the class how they might identify the owner of unknown fingerprints. What would you look for? How could you differentiate between two similar prints? What sorts of careers might involve activities such as this? Make hand lenses available to the class, have students work in pairs or small groups. Give each work group an unknown selected tape-print. Challenge them to compare the unknown print with the known prints (the set the students kept and marked with their names) and to identify the owner.

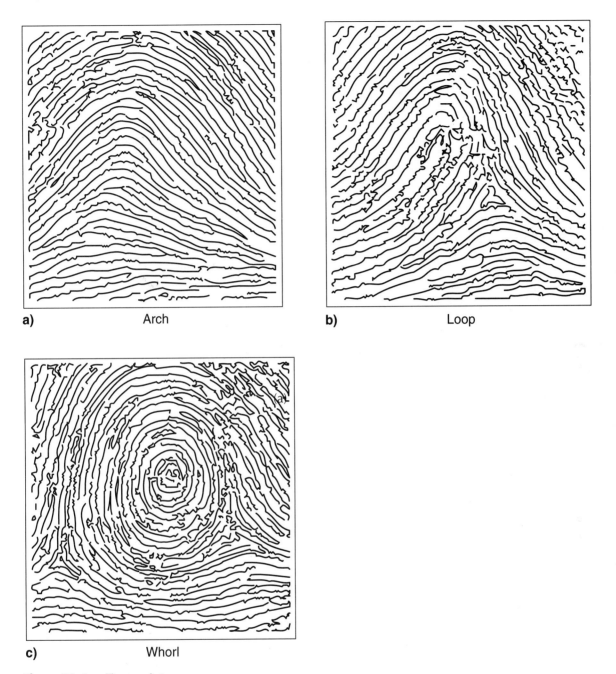

a)                    Arch                    b)                    Loop

c)                    Whorl

**Figure 25–1.**  Fingerprints

When all have completed the task, ask how they went about comparing and identifying. Which groups were successful and why? Which techniques or strategies worked and which didn't? Keep the first set of prints (those marked with names) for the following activity.

5.  Ask the students to imagine that a crime has been committed in the classroom and that we need to identify the "culprits" by locating their fingerprints. Have the class predict where in the classroom they would expect to find lots of fingerprints. Also, where would they expect to find few prints? Have them explain their predictions. Using graphite powder (extra fine; this is a lubricant that is available in hardware stores) and wide pieces of clear, adhesive tape (packing tape works well for this), send groups around the classroom to collect quantities of fingerprints.

To collect prints: (a) lightly dust the area identified area with graphite powder, (b) gently dust away the excess powder with a soft-bristled paint brush, (c) lightly press a piece of tape onto the dusted area, (d) press the tape onto a piece of white paper, (e) label the paper with the location from which the prints were lifted and the investigators' names. Check the places thought likely to have prints; these results would support the predictions if prints are common here. Also check the places thought unlikely to have prints; these results would falsify the predictions if there were many prints here. Make a bar graph of prints per location using the class results. Discuss the relationship of fingerprint presence to classroom activity. Where were prints not found? What surfaces would be unlikely to "hold" clear prints? What surfaces "hold" prints well? Attempt to identify some of the lifted prints using the known set from Step 4. What factors influence an investigator's ability to identify fingerprints? If you were a detective investigating a burglary in someone's home, where would you first dust for fingerprints? Why? In what other jobs would fingerprinting and fingerprints be useful? How could fingerprinting be useful in your day-to-day life?

## Questions for Discussion

1. Can you think of any other ways to make a set of fingerprints? Explain.

2. How were you able to tell one person's prints from another's? What specific techniques did you use to identify them?

3. What do your observations and results from these activities tell you about fingerprints? About fingers?

## Assessment

1. Were students able to identify patterns in their own prints and see similarities between their prints and the prints of others? [embedded, performance tasks, journal entries]

2. Were they able to identify loop, arch, and whorl prints? Could they graphically portray the classroom frequencies of these three categories? [embedded, performance tasks]

3. Were students able to accurately identify the bearers of unknown prints? [embedded, performance tasks]

4. Were they able to effectively locate and "lift" prints from various locations in the classroom or school? [embedded, performance tasks]

5. Could students see the value of fingerprints in various jobs (e.g., detectives) and possibly in their everyday lives? [embedded, journal entries]

6. Were they able to work together effectively? [embedded]

## Connecting Activity

Students can make paintings using their finger and thumb prints (maybe even footprints) as "printing stamps" (see Figure 25–2). Use tempera paint on wet sponges, dry tempera paint on sponge-moistened fingers, finger paints, or even ink from stamp pads. You may want to experiment with other color sources and/or try various colors and weights of paper. Some students might want to make this project into a collage, a mosaic, or a mobile. Encourage creativity, experimentation, and playfulness.

## Other Options and Extensions

1. Replicate the basic activities using toe prints. How do the results compare with fingerprints?

2. Are fingerprints genetically inherited traits? Collect the prints of family members and compare class results.

**Figure 25–2.** Fingerprint painting

3. Challenge students to find out: What forms the fingerprint? How do you know? Can you discover ways to keep from leaving prints without covering your fingers with gloves? How can you make heavier prints?

4. Make prints of other areas of skin, such as the elbow, knee, back of the hand, etc., and compare them with fingerprints.

5. To make Procedure 5 more discovery oriented, have students try to pick up prints using a variety of substances: baby powder, flour, talcum powder, baking powder, etc., after making predictions about which will work, which won't, and why or why not. They may also explore the feasibility of lifting prints from different surfaces (e.g., smooth, rough, porous): What types of surfaces are best/worst for picking up prints, and how do they explain their results?

6. Encourage students to find out what *criminology* and *forensics* mean. What sorts of jobs might involve activities such as fingerprinting? Are there any other aspects of criminology or forensics that interest you?

7. Another possibility would be to create a large *fractal* fingerprint. A fractal is a shape made up of smaller, identical versions of itself. This "fingerprint fractal" can be created by forming small prints into the shape of one giant print. That is, have students make a painting of a giant print, a loop shape

for instance, made up entirely of their finger print "stamps." This mural-like giant print could be a group project.

## *Resources and Further Information*

Beisel, R. W., & Hechtman, J. (1989). Sleuthing is elementary. *Science and Children, 26* (8), 17–19.

Gillespie, D. C. (1984). Science at your fingerprints. *Science and Children, 22* (1), 8–10.

Solomon, A. C. (1978). Fingerprints. *Science and Children, 15* (4), 30.

Twiest, M. M. (1986). Skin prints. *Science and Children, 23* (8), 26–27.

### Activity Sheet 25. Exploring the Mysteries of Fingerprints

1.  What I know about fingerprints:

2.  What I want to know about fingerprints:

3.  Collect your fingerprints here:

|  | *Thumb* | *Index Finger* | *Middle Finger* | *Ring Finger* | *Little Finger* |
|---|---|---|---|---|---|
| Right Hand |  |  |  |  |  |
| Left Hand |  |  |  |  |  |

4.  What conclusions can you draw about the shapes of your own fingerprints?

5.  What patterns can you identify when you compare your prints with those of your classmates?

6.  In the space below, make a bar graph of students in each fingerprint category:

7.  What I learned about fingerprints:

# 26 Determining the Relationship Between Height and Hand Length

 ## Overview

In this calculation-rich activity, students determine whether a mathematical relationship exists between their personal height and hand length. Designed for older students, this lesson promotes mathematical reasoning, including the use and interpretation of bar and line graphs. The process doesn't become too abstract, however, because all data are based on students' own measurements of their own bodies. The activity integrates applied mathematics with scientific inquiry and the visual arts.

## Concepts

Students find that body structure, including height and hand length, differs significantly from person to person and that real-world measurements may be related in ways that can be expressed mathematically.

 ## Processes/Skills

- Observing
- Measuring
- Predicting
- Describing
- Comparing
- Inferring from data
- Designing investigations
- Communicating
- Graphing
- Recognizing mathematical relationships
- Problem solving
- Cooperating
- Creating
- Reflecting

## Recommended for

| | |
|---|---|
| K–2 | Individual ✔ |
| 3–5 | Small Group ✔ |
| 6–8 ✔ | Whole Class |

## Time Required

3–4 hours

## Materials Required

- Butcher paper
- Crayons/pencils
- Paint or other means of decorating body outline
- Plaster of Paris/clay
- Meter sticks
- Graph paper

## Standards

**SCIENCE**
- Abilities Necessary to Do Scientific Inquiry
- Understanding About Scientific Inquiry
- Structure and Function in Living Systems

**MATH**
- Problem Solving
- Reasoning and Proof
- Communication
- Numbers and Operations
- Measurement
- Data Analysis and Probability

## Objectives

- Students will measure and document the two variables, height and hand length, by making a body outline and a hand cast.

- Students will successfully determine the quantitative and graphic relationship between height and hand length and will be able to explain their conclusions.

## Background Information

Any investigation of body measurement may bring up difficult, even painful, issues of body image, even with young children. The sensitive teacher will be careful to avoid placing any child "on the spot," especially in front of the child's peers. It is strongly recommended that personal references, direct student-to-student comparisons, and generalizations related to body aesthetics be carefully avoided throughout this activity.

## Main Activity, Step-by-Step

1. Ask the students to look around the classroom and silently notice how our bodies differ. For instance, everyone is a different height. Then ask, "What are some predictors of a person's height?" That is, what are some things that, if you knew them about a person would tell you something about how tall they are? Encourage a variety of answers.

2. Ask students to predict how a person's height may be related to the length of their hand. Will longer hands belong to taller people, vice versa, or neither? How do they explain their responses? How could we test these hypotheses? Students will probably suggest that we measure and find out for ourselves.

3. Working in small groups, have students outline each other's bodies as they lie down on a sheet of butcher paper. Arms should rest comfortably at sides and toes should point straight up. The body outlines can then be decorated with paint, crayons, or colored pencils. Better yet, consider decorating the outlines in new ways, for instance, with cut up bits of colored paper in mosaic fashion, using magazine illustrations and photos to make human collages, or painting with watercolors.

4. When all the body portraits are completed, have each student measure the head-to-toe length of his or her outline in centimeters and record the length on Activity Sheet 26. Document everyone's data on the chalkboard. As a class, or in small groups, have students compute the range (lowest and highest values), mean (the average), median (the middle measurement in the set of data), and mode (the most frequently occurring value) from the data. Make a bar graph of student heights, using height intervals (for instance, under 70 cm, 71–100 cm, 101–130 cm, 131–160 cm, over 160 cm). Recall the original question about the relationship between height and hand length. What data do we need now? Hand length, of course!

5. To better observe overall hand structure, make casts of right hands (or left if you prefer, or the individual's dominant hand, as long as all students cast the same thing) in plaster or some similar substance (clay, flour/water dough). Hands should be cast flat, a centimeter or two deep, with fingers and thumb pointing directly forward (see Figure 26–1). That described a negative hand cast; a positive cast could also be used for this investigation by making a negative cast in damp sand and filling the "hand" with plaster or wax. If time is limited, simply measure hand length using a pencil-and-paper outline of the hand. After allowing the cast (either negative or positive) to harden, students should begin noting and recording (on Activity Sheet 26) observations regarding their hand structure. Which finger extends farthest? Which is longer, the ring or index finger? How long is each finger, in centimeters? How does the thumb length compare with finger lengths? And of course, how long is the entire hand, in centimeters, from the heel to the tip of the longest finger (see Figure 26–2)? Students should also compare their own hand structure with that of their peers. How great was the variation in finger length between individuals? In hand length? Share and discuss findings as a class activity. Record class hand length data on the chalkboard. Compute mean, median, and mode. Have students make bar graphs of class hand lengths, using length intervals (for instance, under 12 cm, 12–14 cm, 14–16 cm, 16–18 cm, over 18 cm).

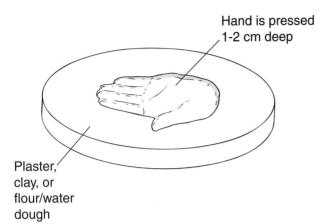

Hand is pressed
1-2 cm deep

Plaster,
clay, or
flour/water
dough

**Figure 26–1.** Hand impression

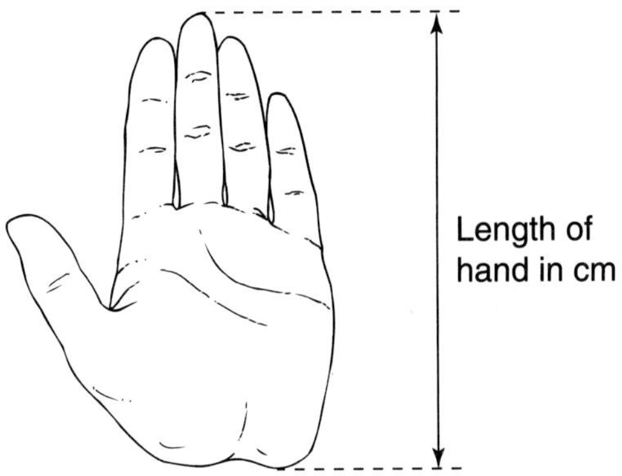

Length of
hand in cm

**Figure 26–2.** Hand length

6. Remind students of the original question in this inquiry: How is height related to hand length? Ask, "Is it easy to see a relationship by just looking at the two lists of data? What could we do to answer our original question? How about a graph? What kind of graph or other portrayal of the data would show us what we want to know?" Consider student responses and their rationale for those responses. Encourage them to reflect on the potential effectiveness of their responses. Let them give it a try, in groups, and see what they come up with. Reflect again.

7. If no one has already done so, suggest generating a coordinate graph of height versus hand length for each student. By looking for a trend (a "line" pointing up, pointing down, lying horizontal, or standing vertical) in the graph's points, this portrayal may show us how the variables (i.e., height and hand length) are related. First, record the heights and associated hand lengths (on Activity Sheet 26). Next, have each student group graph the students' data, using height as abscissa (x axis) and the associated hand length as ordinate (y axis). Now, look for a trend in the "cloud" of points on the graph. If the graph is drawn on the chalkboard or via overhead projector, use a meter stick to find the "best" approximation of the line that "summarizes" the data point cloud, if such a line seems to exist (that is, if the points are really scattered, no linear approximation may be feasible). If you and your class are up to it, consider computing the intercept and slope for the data and drawing the resulting line. For the really advanced groups, this investigation is a good introduction to studies of correlation and regression.

8. In groups, encourage students to examine their graphs and to determine the answer to the original query: How *is* height related to hand length, if it is quantitatively related at all? What responses do they have, and how do they explain their thinking? Do the statistics (mean, median, mode) help? Does the graph help? If so, how? Once the groups have come to their conclusions, individuals may clarify their thoughts and reflections in a journal writing assignment. Be sure to have students reflect on their predictions regarding these measurements. Whether they were "right" or "wrong" they still learned about the association between height and hand length. The value of a working hypothesis is in how it helps us proceed with our inquiry (it directs methods, analysis, and conclusions); it acts as a reference point and gives us direction. Once the study is concluded, whether we were initially "right" doesn't matter.

## *Questions for Discussion*

1. How are human bodies similar in terms of their basic structure? How do they differ?

2. According to your data, was height associated with hand length? How do you know? Did one seem to *cause* the other? How do you know?

3. How did the graphs help you reach your conclusions?

4. Why do we want to collect as many data points as possible in a study like this? That is, why would it have been difficult to reach a believable conclusion if we had studied only two or three students?

## Assessment

1. Were students able to document and measure the two variables, height and hand length, by making a body outline and hand cast, respectively? [embedded, performance]

2. Were students able to determine the quantitative and graphic relationship between height and hand length? Could they explain their conclusions effectively? [embedded, performance, journal entries]

## Other Options and Extensions

1. How would adult data of heights and hand lengths compare with the student data they collected and analyzed? Have students hypothesize (consider hypothesizing not only in words, but graphically, by predicting what the adult height/hand length "best fit" line would look like), then test their predictions by collecting data from significant adults in their lives (measuring height and hand length at home with paper meter sticks that can be made in class). Make another data table using student-collected data and make another graph. Compare the "best fit" line with that of the student-based graph (from Procedure 7, above). How accurate were the predictions?

2. What about other species? Examine the relationship between dogs' body length and hind leg length, or between cats' height and tail length, for instance. What other relationships can the students come up with?

## Resources and Further Information

Burns, M. (1974). Ideas. *The Arithemtic Teacher, 21* (6), 506–518.

Horak, V. M., & Horak, W. J. (1982). Let's do it: Making measurement meaningful. *Arithmetic Teacher, 30* (3), 18–23.

Parker, S. (1988). *Eyewitness books: Skeleton.* New York: Knopf.

Phillips, J. (1983). Space age meter. *Science and Children, 21* (2), 9–11.

Rezba, R. J., Sprague, C., Fiel, R. L., & Funk, H. J. (1995). *Learning and assessing science process skills.* Dubuque, IA: Kendall/Hunt.

Ruggles, J., & Slenger, B. S. (1998). The measure me doll. *Teaching Children Mathematics, 5,* 40–44.

Slesnick, I. L. (1982). Investigating the human skeleton. *Science and Children, 20* (1), 24, 37–38.

Williams, D. (1995). *Teaching mathematics through children's art.* Portsmouth, NH: Heineman.

## Activity Sheet 26. Determining the Relationship Between Height and Hand Length

1. Prediction: Do you think that height is related to hand length? If so, how is it related? What makes you think so?

2. What is your height, head to toe, in cm? _____ cm Class height data:

   Range _____ Mean _____ Median _____ Mode _____

   Make a bar graph of the class height data.

3. How long is your hand, from heel to the tip of the longest finger, in cm? _____cm

   Class hand length data:

   Range _____ Mean _____ Median _____ Mode _____

   Make a bar graph of the class hand length data.

4. Make a coordinate graph of height (x axis) versus hand length (y axis), using data from the table below. Enter class data for each student:

| *Student Height* | *Student Hand Length* |
|---|---|
|  |  |
|  |  |
|  |  |
|  |  |
|  |  |
|  |  |
|  |  |
|  |  |
|  |  |
|  |  |
|  |  |
|  |  |
|  |  |
|  |  |

5. Based on your analysis of the data, is student height related to hand length? If so, how? How do you know?

# Exploring Cellular Shape Using Area

 **Overview**

Students are challenged to maximize the area enclosed within the limited perimeter of a string "cell membrane." They will use area formulas as they do so, making this activity appropriate for upper grades. This is a very open-ended activity that will challenge groups of students to apply mathematical thinking to a problem in cell biology. They will confront the issue of cellular shape and the differences between area and volume in a practical setting.

 **Concepts**

Students examine cell theory and cell shape while applying area formulas and developing spatial thinking.

## Processes/Skills

- Observing
- Measuring
- Communicating
- Developing spatial and geometric reasoning
- Comparing
- Reflecting
- Recognizing shapes and patterns

- Problem solving
- Analyzing
- Designing
- Applying area formulas
- Communicating
- Cooperating

## Recommended for

| K–2 | Individual |
| 3–5 | Small Group ✔ |
| 6–8 ✔ | Whole Class |

 **Time Required**

1–2 hours

## Materials Required

- String
- Metric rulers
- Calculators

## Standards

**SCIENCE**

- Abilities Necessary to Do Scientific Inquiry
- Understanding About Scientific Inquiry
- Structure and Function in Living Systems
- Regulation and Behavior in Living Systems

**MATH**

- Problem Solving
- Reasoning and Proof
- Numbers and Operations
- Geometry
- Measurement

## Objectives

- Students will use area formulas of circle, square, rectangle, and triangle to maximize the surface area of a cell.

- Students will understand why cells tend to be round.

## Main Activity, Step-by-Step

1. Explain that all living things are made of cells (this concept is known as the *cell theory*). Check for students' background understanding of cells by asking them to draw some cells and to describe their shapes to the class. Explain that cells usually need maximal surface area for transfer and exchange of materials across the *cell membrane* (the outer surface of the cell). Given a certain amount of surface area for a particular, single cell, what general shape must the cell be to maximize its volume? This is a particularly important point for cells that store materials, such as fat cells. The answer to the question lies in the cell's general shape. We'll solve this problem, though, in two dimensions rather than three for the sake of simplicity (this is, working with two-dimensional *area* rather than in three-dimensional *volume*).

2. In this activity, students should work in groups of three or four. Each group receives a one-meter length of string, a meter stick, and a calculator. The string represents the cell membrane (in two dimensions) of a cell they're going to "build." The challenge: Each group must make as large a cell as possible with the string, using any of four basic geometric shapes (circle, square, rectangle, or triangle) They may solve the problem any way that they like, but they must be able to prove that their shape solution is largest using the formulas for area ($\pi r^2$, length × width, or ½ length × width). (The circle encloses the largest area for any given perimeter, as student calculations should show.)

3. When all groups have completed the task, have each report their approach to solving the problem, their solution, and their computational evidence. The ensuing discussion may become lively, particularly if some students disagree about the round shape being best. Be sure to base the evidence in area formulas and calculations. Encourage them to reflect on their methods, their grasp of the area formulas, and their calculations.

## Questions for Discussion

1. Would you be surprised to find that many cells are rounded or oval shaped? Explain your answer.

2. How are area formulas useful? Can you think of some ways that they might be useful to you or to people that you know?

3. How do real cells different from the one you "made" with your string membrane?

## Assessment

1. Were students able to use the area formulas to either solve the problem or act as evidence of their decision? [embedded, performance]

2. Did students understand why many cells tend to be rounded? [embedded, journal entries]

## Options and Extensions

1. Certainly not all cells are round or oval. Can you discover some cells that have other shapes? Is their shape related to their function, and if so, how? (Consider epithelial cells, neurons, or red blood cells.)

2. Look at some cells under a microscope. Prepared slides and/or pond life, fresh water samples, and so forth.

3. If you wanted to make a chicken coop and you had only 10 yards of chicken wire to use, what shape would you make the coop as big as possible?

## *Resources and Further Information*

Burns, M. (1976). Ideas. *The Arithmetic Teacher, 23,* 112–117.

Cantlon, D. (1998). Kids + conjecture + mathematics power. *Teaching Children Mathematics, 5,* 108–112.

Hopkins, M. (1996). Picket fences. *Teaching Children Mathematics, 3,* 86–90.

Nitabach, E., & Lehrer, R. (1996). Developing spatial sense through area measurement. *Teaching Children Mathematics, 2,* 473–476.

Ritter, D. (1995). *Math art.* Cypress, CA: Creative Teaching Press.

Way, V. (1982). Sculpting cells with Play Doh. *Science and Children, 20* (2), 25.

Whitin, D. J. (1993). Looking at the world from a mathematical perspective. *The Arithemtic Teacher, 40,* 438–441.

Williams, D. (1995). *Teaching mathematics through children's art.* Portsmouth, NH: Heineman.

# Making Prints From Fruits and Vegetables

## Overview

Students may be familiar with eating fruits and vegetables, but have they ever taken a really close look at the anatomy of those specimens? In this activity, they will have an opportunity to explore aspects of the internal and external anatomy of produce by making prints of fruits and vegetables. As students discover the fun of printmaking, they will observe and compare botanical shapes, patterns, and textures in the resulting prints. By adding or limiting the degree and complexity of concept introduction, altering the required amount of student tool use, and modifying questioning technique, this activity is easily adapted to all grades in the K–8 range.

## Concepts

Students find that fruits and vegetables are different inside and out as they study botanical anatomy, including arithmetic and geometric aspects, via specimen prints.

## Processes/Skills

- Observing
- Counting
- Predicting
- Describing
- Inferring from data
- Inquiring
- Communicating
- Printing
- Recognizing shapes and patterns
- Problem solving
- Innovating

## Recommended For

| | |
|---|---|
| K–2 ✔ | Individual |
| 3–5 ✔ | Small Group ✔ |
| 6–8 ✔ | Whole Class |

## Time Required

1–3 hours

## Materials Required

- An assortment of fresh produce
- A sharp knife (for teacher use *only*)
- Plastic knives (for student use)
- Paper
- Newspaper
- Tempera paints in a variety of colors
- A means of inking the stamps (brushes, sponges, cloths, plastic dishes, paper towels, small brayers)

## Standards

**SCIENCE**
- Abilities Necessary to Do Scientific Inquiry
- Understanding About Scientific Inquiry
- Characteristics of Organisms
- Structure and Function in Living Systems
- Diversity and Adaptation of Organisms

**MATH**
- Problem Solving
- Connections
- Numbers and Operations
- Geometry
- Algebra

*Objectives*

- Students will successfully make, observe, and analyze prints from a variety of fruit and vegetable specimens.

- Students will identify geometric shapes, numbers, and numeric patterns within the fruits and vegetables by observing the prints that they make.

## Main Activity, Step-by-Step

1. Collect an assortment of fruits and vegetables: apples, oranges, mushrooms, carrots, lemons, cucumbers, onions, potatoes, peppers, turnips, celery, lettuce and cabbage leaves, tomatoes, garlic, bananas, squash, grapes, snow peas, etc. You can encourage diversity and involvement by requesting that students each bring in at least one piece of produce themselves. Ask students to identify the various fruits and vegetables and to describe the inner structure of each. Explain that these objects will be used to make prints, and ask the class to suggest ways to make prints from these fruits and vegetables. Demonstrate how to make a basic print, using either the outside or the inside of the specimen. Ask, "What do you think we might see if we make prints of these fruits and vegetables?" This would be an opportune time to introduce the terms *botany* and *anatomy*.

2. Ask for predictions, "Which fruits or vegetables will make good prints? Which will not? Why or why not? What qualities make a 'good' print?"

3. With a sharp knife, cut the harder produce into various sections. For the softer specimens, allow students to make their own cuts with plastic knives. Cut the specimens in a variety of directions, cross sections, longitudinal sections, at different angles, in halves, in quarters, etc. For items such as cabbage leaves, make prints from the entire specimen. Make the specimens available to all of the student groups.

4. Allow students to experiment with the various shapes and print technique possibilities. Instruct them to keep all their work and to pay attention to texture, shape, and pattern within each fruit or vegetable print. Demonstrate what you mean by "texture, shape, and pattern" with an example or two.

5. Provide plenty of paper for this project. For clearer printing, cushion the stamped paper with an underlying layer of newspaper. You can ink the stamps in any of three ways: (a) apply paint (tempera) directly to the specimen using a brush, (b) make a stamp pad by placing a sponge, folded cloth, or paper towel in a shallow dish or lid and saturating it with thick tempera paint, or (c) spread paint on larger stamps with a brayer (a small paint roller, available at arts or crafts stores). Offer a variety of tempera paint colors.

6. Encourage students to identify shapes (e.g., lines, circles, rectangles), numbers (e.g., number of seeds visible in the split apple), or patterns (arrangement of seeds in the split apple). They can even outline or otherwise mark shapes, numbers, or patterns observed in the dried print with charcoal, chalk, or pencil. Direct students to estimate the number of seeds in a pepper, banana, or watermelon, and then to determine how to check their estimation for accuracy.

7. Display examples of student prints on the bulletin board. Discuss as a class or in small groups the variety of printing techniques, artistic results, and anatomical/structural/mathematical observations.

## Questions for Discussion

1. What did you notice about the various fruits and vegetables regarding their inner or outer texture, anatomy, form, or structure?

2. What geometric shapes, numbers, and/or numeric patterns did you find in the fruits or vegetables? What shapes, numbers, or patterns are most common? Least common? How do you know that they are most or least common?

3. What surprised you about this activity? Why?

4. Ask students to write about this in their science journal: When it comes to printmaking, the part I like best is ———.

## Assessment

1. Were students able to successfully make prints from the various specimens? [embedded, performance, portfolio]

2. Were they able to identify regularities or abnormalities in internal and external texture, anatomy, and overall structure in these botanical specimens? Could they explain something about the diversity of botanical structure? [embedded, journal entries]

3. Did students identify geometric shapes, numbers, and/or numeric patterns in their fruit and vegetable prints? [embedded, journal entries]

## Other Options and Extensions

1. Use printmaking and library or Internet research to investigate the anatomical differences between fruits and vegetables.

2. Experiment with the printing method: more paint, less paint, different paint, different ways of inking the stamp, different types of paper, etc.

3. Extend the printing process to other specimens: leaves, branches, whole fish, sponge, wood blocks, rocks, dried seaweed, etc.

4. Make an environmental mural (e.g., rainforest, underwater, desert) using stamps.

5. Extend the mathematical component of the activity by collecting data via the prints, e.g., measure and compute class averages of lemon diameters, lime circumferences, apple weight versus apple diameter, average number of peas in a pod, and so on. Data can be graphed, analyzed, and/or discussed.

6. For a social studies connection, examine fruits and vegetables from around the world, if available in your community, and allow students to find out how different cultures use them.

## Resources and Further Information

Gerber, B. (1995). These plants have potential. *Science and Children, 32* (1), 32–34.

Jenkins, P. D. (1980). *Art for the fun of it.* New York: Fireside.

Miller, J. (1973). Ozalid printing. *Science and Children, 10* (7), 35.

Mitchell, C. W. (1985). Leaf printing. *Science and Children, 23* (2), 24–26.

# Examining Serial Sections of an Apple

## Overview

In this activity the students will make *serial sections* of a familiar fruit, the apple. That is, they will begin with a print made from a cross section taken the very top portion of the specimen, then a print made from a slightly deeper cut, and so on until the final print is from the very lowest portion of the specimen. This serial sectioning technique provides almost a three-dimensional view of the inside of the apple, and serves as a very good aid in discerning the complete internal anatomy of the fruit. They can use their new-found knowledge of fruit anatomy to label their completed serial prints.

The apple is a sort of fruit known as a *pome.* A pome is defined as a fruit whose fleshy parts are all derived from the flower and enclose the portions produced by the pericarp (see Figure 29–2). The pear is also a pome.

## Concepts

Students develop their spatial sense and practice pattern recognition as they explore fruit anatomy and function.

## Processes/Skills

- Observing
- Predicting
- Describing
- Analyzing
- Concluding
- Measuring
- Calculating
- Inquiring
- Communicating
- Recognizing shapes and patterns
- Developing spatial sense
- Cooperating

## Recommended For

| | |
|---|---|
| K–2 ✔ | Individual |
| 3–5 ✔ | Small Group ✔ |
| 6–8 ✔ | Whole Class |

## Time Required

1–2 hours

## Materials Required

- Apples
- A sharp knife (for teacher use *only*) or plastic knives (for student use)
- Paper
- Newspaper
- Tempera paints in a variety of colors
- A means of inking the stamps (brushes, sponges, cloths, plastic dishes, paper towels, small brayers)

## Standards

**SCIENCE**
- Characteristics of Organisms
- Structure and Function in Living Systems
- Diversity and Adaptation of Organisms

**MATH**
- Connections
- Numbers and Operations
- Geometry
- Representation

## ● *Objectives*

- Students will successfully make prints from serial sections of an apple and will be able to explain how that series of prints provides a three-dimensional view of the inner apple.

- Students will observe, discuss, and compare the internal characteristics of apples, including number-related and shape-related patterns.

## *Main Activity, Step-by-Step*

1. Begin by asking students if they have ever seen the inside of a fruit of vegetable. When they confirm that they have, ask if they have ever seen the entire inside *all at once.* Not likely. X rays allow us to see inside things, but we don't have X-ray equipment in the classroom. Explain that they are going to create serial sections of an apple, and that a serial section is like a sliced up loaf of bread, i.e., a series of cross sections through a single specimen. What would they like to know about the inside of an apple? Note their responses on the chalkboard.

2. Assemble the students into small groups, and provide each group with a specimen. Have each group make and document predictions about what they think they'll find inside the apple. Students must then measure the length of the apple, in millimeters, and decide how many slices are appropriate for the size of their particular specimen. Four to seven slices should be reasonable. With longer specimens (such as cucumbers), or with older students, more slices can be made. Once they decide on the number of cross sections to make, they must divide the entire length by the number of slices plus one (we add one because we're really dividing the length by the number of *sections* into which the specimen is to be cut) to determine how far apart each section must be for all sections to be of equal depth. For example, a 100 mm apple with four slices will have a cut every 20 mm (see Figure 29–1).

3. Students can then make the first slice, using a plastic knife, or you can slice it for them with a metal knife. In either case, each group should proceed just one section at a time. Finish printing one section before moving on to the next so that the inside of the specimen remains fresh. Using the same printmaking techniques outlined in Activity 28, students produce a series of internal views of their apple. When all prints are completed and the paint has dried, the views should be labeled thoroughly. Labels should include information about the specimen (type of specimen, total length, thickness of sections, any unusual characteristics of the entire specimen), the internal anatomy (basic features; see Figure 29–2), and the investigators (names and responsibilities).

    Students can then examine their illustrations for patterns and regularities, comparing their serial views with those of other groups. What generalizations can they make about the internal

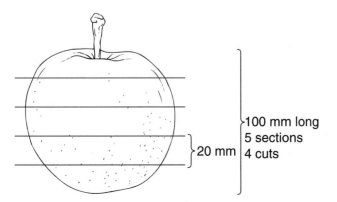

**Figure 29–1.**   Apple sections

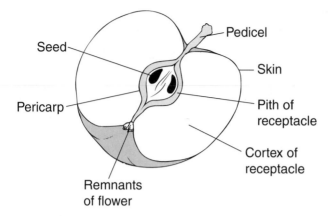

**Figure 29–2.**   Apple anatomy

anatomy of apples? Consider the location of seeds, the size of the receptacle, the location of the pericarp, and any student questions noted earlier on the chalkboard. Have them reflect on the accuracy of their predictions. What have they learned about the internal anatomy of the apple?

## Questions for Discussion

1.  How is the set of serial views like looking at an X ray of the apple's insides? How is it different than an X ray?

2.  What arithmetic or geometric patterns did you identify within the apple?

3.  In terms of their internal anatomy, how are apples similar? How do they differ?

## Assessment

1.  Were students able to successfully make a series of prints from serial sections of the apple? [embedded, performance]

2.  Were they able to observe, discuss, and compare the internal characteristics of apples, including shape-related patterns? [embedded, journal entries]

3.  Did they get a sense of how the serial sections provide an X ray or three-dimensional perspective of the inner apple? [embedded, journal entries]

## Other Options and Extensions

1.  Investigate the anatomy of other kind of fruits: *Berries* (tomato, grape, date, avocado, and citrus fruits), *drupes* (peaches, plums, cherries, olives, and apricots), and *false berries* (cucumber, squash, banana, cantaloupe, and cranberry).

2.  The activity can be done with printmaking, as suggested, or by having students make their own pencil illustrations of the serial sections. It is recommended that you choose hard specimens (pepper, apple, cucumber, squash), because they are more easily cut into thin sections and are much less messy. Advantages of the printmaking option are that it is quicker and offers more connections to the visual arts (the actual serial prints can be quite beautiful). Advantages of the illustration option are that it requires students to observe the cross sections more closely and that it tends to require less clean up.

## *Resources and Further Information*

Gerber, B. (1995). These plants have potential. *Science and Children, 33* (1), 32–34.

Jenkins, P. D. (1980). *Art for the fun of it.* New York: Fireside.

Miller, J. (1973). Ozalid printing. *Science and Children, 10* (7), 35.

Tolley, K. (1994). *The art and science connection.* Menlo Park, CA: Addison-Wesley.

Tortora, G. J., Cicero, D. R., & Parish, H. I. (1970). *Plant form and function.* New York:Macmillan.

# Please Pass the Pollen: Flowering Plants, Pollination, and Insect Pollinators

 ## Overview

This high-interest activity, designed for grades 6 through 8, will provide an opportunity for your students to learn more about the natural world, while they hone their investigatory skills. In this procedure, student groups investigate pollination, insect behavior, and flower structure. They will design and carry out experiments of their choosing, as they apply the inquiry skills learned in other *SISMI* activities. In a connecting activity, they then "build" an artificial flower that will attract pollinators.

## Concepts

Students explore angiosperm (flowering plant) pollination via insects, with a mathematical focus on data analysis and pattern recognition.

## Processes/Skills

- Observing
- Counting
- Predicting
- Describing
- Inferring
- Recognizing mathematical relationships
- Experimenting
- Communicating
- Reflecting
- Recognizing patterns
- Problem solving
- Analyzing
- Inquiring
- Creating
- Cooperating

## Recommended For

| | |
|---|---|
| K–2 | Individual |
| 3–5 | Small Group ✔ |
| 6–8 ✔ | Whole Class |

 ## Time Required

2–4 hours

 ## Materials Required

**MAIN ACTIVITY**

- Flowering plants
- Hand lenses (and/or microscopes or dissecting scopes if available)
- Calculators

**CONNECTING ACTIVITY**

- A variety of materials for creating artificial flowers (including various types of paper, inks, paints, pens, tape, glue, and fragrances)
- Wire
- Bamboo plant supports or bamboo skewers to serve as artificial flower "stems"

## Standards

**SCIENCE**

- Abilities Necessary to Do Scientific Inquiry
- Understanding About Scientific Inquiry
- Characteristics of Organisms
- Structure and Function of Living Systems
- Regulation and Behavior of Living Systems
- Diversity and Adaptation of Organisms

**MATH**

- Problem Solving
- Reasoning and Proof
- Communication
- Connections
- Data Analysis and Probability

##  *Objectives*

- Students will design experiments to test their ideas and predictions about pollination.

- Students will reach accurate and thoughtful conclusions regarding pollination based on their observations.

- Students will successfully apply mathematical thinking to their pollination investigations.

## *Background Information*

This lesson differs somewhat from the other 40 *SISMI* lessons, because a great deal of the investigation occurs outside the classroom, and because it requires some special materials, i.e., a fairly large number of living, flowering plants (either plants that you find on campus or those that you and/or the class plant yourselves). It could be undertaken on a smaller scale using several potted plants, however. In any case, you'll want to check ahead to be sure that you have a sufficient number of pollinators visiting whatever flowers you have available. Weather will also affect the number of pollinators visiting your flowers and, as happens so often in scientific investigation, you'll have to adjust and adapt your plans accordingly.

Pollen grains are the dustlike particles produced by the male reproductive organ, the anther, of flowering plants (i.e., angiosperms). Pollination is the deposition of pollen grains on the stigma of the flower's female reproductive organ (see Figure 30–1). Some flowering plants are self-pollinated and others are cross-pollinated, i.e., pollen is transferred from the anther of one flower to the stigma of another. Cross-pollination is usually accomplished by wind or by insects (often moths, bees, and butterflies). Once pollination occurs, the pollen grains release sperm cells that fertilize eggs, which develop into seeds.

## Main Activity, Step-by-Step

1. Begin by asking students to name foods we eat that come from plants. List their responses on the board; the list will certainly be long. Point out that many of those plants would not grow if it weren't for pollinators, which spread the plants' pollen from flower to flower and allow the plants to reproduce and grow fruits, vegetables, etc. We therefore rely on pollinators for much of our food, and many flowering plants rely on pollinators for their very survival. Ask the students what they know about pollinators and pollination.

    Take the class out to observe some flowers on campus (these can be in the ground or in pots, but the more the better). Have students record their observations of any pollination activity that they can see: what sorts of pollinators, which flowers are most often visited, etc. For safety's sake,

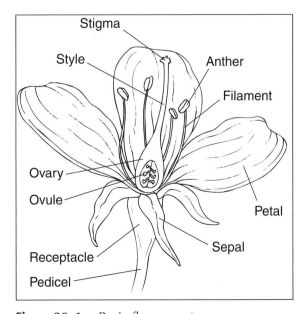

**Figure 30–1.** Basic flower anatomy

inform students ahead of time that they must not disturb the pollinators (especially those that are members of Order Hymenoptera, i.e., bees and wasps—by keeping calm and remaining at a respectful distance (a meter or so), there is little need to worry about stings. For safety's sake, it would also be wise to identify any students who have allergies to stinging insects; be sure that they stay far out of harm's way. Return to the classroom and have students report their findings. What do they want to know about flowers, pollen, and pollinators? Ask, how can we investigate and find answers to your questions? Be sure to adjust the following activities to their own notions of experimentation in order to offer opportunities for them to understand effective experimental technique through trial and error.

2. Devise investigations to encourage students to find out more about their questions regarding pollination and pollinators by direct observation. This process will be much more valuable if you allow the student groups to devise their own investigations, scaffolded by your comments and suggestions. They will practice determining the empirical means to answer their own questions.

   For instance, how often are flowers visited by pollinators?

   Predict and count the number of pollinators visiting a particular flower or a particular area of flowers within a certain time (e.g., in 10 minutes).

   How many pollinators would we expect to visit that flower or area in an hour? In a day?

   Is pollination more likely to occur in morning or afternoon? Students can make observations at different times of the day and compare their results.

   Are different pollinators active at different times of the day (e.g., morning versus afternoon)? Again, observations made throughout the day may be compared to provide insight.

   Do different flowers attract different pollinators? Does flower color seem to have anything to do with pollinator type or number of visits? Compare data to find out.

   Bring some flowers, both large and small, into the classroom for observation with hand lenses, microscopes, and/or dissecting scopes. Carefully dissect the flowers under a lens and watch for small or hidden insects. Are there any insect pollinators present that you might have missed seeing in the field?

   Clearly, students have unlimited opportunities to use math to analyze pollinator behavior: How long does a bee remain on a particular flower? What does it do while it's on the flower? Does it move on to a nearby flower or fly away, and approximately how far does it move? How many flowers does it visit before leaving the area? Within a given time on a particular flower, how many insects are present? (Consider comparing the *mean* and the *mode*, i.e., the most frequently occurring number of insects on a particular flower.) Data can also be used to create bar graphs, such as three bars comparing the number of insects seen on three different types of flowers. Students should see that by combining individual data they have more evidence on which to base their conclusions. They should also be encouraged to reflect on their methodologies, before and after carrying out their investigations. For instance, do you foresee any problems with this experimental technique? What were some sources of error in their investigations? How would they proceed differently if they were to do the investigations again?

## Questions for Discussion

1. For what foods do we depend on pollinators? In what other ways do pollinators affect our lives?

2. Pollination can be thought of like an "arranged deal" between the flower and the pollinator, with both parties benefiting from the relationship. How does the flower benefit? How does the pollinator benefit? Who or what else benefits? (In scientific jargon, we might call the relationship in which both parties benefit a *mutualistic* instance of *symbiosis*.)

3. How are flowers adapted for insect pollination? How are the insect pollinators adapted for pollinating flowers?

4. How did you use mathematics in your studies of pollination? How would your pollination experiments and/or investigations been different if you had not used math?

5. How would our lives be different without insect pollinators? What can we do to ensure that insect pollinators survive and thrive?

## Assessment

1. Were students able to effectively design experiments to test their ideas and predictions about pollination? [embedded]

2. Did they reach accurate and thoughtful conclusions regarding pollination based on their observations? [embedded, journal entries]

3. Were they able to successfully apply mathematics to their investigations of pollinators and pollination? [embedded]

## Connecting Activity

Begin this art connection by asking, "What sorts of flowers seem to attract insect pollinators? What are the characteristics of an insect-attractive flower?" Consider primary attractants (e.g., nectar and pollen availability, that is, nutrition) and secondary attractants (e.g., color, odor, shape, temperature, motion, placement/location). Direct the student groups to design and build a flower that will attract as many insects as possible, or that will attract an particular type of insect (most flowers are at least somewhat specific about attracting only a few types of pollinators, whereas some are linked to a single species of insect). Offer a variety of materials for flower building, including various types of paper, inks, paints, pens, tape, glue, fragrances. Wire, bamboo plant supports, or bamboo skewers will work well as flower stems. Or you could simplify the process by providing artificial flowers that the students can embellish with paint, fragrance, etc. Ask the students to predict the types of insects that will be attracted to their flower. Take the completed flowers outside and "plant" them. Have students record the type and number of pollinators that visit within a certain time period. On average, how long did insects remain on these artificial flowers? Return to the classroom and discuss the data. What conclusions can be reached? What sorts of attractants were effective? Which were ineffective? How did "time on artificial flower" compare with "time on real flower"? What surprised you about this investigation? What else do you want to know about this topic?

## Other Options and Extensions

1. Options and extensions here are nearly limitless. Students could find out more about flower structure, pollen structure and function, life cycles of the insect pollinators, angiosperms, coevolution (that is, the joint evolution of two or more different species in which selection pressure operates to make the evolution of either species partially dependent on the evolution of the other) of flowers and their pollinators (consider the passion flower and the *Heliaconius* butterfly, the *Yucca* flower and the yucca moth, or the hummingbird and the chuparosa [*Beloperone californica*] or *Penstemon* flowers), carnivorous plants, bees and beekeeping, the significant loss of bee pollinators in North America, and the dispersal of "killer bees" (Africanized Bees) into the United States from Central and South America.

2. Students can do more in-depth studies of flower anatomy, which might include pressing various flowers (in a plant press, see Figure 30–2, or between pieces of newsprint placed between the pages of a heavy book). Pressed flowers make beautiful and useful displays when glued onto paper.

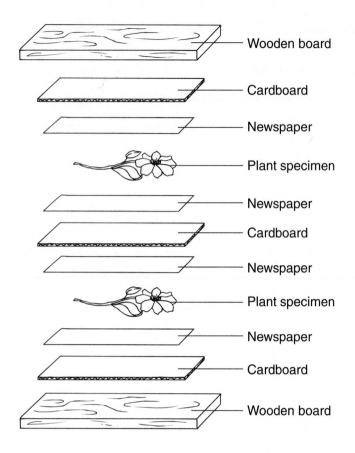

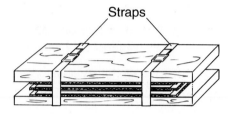

Straps

You can stack many plant specimens in a single press, which is cinched tightly together with straps. Remove specimens when completely dry.

A smaller version of the plant press can be cinched together using heavy rubber bands.

For each specimen, collect part of stem and foliage along with the flower, keeping all parts intact and connected. Record collection location, date, specimen name, and pollinators observed on the flowers.

**Figure 30–2.** Plant press

## Resources and Further Information

Faegri, K., & van der Pil, L. (1979). *Pollination ecology.* New York: Pergammon Press.

Moore, G. J. (1991). Flowering in Fairbanks. *Science and Children, 29* (3), 29–30.

Pianka, E. R. (1983). *Evolutionary ecology.* New York: Harper & Row.

Radue, A. K. (1991). The amaryllis—From bulb to blossom. *Science and Children, 29* (3), 27–28.

Seidel, J. D. (1998). Symmetry in season. *Teaching Children Mathematics, 4,* 244–249.

# Digging Into Soil

##  Overview

Here is an exciting, hands-on, earth science investigation that is adaptable to all grades. Students examine the composition of soil samples taken from the same location, but from three different depths. How do the three samples compare? How does the soil feel? Look? Smell? What sorts of things are included in it? Are there any living creatures? Will a hand lens help me find out? Students will then measure, count, and graph the number of rocks more than 3 cm in diameter. Finally, they will estimate the percentages of seven soil components for each of the three samples. All in all, your class will probably take a closer look at soil than they ever have before.

##  Concepts

Students count, measure, and estimate percentages as they learn about soil composition.

## Processes/Skills

- Observing
- Predicting
- Measuring
- Counting
- Describing
- Graphing
- Analyzing
- Comparing
- Concluding
- Cooperating
- Communicating

## Recommended for

K–2 ✔        Individual

3–5 ✔        Small Group ✔

6–8 ✔        Whole Class ✔

## Time Required

1–2 hours

## Materials Required

- Soil samples (from the surface 3 cm, 50 cm deep, and 1 m deep)
- Beaker or other measuring device
- Hand lenses
- Marking pens
- Large plastic cups
- Metric rulers
- Graph paper
- Newsprint or butcher paper

## Standards

**SCIENCE**
- Properties of Earth Materials
- Structure of the Earth System

**MATH**
- Reasoning and Proof
- Communication
- Numbers and Operations
- Representation

## Objectives

- Students will effectively describe, compare, and reach conclusions about the composition of the three soil samples.

● Students will successfully estimate component percentages of the three soil samples.

---

### ◉ *Background Information*

The *texture* of a *soil* is determined by the size of its constituent particles, which are classified based on size as *gravel, sand, silt,* or *clay.* Gravel particles are larger than 2.0 mm in diameter. Sand particles are easily seen, feel gritty, and range in size from 0.05 to 2.0 mm. Silt particles feel like flour and can barely be seen by the unaided eye, and range in size from 0.002 to 0.05 mm. Clay particles are too fine to be seen with the unaided eye and are difficult to see even under a microscope.

Collect the soil samples at school if possible, with students helping to dig and measure depth. If this is not feasible, collect the soil yourself and bring in sufficient samples from the three depths.

---

## *Main Activity, Step-by-Step*

1. Ask the students what they know about soil. Is it the same thing as dirt? Does soil matter to us? Why or why not? Have they ever taken a close look at soil? Today they will look closely at soil from the same location but from three different depths: the top 3 cm, from a 50-cm depth, and from a 1-m depth. What do they think they'll observe? Will the soil samples vary at the three depths? How will they vary? Have students fill in their predictions in Table 31–1 on Activity Sheet 31. What do they expect to find in terms of texture, color, odor, inclusions (rocks, sticks, etc.), life forms, and other factors?

   Give each group a hand lens and a 250-ml sample (use a beaker to measure, loosely packed) of the surface soil (top 3 cm) in a large plastic cup or other suitable container and have them make and record their observations using the first data table on the Activity Sheet. Repeat with the 50-cm depth and 1-m depth soil samples. Be sure that groups keep all three samples (mark the cups accordingly). After observing all three, ask students to describe what they found in the soil samples. Did they see what they expected to see? How did their predictions differ from their actual observations?

2. Were there any rocks in the samples? In this procedure they will count and compare the number of rock inclusions in each of the three samples. Direct student groups to count the number of rocks more than 3 cm in diameter (they'll need a metric ruler) in each sample. Record the data in Table 31–2. Have each group make a bar graph of the number of rocks counted in each sample. What conclusions can they reach by looking at their data?

3. Ask the students to describe the components of the soil samples. Encourage qualitative and quantitative responses. Offer descriptions of *gravel, silt, sand,* and *clay* (see Background Information above). Direct each group to spread each sample out, one sample at a time, on a large sheet of plain paper (newsprint or butcher paper). For each sample, have the students estimate the percentage that is rock, gravel, sand, silt, clay, organic material, and other substances. They should record their estimates in Table 31–3. What can they conclude from their data? What else would your students like to know about soil?

---

## *Questions for Discussion*

1. How were your observations of the soil different from what you expected to find?

2. Which soil depth contained the most rocks? How do you know?

3. How can you tell the difference between the different soil components?

---

## *Assessment*

1. Were the students able to effectively describe what they observed in the soil samples and compare their predictions to what they actually observed? [embedded, journal entries]

2. Could students reach meaningful conclusions about the differences between the three different samples? [embedded, journal entries]

3. Were the students able to successfully estimate component percentages of the samples? [embedded, performance]

## *Other Options and Extensions*

1. Students can collect and compare soil samples from different locations: various spots around the school grounds, the neighborhood, students' yards, and/or nearby natural areas. Expand this investigation to find out how soil varies around the world.

2. Use the Internet and/or library to investigate the importance of soil in agriculture.

3. Find out what sorts of organisms live in the soil.

## *Resources and Further Information*

Barcus, S., & Patton, M. M. (1996). What's the matter? *Science and Children, 34* (1), 49.

Smith, R. L. (1966). *Ecology and field biology.* New York: Harper & Row.

Tolley, K. (1994). *The art and science connection.* Menlo Park, CA: Addison-Wesley.

Tolman, M. N., & Morton, J. O. (1986). *Earth science activities for grades 2–8.* West Nyack, NY: Parker.

## Activity Sheet 31. Digging Into Soil

1. Table 31–1

| Soil Sample | Predictions. What do you think you'll observe? | Actual Observations | | | | | |
|---|---|---|---|---|---|---|---|
| | | *Texture* | *Color* | *Odor* | *Inclusions* | *Life Forms* | *Other* |
| Top 3 cm | | | | | | | |
| 50 cm deep | | | | | | | |
| 1 m deep | | | | | | | |

How did your predictions differ from your actual observations?

2. Table 31–2. How many rocks (> 3 cm in diameter) were in each sample?

| Soil Sample | Number of Rocks |
|---|---|
| Top 3 cm | |
| 50 cm deep | |
| 1 m deep | |

Make a bar graph of your data.

3. Table 31–3 Estimate the component percentages of each sample.

| Soil Sample | Estimated Percentages | | | | | | |
|---|---|---|---|---|---|---|---|
| | Rock | Gravel | Sand | Silt | Clay | Organic | Other |
| Top 3 cm | | | | | | | |
| 50 cm deep | | | | | | | |
| 1 m deep | | | | | | | |

What are your conclusions about the composition of the three soil samples?

# Observing and Sorting Rocks

 **Overview**

In this activity students examine garden variety rocks, classifying them based on observable properties. This lesson teaches them not only about rocks, but also about how to take a closer look at objects and materials that they encounter every day. They are encouraged to notice details that they may have previously overlooked. Students observe, test, and sort a collection of rocks using a variety of criteria including hardness, texture, luster, reaction to weak acid, magnetic attraction, and density. They will then use Venn diagrams to group similar rocks. This activity was designed for the middle and upper grades, although it could be simplified for primary students.

 **Concepts**

Students find out about properties of rocks and use Venn diagrams to classify rocks.

**Processes/Skill**

- Observing
- Describing
- Measuring
- Classifying
- Analyzing
- Recognizing patterns
- Problem solving
- Comparing
- Cooperating

**Recommended for**

| | |
|---|---|
| K–2 | Individual |
| 3–5 ✔ | Small Group ✔ |
| 6–8 ✔ | Whole Class ✔ |

**Time Required**

2–3 hours

**Materials Required**

**MAIN ACTIVITY**

- Several sets of 5 to 10 different rocks (garden variety specimens are fine, as long as they're easily distinguishable from one another).
- Hand lenses
- Masking tape
- Metric rulers
- Vinegar
- Droppers or drinking straws
- Magnets
- Metric balances
- Beaker or graduated cylinder

**CONNECTING ACTIVITY**

- Rocks
- A variety of construction materials such as tape, cardboard, paper, scissors, sticks, glue, and string

 **Standards**

**SCIENCE**

- Abilities Necessary to Do Scientific Inquiry
- Understanding About Scientific Inquiry
- Properties of Earth Materials
- Structure of the Earth System

**MATH**

- Communication
- Numbers and Operations
- Representation

##  Objectives

- Students will sort rocks into several categories based on their own criteria.

- Students will test rocks for various properties, including hardness, reaction to acid, magnetic attraction, luster, texture, and density.

- Students will successfully use Venn diagrams to group rocks.

## Background Information

Rocks are *aggregates* (combinations or composites) of *minerals* (naturally occurring inorganic [i.e., nonliving] substances, each with a definite chemical composition). Rocks are often classified into three main groups: (1) *igneous rocks*—formed from molten magma; make up most of the continental crust; examples: pumice, granite; (2) *sedimentary rocks*—rocks formed on the earth's surface, usually as products of erosion from other rocks; i.e., rocks erode, the debris becomes deposited into low lying areas where in time it is compacted into new sorts of rocks; examples: sandstone, shale, limestone; (3) *metamorphic rocks*—rocks formed by alteration of other rocks by heat, pressure, and other natural forces; example: mica.

## Main Activity, Step-by-Step

1. Ask, "Are rocks important to people? How do we use rocks?" As students respond, be sure that they realize that humans have long used rocks for many purposes including tools, ornaments, and building materials. Can the students think of any other uses for rocks? Where have you seen rocks? Describe some rocks that you've seen. Generally consider the following questions: How do the rocks differ from one another? What do rocks have in common? What size? Color? Other characteristics? Where do you think rocks come from? Why are rocks important to us? In this activity the class will have a chance to take a much closer look at some rocks.

2. Give each student group a collection of 5 to 10 different rocks, a metric ruler, and a hand lens. Each rock should have its own number (marked on a small piece of masking tape). It is quite all right for each group's collection to contain different types of rocks, as long as there is a variety in each set. Give them a few minutes to just observe their rocks, then ask them to sort the rocks into two piles, based on some characteristic they notice about the rocks. One student from each group should document the sorting criteria. Discuss their ideas: maybe they sorted the rocks based on size (large or small), color (black or white), shape (flat or round) or another observable property (striped or not). There are no wrong answers here, so you can encourage diverse and creative responses. Have each group do this sorting process several more times, being sure to keep a written record of their sorting criteria. Have groups share and discuss their schemes.

3. Next, the groups can test the rocks in several ways. These tests serve as ways to classify rocks. They should keep a written record of their test results using Activity Sheet 32.

   *Hardness.* Test the rock specimens for hardness. Select any two. Scratch one against the other. The one that can scratch the other is the hardest. Now test the harder of the two against another specimen from the collection, and so on until you find the hardest rock. Then find the second hardest, the third, and so on until you know the order of hardness for all the rocks.

   *Reaction to acid.* If you have included a rock containing calcium carbonate, such as limestone, marble, calcite, or chalk, you can include this test. Place a few drops of vinegar, a weak acid, on each rock. Rocks containing calcium carbonate will fizz in the presence of vinegar, indicating a positive test.

   *Magnetic Attraction.* Does a magnet react to any of the rocks? If you have included an iron-containing rock such as galena, it will. Better yet; include a lodestone if you can. A lodestone is made of magnetite and is a naturally occurring magnetic rock.

*Luster.* Luster refers to the rock's shininess, that is, its ability to reflect light. Check each rock to judge whether it is shiny or dull.

*Texture.* Look at the crystals or particles in the rocks. If they are ≥3 mm in size, the rock is "rough." If they are < 3 mm in size, the rock is "smooth."

*Density.* This test is offered as an adaptation for older students. The density of an object refers to its relative weight and is calculated by dividing the object's mass by its volume (see Activity 20, Layered Liquids). For each rock in the collection, find its mass in grams using a balance, and divide that number by the specimen's volume in ml, determined by completely immersing the rock in a beaker or graduated cylinder of water and finding out how many ml it displaces. (In other words, how much higher did the water go when the rock was placed into the container? If the water was at a level of 100 ml and rose to 200 ml when the rock was immersed, the rock has a volume of 100 ml.) Rank order (first, second, third, etc.) the rock specimens based on their densities.

4. Use the information gathered in Procedure 3, to decide where the rocks fit into the Venn diagram on Activity Sheet 32. Students write each rock's number in the proper circle, or junction of circles, based on whether it has a rough or smooth texture, is shiny or dull in luster, and/or reacts to vinegar. Some rocks (those that are smooth, dull, and do not react to vinegar) might not fit into any circles; they should be placed outside all three Venn circles. When they have finished, discuss their completed Venn diagrams. Which rocks in the collection were most similar? How do you know? Why is the Venn diagram helpful in determining similarities and differences?

5. Finally, student groups can make their own Venn diagrams using any bimodal (either-or) characteristics that they noticed and recorded in Procedure 2: large or small, light or dark, striped or not, single color or multiple colors, etc. For younger students, a Venn diagram with two intersecting circles is appropriate. Older students can try three or even four circles at once.

   Discuss their results as a class. What have they learned about rocks? What else would they like to know? Ask each student group to write their own definition of the word *rock*. Introduce the concept of igneous, sedimentary, and metamorphic rocks. Determine which of those three categories the rocks in the collections belong to.

## Questions for Discussion

1. What sorts of characteristics do rocks have in common?

2. Which rock from the collection is your favorite, and why?

3. What other objects could you sort using a Venn diagram?

## Assessment

1. Were the students able to sort the rocks into several categories based on their own criteria? [embedded, performance]

2. Did students successfully test the rocks for hardness, reaction to acid, magnetic attraction, luster, texture, and density? [embedded, performance]

3. Were students able to comprehend and use the Venn diagrams? [embedded, performance]

## Connecting Activity

For a social studies connection, have each student group choose one of their rocks and make it into a tool that an ancient person might have used. Offer a variety of materials for tool construction: tape, cardboard, paper, scissors, sticks, glue, string, etc. When completed, each group can explain to the class how their tool was constructed and how it would be used. Look into the history of rock tools.

## Other Options and Extensions

1.  Students can begin their own rock collections, keeping track of where and when they found each specimen. Display their collections in the classroom.

2.  Using reference materials from the library and/or Internet, identify the types of rocks found in the classroom rock collections.

3.  Find rocks that look like other things: people's faces, cars, boats, houses, etc.

4.  Investigate Mohs' scale, developed about 150 years ago to determine the hardness of minerals and rocks. In increasing order of hardness: (1) talc, (2) gypsum, (3) calcite, (4) fluorite, (5) apatite, (6) orthoclase feldspar, (7) quartz, (8) topaz, (9) corundum, (10) diamond.

## Resources and Further Information

Barcus, S., & Patton, M. M. (1996). What's the matter? *Science and Children, 34* (1), 49.

Gaylen, N. (1998). Encouraging curiosity at home. *Science and Children, 35* (4), 24–25.

MacFall, R. P. (1980). *Rock hunter's guide.* New York; Crowell.

Pearlman, S., & Pericak-Spector, K. (1994). A series of seriation activities. *Science and Children, 31* (4), 37–39.

Tolman, M. N., & Morton, J. O. (1986). *Earth science activities for grades 2–8.* West Nyack, NY: Parker.

Williams, D. (1995). *Teaching mathematics through children's art.* Portsmouth, NH: Heineman.

## Activity Sheet 32. Observing and Sorting Rocks

List the rocks (by their number) in order from softest to hardest:

1.     2.     3.     4.     5.     6.     7.     8.     9.     10.

Which rock(s) reacted to the vinegar?

To which rock(s) did a magnet react?

Luster:

| *Shiny Rocks* | *Dull Rocks* |
|---|---|
|  |  |

Texture:     Rough = crystals or particles ≥ 3 mm
Smooth = crystals or particles < 3 mm

| *Rough Rocks* | *Smooth Rocks* |
|---|---|
|  |  |

Density:

| *Rock #* | *Mass (g)* | *Volume (ml)* | *Density (Mass/Vol.)* | *Rank Order* |
|---|---|---|---|---|
|  |  |  |  |  |
|  |  |  |  |  |
|  |  |  |  |  |
|  |  |  |  |  |
|  |  |  |  |  |
|  |  |  |  |  |
|  |  |  |  |  |
|  |  |  |  |  |
|  |  |  |  |  |
|  |  |  |  |  |

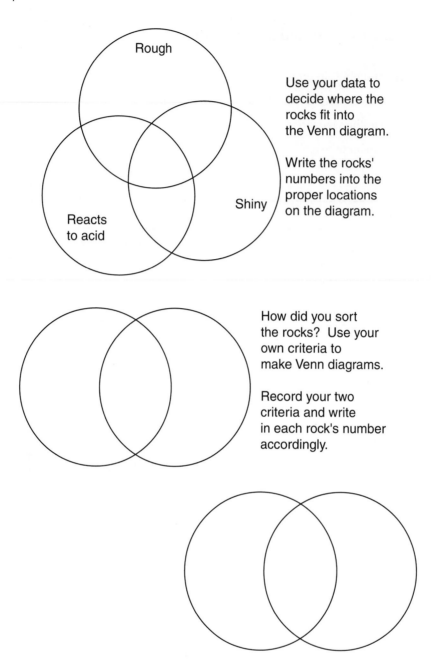

Use your data to decide where the rocks fit into the Venn diagram.

Write the rocks' numbers into the proper locations on the diagram.

How did you sort the rocks? Use your own criteria to make Venn diagrams.

Record your two criteria and write in each rock's number accordingly.

# 33 Discovering Sand and Sand Paintings

## Overview

This activity blends social studies and art with math and science. First, students will explore the visible characteristics of sand, then they will make Navajo-style sand paintings with paper, glue, and colored sand. In the process, they'll hone their estimation skills by assessing the number of sand grains on their paintings, as well as in a small bag of sand. They will gain an appreciation for the meaning, beauty, and utility of Navajo sand paintings.

## Concepts

Students observe sand grains, comparing them to one another and to other substances. They design and create a Navajo-style sand painting and estimate the number of sand grains on the sand painting (area) and in a small container displayed by the teacher (volume).

## Processes/Skills

- Observing
- Using the hand lens
- Estimating
- Describing
- Comparing
- Counting
- Measuring
- Weighing
- Inferring
- Analyzing
- Recognizing shapes and patterns
- Problem solving
- Inquiring
- Designing
- Creating
- Reflecting
- Communicating

## Recommended for

| | |
|---|---|
| K–2 | Individual ✔ |
| 3–5 ✔ | Small Group ✔ |
| 6–8 ✔ | Whole Class |

## Time Required

2–3 hours

## Materials Required

- Sand
- Hand lenses
- Photos of Navajo sand paintings (or actual sand paintings)
- Paper
- Glue sticks
- Food coloring
- Newspaper
- Scales or balances

## Standards

SCIENCE
- Abilities Necessary to Do Scientific Inquiry
- Understanding About Scientific Inquiry
- Properties of Earth Materials
- Structure of the Earth System

**MATH**

- Problem Solving
- Numbers and Operations

##  *Objectives*

- Students will successfully observe, describe, and compare sand grains.

- Students will estimate the number of sand grains on their paintings (area) and in a small container displayed by the teacher (volume), thus contrasting area and volume.

- Students will create, observe, compare, and reflect on Navajo-style sand paintings.

##  *Background Information*

Traditionally, Navajo sand paintings are used in healing and other important spiritual rituals. They are often used in conjunction with prayers, chants, and dances in ceremonies that may last several days. The paintings represent the supernatural spirits and invoke the power of those beings. Sand paintings are made directly on the earth and are swept up soon after completion. Their size ranges from 4 to 18 feet wide, and their shape can be square, oblong, or round. They often incorporate the four cardinal directions (east, white; south, yellow; west, blue; north, black). The pigments are taken from the earth: white from rock, red and yellow from ochre, black from charcoal mixed with sand, blue/gray from a mixture of white and black, pink from red and white.

## *Main Activity, Step-by-Step*

1. Ask, "What is sand?" Brainstorm answers as a class or in small groups. Encourage a variety of responses, documenting them all. How could we find out more about sand? What are some things we could do with sand? What would you like to know about sand? Again, encourage a variety of student responses, first by having everyone record their responses in their science journals, then by offering their ideas publicly, in small groups.

2. For each group of students, provide a small dish or plastic bag of sand, some newspapers or paper towels, and a hand lens. Also helpful, but not necessary, would be a small flashlight, as an aid in viewing sand under the lens. Ask, "How many grains of sand do you think are in this bag/dish? How did you decide on that number? What are some other ways to estimate?" Record their rough estimations and brainstormed techniques for estimating.

3. Now conduct general research on the sand samples. Challenge student groups to learn as much as they can about the sand. No observation would be considered too big or too small. All observations must be recorded on a data sheet or in a science journal. They can also compare the sand to a small sample of dirt, potting soil, or other similar substance. Share all research findings in a classwide "symposium" or "scientific conference" on sand. Again ask, "What else would you like to know about sand?" Their responses could form the basis for extension activities to be conducted later.

4. Show photos of Navajo sand paintings, or actual sand paintings if you have them or can find them on the Internet (see Figure 33–1 for several design examples). Ask, "What do the paintings have in common? Why do you suppose that the artists chose these designs? What other art forms are the Navajo known for (e.g., woven rugs)? What designs would *you* make in a sand painting?" During the discussion of the sand paintings, you can share information about the Navajo people and their arts, perhaps including a story like *Knots in a Counting Rope.* What other questions do students have about the Navajo? Here is an opportunity for inquiry-based research on the tribe's history, sociology, geography, art, philosophy, and general way of life.

5. Next, students will have a chance to make their own sand paintings. Although Navajo sand paintings were traditionally made on the ground with loose sand, using no glue or other fixative (Why would they make such intricate art in such a fragile form?), students can make a more permanent product on paper. You'll need to color the sand ahead of time by soaking plain sand in

**Figure 33–1.**    Navajo designs

water tinted with food coloring for an hour, pouring off the water, and letting the sand dry overnight. The basic technique for making the sand painting itself is this: On a piece of clean white paper sketch the desired design lightly in pencil, apply glue to a portion of the painting and sprinkle with sand, shake off the excess sand, apply glue and sand to another area, and so on until the piece is completed.

6. Provide students with materials (paper, glue sticks, various colors of sand, newspaper to cover the work surface) and let them create their own sand paintings.

7. When all students have completed their projects, analyze the sand-painting process (what worked, what didn't, what problems did you have, what surprises, what did you enjoy, etc.?) and allow each group present their work. Discuss or write about reactions to the various sand paintings. How are they like traditional Navajo art? How are they different?

8. Now let's estimate the number of sand grains in a given area or volume. As an introduction ask, "When have you wanted to know the approximate number of a large number of objects?" Ask, "Can you think of any situations where people might want to estimate amounts or numbers?" Encourage variety in responses; you may want to offer a "warm up" example or two (e.g., How much pet food would you need to leave behind if you went away on a week-long trip?). Challenge students to estimate the number of sand grains on their sand painting. Resist the temptation to offer specific hints; let them work it out in groups, but do make sure that they have access to hand lenses, rulers, and scales or balances. They *could* estimate the sand grains on a painting by counting the grains within a small (e.g., one square centimeter) area and multiplying by the estimated number of square centimeters covered in sand on the entire painting. If the working groups are getting too frustrated, you can gently "encourage" them with hints to send them in this direction. The less you suggest, in terms of technique, the better. When the time is right, ask groups to explain how they proceeded to solve this problem. Ask them to reflect on the process, "Which techniques were effective? Why? Which weren't? Why? How do these estimations compare with those made earlier [in Procedure 2]?" Point out that the first was an estimate of volume (height x width x depth; three-dimensional space) and the second was an estimate of area (height x width; two-dimensional surface).

9. Now revisit the question posed in Procedure 2; challenge them to estimate the number of grains in the bag, dish, or other container, after considering the methods used in the sand-painting estimations. Provide each group with a similar container of sand. Again, don't succumb to temptation; let the groups work it out on their own. If, after a time, students are too frustrated, you can offer hints leading to any of several solutions: counting the number of grains in a pinch or a small spoonful (unit of volume) and multiplying, or weighing (mass) a pinch or small spoonful and counting its grains, then multiplying, etc. The idea here is to encourage the development of problem-solving skills and to allow students to "own" their solutions, possibly using you, the teacher, as a resource person. When the task is completed, analyze and reflect on the various methods used. How could estimation be usefully applied to their own lives?

## Questions for Discussion

1. How are sand grains similar to one another? How do they differ? What have you learned about sand?

2. Can you think of a situation in which you or someone else might need to estimate a large quantity of sand or other substance?

3. How is *estimating* like *counting*? How is it different?

4. Can you think of ways in which *area* and *volume* are alike? Ways in which they are different?

5. Why do you think that sand paintings are important to the Navajo people? What else would you like to find out about the Navajo?

## Assessment

1. Were students able to successfully observe, describe, and compare sand grains? [embedded]

2. Were they able to estimate the number of sand grains in area and in volume? Did they explore a variety of estimation methods, choosing (with or without teacher facilitation) the most effective techniques? [ebmedded, performance]

3. Did they create, observe, and compare Navajo-style sand paintings? [embedded, journal entries]

## Other Options and Extensions

1. Homework: Go home and estimate at least three large amounts (these could be in the actual home or somewhere in the community). Work can be done with family members.

2. Conduct research on sand paintings in other cultures, such as Tibetan mandalas. Make one yourself.

3. Have the entire class produce a mural-sized sand painting.

4. Make sand paintings using geometric designs only (e.g., angles, shapes, repeating patterns) then ask students to describe their work in geometric and mathematical terms.

## Resources and Further Information

Alexander, D. (1994). The dirt finders. *Science and Children, 31* (7), 12–14.

Carp, K. S. (1994). Telling tales: Creating graphs using multicultural literature. *Teaching Children Mathematics, 1,* 87–91.

Martin, B., Jr., & Archambault, J. (1987). *Knots in counting rope.* New York: Holt.

Stroud, S. (1980). An affair with sand. *Science and Children, 18* (2), 22–25.

Underhill, R. M. (1965). *Red man's religion.* Chicago: University of Chicago Press.

# 34

# Heat Exchange in Air, Water, and Soil

 ## Overview

The earth is composed, at least at the surface, of soil/rock, water, and air. How do the heat exchange properties of these three very different substances compare, and what effect, if any, do they have on our climate and weather? This represents a somewhat more advanced investigation of a complex subject, designed for grades 5 through 8 but easily adapted to lower grades.

 ## Concepts

Students discover how air, soil, and water compare in terms of heat absorption and radiation. Data are collected and analyzed for patterns.

## Processes/Skills

- Observing
- Inquiring
- Describing
- Counting
- Measuring
- Graphing
- Analyzing data
- Problem solving
- Concluding
- Applying conclusions
- Communicating

## Recommended for

| | |
|---|---|
| K–2 | Individual |
| 3–5 | Small Group ✔ |
| 6–8 ✔ | Whole Class ✔ |

 ## Time Required

1–2 hours

## Materials Required

- Plastic cups
- Thermometers
- Soil (or sand)
- Water
- Desk lamp(s)
- Graph paper

 ## Standards

**SCIENCE**

- Structure of the Earth System

**MATH**

- Reasoning and Proof
- Connections
- Measurement
- Representation

## Objectives

- Students will successfully explore the heat exchange properties of the three substances (air, soil, water).
- Students will make thoughtful connections between heat exchange and climate/weather patterns.
- Students will successfully collect, display, and analyze their numerical data regarding heat exchange.

## *Main Activity, Step-by-Step*

1.  Ask the students to recall a time when they sat outside in the sunlight—maybe at the beach or out for a walk. Better yet, if it is in fact a sunny day, go outside and let everyone stand in the sunlight for a few minutes. How do the students describe their experience, especially in terms of temperature changes? They will probably say that they became warm. This is an example of *heat exchange*, in particular *heat conduction*, which is when heat flows from one object or substance (in this case, the air) to another (in this case, the students themselves). What do they do when they become too warm? They leave the sunlight and somehow find shelter. But the sun shines 24 hours a day, 7 days a week, and the earth itself cannot find shelter from the sun's light and warmth. How do the substances of the earth (air, soil, water) react to the warmth of the sun? Are they all the same, or do they react differently? Do they differ in how they conduct heat? Do some of the earth's substances retain heat better than others? That is, do some substances lose, or *radiate*, heat more slowly than others? How could we find out? Encourage diverse responses, and try them out. One particular means of inquiry follows.

2.  Divide the class into three groups (or multiples of three), one for each of the three substances mentioned. Provide each group with a large plastic cup filled with a single substance; that is, either a cup of air, soil (or sand), or water. Each group also receives a thermometer, which is placed into the central portion of their substance. Students should predict which substance will heat up fastest, and which will lose heat the fastest. That is, which substances will conduct and radiate heat most quickly. Be sure that all substances are initially at room temperature, and record that temperature. Immediately place each of the three cups directly under identical desk lamps and record each substance's temperature every minute for 15 minutes, using Activity Sheet 34 to record data. At the end of that 15-minute period, turn off the lamps and continue recording temperature readings each minute for the next 15 minutes. Results will vary significantly depending on how deeply the thermometer is inserted into the soil/sand and on how close the three substances are to the lamp.

3.  All groups then share data so that everyone has results for all three of the substances. In the last column of the data table (Activity Sheet 34) students can calculate the heat retained, if any, by each of the substances (find the difference between Temperature Reading #15 and Temperature Reading #30). How else could we decide which substance retains heat best, worst, and so on? Why not plot temperature (y axis) versus time (x axis) for all three substances on a single graph so that they can be easily compared throughout the 30-minute time period? (Make sure to label each of the three resulting lines so that students can tell them apart.)

    According to the graph, which substance gained heat the fastest? Which lost heat quickest? How do you know? Which substance retained heat most effectively? That is, which lost its heat most slowly? How close were your predictions to the actual results? For older students, the inquiry can expand into actual rates of heat gain and loss in degrees per minute.

    Ideally, water generally retains heat most efficiently, followed by soil (or sand), and air. Water retains heat well and acts like a heat reservoir: it heats up slowly and cools off slowly. Air, like most gases, is a poor conductor of heat because it has few molecules per unit of volume with which to transfer heat energy. Air (and water) can transport heat effectively via *convection*, however. Convection refers to the transport of heat energy by the actual motion of the heated gas (or liquid). Currents caused by convection are easily seen in boiling water. Solid land (e.g., rock, clay, sand, and soil) conducts and radiates heat efficiently, allowing it to heat up *and* cool off quickly. Heat exchange in real systems is quite complex, because it is influenced by many variables, including mass, evaporation, and reflectivity of the substances being heated.

    The interplay among the temperature differentials of atmosphere, water (especially oceans), and land (especially continents) has a huge impact on the climate, weather, and the general circulation of the earth's atmosphere. For instance, in coastal areas during the day the land tends to be warmer than the adjacent ocean, and the opposite is true at night. This effect tends to stabilize the region's temperature and often causes daytime onshore breezes and nighttime offshore breezes, which affect the level of comfort for residents. On the other hand, continental heartlands, far from the influence of sea or ocean, tend to be very hot in the summer and very cold in the winter.

## Questions for Discussion

1. How do the thermal properties of air, soil, and water affect climate and/or weather?

2. How did mathematics help you determine the differences in heat exchange of the three substances (air, soil, water)? Could you have reached a meaningful conclusion without using math?

3. Why do some people want to live near an ocean or sea, in terms of the water source's affect on weather/climate? Where would you like to live, and why?

## Assessment

1. Did students successfully explore the heat exchange properties of the three substances (air, soil, water)? [embedded, performance]

2. Were students able to make thoughtful connections between heat exchange and climate and/or weather patterns? [embedded, performance, journal entries]

3. Could students successfully collect, display, and analyze their numerical data regarding heat exchange? [embedded]

## Other Options and Extensions

1. Have students design and build model houses of different substances (clay, cardboard, paper, etc.). Test the heat retention of the houses, using a lamp as a heat source. Record the temperature data and find out which home material insulates best. Also, test different designs for thermal differences.

2. Give each student group an ice cube (in the bottom of a clear plastic cup so that it is visible and you can see when it has melted) and challenge them to insulate the cube so that it lasts as long as possible under a desk lamp. Offer a variety of materials (cotton, paper, cardboard, packing bubbles, etc.) to lay over the cube for insulation against the heat of the lamp.

3. Test the thermal properties of salt water (using the basic procedure noted above), and compare the thermal properties of salt water to those of fresh water. Compare the thermal properties of different types of soil, and/or compare moist air (put a damp paper towel in the bottom of the cup) with dry air for heat gain and loss.

## Resources and Further Information

Critchfield, H. J. (1983). *General climatology.* Englewood Cliffs, NJ: Prentice-Hall.

Gates, D. M. (1972). *Man and his environment: Climate.* New York: Harper & Row.

Lockwood, J. G. (1979). *Causes of climate.* New York: Wiley.

Pearlman, S., & Pericak-Spector, K. (1994). A series of seriation activities. *Science and Children, 31* (4), 37–39.

Pearlman, S., & Pericak-Spector, K. (1995). Graph that data. *Science and Children, 32* (4), 35–37.

Rezba, R. J., Sprague, C., Fiel, R. L., & Funk, H. J. (1995). *Learning and assessing science process skills.* Dubuque, IA: Kendall/Hunt.

Tolley, K. (1994). *The art and science connection.* Menlo Park, CA: Addison-Wesley.

Tolman, M. N., & Morton, J. O. (1986). *Earth science activities for grades 2–8.* West Nyack, NY: Parker.

## Activity Sheet 34. Heat Exchange in Air, Water, and Soil

Predict: Rank order the three substances (air, soil, water) in terms of how well you think they will be able to retain heat.

| Ranking | Prediction | Actual |
|---------|------------|--------|
| Most Effective | | |
| Second | | |
| Least Effective | | |

Record heat gain (conduction) and heat loss (radiation) data for all three substances. Each group will experiment with a single substance. Room Temperature (initial temperature of all three substances) = _____ °C

| | Lamp On (by minutes; record temperature) | | | | | | | | | | | | | | | Lamp Off (by minutes; record temperature) | | | | | | | | | | | | | | | Heat Retained |
|---|---|---|---|---|---|---|---|---|---|---|---|---|---|---|---|---|---|---|---|---|---|---|---|---|---|---|---|---|---|---|---|
| | 1 | 2 | 3 | 4 | 5 | 6 | 7 | 8 | 9 | 10 | 11 | 12 | 13 | 14 | 15 | 16 | 17 | 18 | 19 | 20 | 21 | 22 | 23 | 24 | 25 | 26 | 27 | 28 | 29 | 30 | #15 minus #30 |
| Air | | | | | | | | | | | | | | | | | | | | | | | | | | | | | | | |
| Soil | | | | | | | | | | | | | | | | | | | | | | | | | | | | | | | |
| Water | | | | | | | | | | | | | | | | | | | | | | | | | | | | | | | |

Graph the class data for all three substances: time (x axis) versus temperature (y axis).

What can you conclude based on the data?

# 35

# Exploring Evaporation

##  Overview

Through a series of hands-on investigations the students learn what evaporation is and how various factors affect it. Designed for grades 5 through 8, but adaptable to lower grades, students will find out how time, heat, surface area, and wind affect evaporation. They'll discover that not all liquids evaporate at the same rate and that saltwater leaves something behind when it evaporates. Finally, they'll apply what they've learned to discover how evaporation affects climate and weather.

In this activity, the "factual information" regarding evaporation is purposely distributed throughout the lesson, with much of it left for the lesson's finish. By investigating first and informing after, student curiosity remains engaged as we build an experiential base on which to construct conceptual/factual knowledge. That is, we begin with concrete, hands-on experiences and later merge those experiences with factual material.

##  Concepts

Students explore aspects of evaporation, using measurement, data analysis, and problem-solving strategies. They eventually consider how evaporation affects climate and weather.

##  Processes/Skills

- Observing
- Inquiring
- Describing
- Measuring
- Graphing
- Analyzing data
- Problem solving
- Concluding
- Communicating

##  Recommended for

| | |
|---|---|
| K–2 | Individual |
| 3–5 | Small Group ✔ |
| 6–8 ✔ | Whole Class ✔ |

##  Time Required

2–3 hours

## Materials Required

- Water
- Beaker and/or graduated cylinder (for measuring)
- Small plastic cups (medicine cups work very well)
- Plastic plates
- Graph paper
- Rubbing alcohol
- Nail polish remover (with acetone)
- Marking pens
- Paper towels
- Desk lamp(s)
- Aluminum foil and/or cookie sheets
- Small fan(s)
- Salt

##  Standards

**SCIENCE**

- Abilities Necessary to Do Scientific Inquiry
- Understanding About Scientific Inquiry

- Properties of Earth Materials
- Structure of the Earth System

**MATH**

- Problem Solving
- Reasoning and Proof
- Measurement
- Data Analysis and Probability

## ◉ *Objectives*

- Students will offer a definition of *evaporation* in their own words and will be able to explain how it may affect climate and weather.

- Students will successfully graph, analyze, and draw conclusions from their data regarding variables that affect evaporation.

- Students will be able to explain evaporation's place in the water cycle.

## *Main Activity, Step-by-Step*

1.  Ask the students whether they have ever left water out for a period of time. What happened to the water? If it disappeared, where did it go? Do other liquids disappear this way? Do all water sources disappear like this? Puddles, lakes, streams, seas, oceans? Explain that this disappearance of liquids is called *evaporation*. *Evaporation* is the process of a liquid changing into a gas. What do your students want to know about evaporation? How can we find out more about evaporation? Explain that in the upcoming series of exercises we are going to explore some aspects of evaporation.

    First we can ask, "How fast does water evaporate?" Provide student groups with graduated cylinders or beakers, water, marking pens, and a small plastic cup. Have each group mark the cup at the 10, 20, 30, and 40 ml points. Then fill the cup to the 40 ml point and place all the groups' cups in an open but protected spot in the room (this will take a few days, so plan ahead). Students should predict how long it will take for one fourth (10 ml), one-half (20 ml), three-fourths (30 ml), and all (40 ml) of the water in their cup to evaporate. Data can be collected daily on Activity Sheet 35. Graph the results (volume of water on the y axis and time on the x axis). What conclusions do student reach? Does evaporation seem fast or slow?

2.  Ask, "Do all liquids evaporate at the same rate?" To find out, try this classroom demonstration. Measure out 5 ml (about one teaspoon) and place into plastic cups each of three liquids: water, rubbing alcohol, and nail polish remover (a brand that contains acetone). Will the liquids evaporate at different rates? Ask for student predictions of which will evaporate first, second, and last. Have three student volunteers each fold a paper towel into quarters; at a signal from you they pour one of the three liquids completely onto the towel, and at a second signal they smear the liquid on the chalkboard. Two safety issues: (a) be sure that the room is well ventilated, and (b) remind students not to touch their hands to their mouths or faces after handling the liquids. The rest of the class observes which liquid evaporates fastest. Repeat as necessary with new volunteers. Compare results with predictions. Be sure that all volunteers wash their hands thoroughly. Discuss the results. Did the liquids evaporate at different rates? Which consistently evaporated fastest? Slowest? How do you explain the differences in evaporation? Were there any sources of error in this experiment (e.g., maybe one student wiped more of the liquid from the towel to the board than another student did)? How could the error be reduced?

    *Hydrogen bonds* between the molecules in a liquid tend to hold it together and keep it from evaporating quickly. Water has many hydrogen bonds, rubbing alcohol has few, and acetone essentially has none. Therefore, water tends to evaporate slowest and acetone fastest.

3.  Ask, "Does heat affect evaporation?" Direct student groups to place 5 ml of water in each of two plates. Place one plate on a desk or countertop under a warm lamp, and the other in similar conditions, but not near the lamp or any other heat source. Which will evaporate first? Students can record the time for each plate of water to evaporate and display the data in a bar graph.

Heat breaks the bonds between the liquid molecules, allowing them to break free and evaporate into the air. The more heat, the more evaporation. Think of several examples of evaporation in real life. What is the source of heat that causes evaporation in the case of each example (e.g., wet hair—heat in the room or even faster evaporation with a hair dryer; rain puddles—sunlight)?

4. Now ask, "What else might affect evaporation?" Have student groups place 5 ml of water in a small plastic cup, and another 5 ml spread out on a cookie sheet or sheet of aluminum foil. Which will evaporate fastest? Students can record the time needed for each source of water to evaporate and display the data in a bar graph. What do their results show?

   *Surface area* is connected to evaporation rate. If the surface area is great, more water molecules are exposed to heat and more can escape from the liquid. Therefore, the greater the surface area, the greater the rate of evaporation. Anyone with long hair will tell you that it takes much longer to dry if it is tied up in a braid, as opposed to being spread out over the shoulders.

5. Consider, "Could any other factor significantly affect evaporation?" Have student groups place 5 ml of water into each of two plates. One plate is placed in front of a small fan and the other is not. Which will evaporate fastest? Again, students can record the time needed for each source of water to evaporate and display the data in a bar graph. What do these results indicate?

   *Moving air* (*wind*) clearly affects evaporation. The wind blows away the escaping water molecules, allowing more to warm and escape. More wind means more evaporation. To return to the hair-drying example, remember that wet hair dries faster in a moving car with the windows down than it does indoors.

6. Most of the world's water is salty, so you might wonder, "What happens when saltwater evaporates?" Mix a tablespoon of salt into 50 ml of water and have student groups place 5 ml of the mixture onto small sheets of aluminum foil. Allow the water to evaporate completely (you could challenge the students to try to speed up the evaporation rate as much as possible using heat, surface area, and/or moving air). The white residue left behind is the salt, because it cannot evaporate into the air along with the water. When salty ocean or sea water evaporates, therefore, the salt stays behind.

7. Ask the class what they learned about evaporation in these exercises. List their responses on the board. But why is evaporation important? Encourage responses from the students. Explain that the chemical process we call evaporation is important to living things (it cools us, which you can feel by wetting your arm and blowing air over it). It is also an important part of the *water cycle* (see Figure 35–1), which keeps all the earth's plants and animals alive. The water cycle also is the basis for *climate* and *weather*. Which has a greater rate of evaporation, a deep lake or a shallow lake? A cool sea or a warm sea? A hot desert or a cool prairie? How might evaporation affect an area's humidity and temperature? Why do we find *monsoons* and *hurricanes* mainly in *tropical regions?* There are many questions that come to mind regarding evaporation. Find out what your students would like to know, and encourage them to investigate further.

## Questions for Discussion

1. How can we slow down the rate of evaporation? How can we speed it up?

2. Do all liquids evaporate at the same rate? How do you know?

3. How might oceans affect an area's climate and weather?

4. Why don't the oceans eventually evaporate completely?

## Assessment

1. Could students provide a definition for evaporation in their own words, as well as discuss its general effect on climate and weather? [embedded, performance, journal entries]

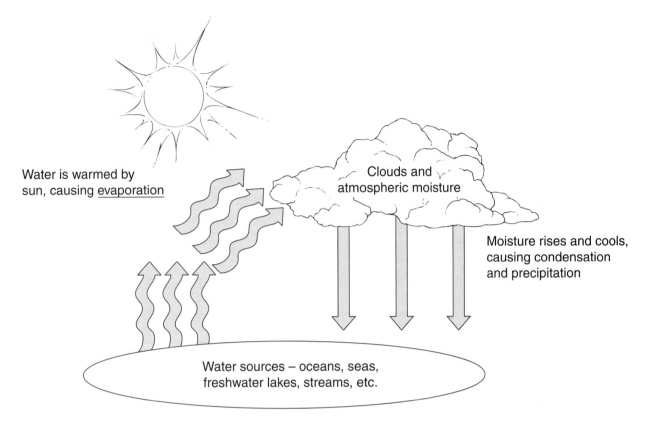

**Figure 35–1.** The water cycle

2. Were students able to successfully graph, analyze, and draw conclusions from their data regarding variables that affect evaporation? [embedded, performance, journal entries]

3. Do students understand evaporation's place in the water cycle? [embedded, journal entries]

## *Other Options and Extensions*

1. Explore the role of *condensation* in the water cycle. One way to do this is by placing ice water in a metal cup and having students observe the water condensing on the cup's outer surface. Can they explain its source? Refer to the *water cycle* diagram (Figure 35–1).

2. Find out more about evaporation's affect on weather and climate in your region.

## *Resources and Further Information*

Gentile, L. (1991). The disappearing act. *Science and Children, 28* (8), 26–27.

Koziel, K. (1994). The water cycler. *Science and Children, 32* (1), 42–43.

Rezba, R. J., Sprague, C., Fiel, R. L., & Funk, H. J. (1995). *Learning and assessing science process skills.* Dubuque, IA: Kendall/Hunt.

Tolley, K. (1994). *The art and science connection.* Menlo Park, CA: Addison-Wesley.

Tolman, M. N., & Morton, J. O. (1986). *Earth science activities for grades 2–8.* West Nyack, NY: Parker.

## Activity Sheet 35. Exploring Evaporation

In the table, *predict* how long it will take for each amount of water to evaporate from the cup. Keep track of how long it *actually* takes, and then find the *difference* between the predicted and actual time by subtracting the smaller from the larger.

| Volume of Water | Fraction of Volume | Time Until Evaporated | | |
| --- | --- | --- | --- | --- |
| | | Predicted Time | Actual Time | Difference |
| 10 ml | 1/4 | | | |
| 20 ml | 1/2 | | | |
| 30 ml | 3/4 | | | |
| 40 ml | 1/1 | | | |

Graph your results: volume of water on the x axis versus time on the y axis.

What conclusions can you draw from your data?

# 36

# Developing a Model of the Earth's Inner Structure

 **Overview**

How much do your students know about the earth's interior? This learning cycle activity will provide them with a hands-on experience, as well as with appropriate terms and concepts. Students discover what makes a good model as they first choose a fruit or vegetable model and then create both a two-dimensional and a three-dimensional model of the earth's interior. They'll use proportion and estimation to build their three-dimensional models. They'll also compare their various models for accuracy and overall utility.

   The learning cycle format (as outlined in Activities 9, "Learning Cycle Studies in Symmetry," and 22, "Investigating the Properties of Magnets"), includes three phases: *exploration* (in which student exploration with concrete materials and problems allows them to make new connections with past experience), *conceptual invention* (in which meaningful term and concepts related to the exploration experience are introduced), and *conceptual expansion* which students use the experience and concepts to progress in their understanding of the subject).

 **Concepts**

Students choose the fruit or vegetable that makes the best model of the earth's inner structure, and then use estimation, proportion, and scale to make a clay model of the planet.

 **Processes/Skills**

- Observing
- Creating
- Describing
- Estimating
- Analyzing
- Measuring
- Calculating

- Communicating
- Reasoning
- Recognizing patterns
- Problem solving
- Developing spatial sense
- Cooperating

 **Recommended for**

| | |
|---|---|
| K–2 | Individual |
| 3–5 ✔ | Small Group ✔ |
| 6–8 ✔ | Whole Class |

 **Time Required**

1–2 hours

 **Materials Required**

- A variety of fruits and vegetables (peach or nectarine, avocado, potato, orange, apple, grape, tomato)
- Paper
- Drawing compasses
- Calculators
- Clay (three different colors)
- Balances

 **Standards**

**SCIENCE**
- Abilities Necessary to Do Scientific Inquiry
- Understanding About Scientific Inquiry

- Properties of Earth Materials
- Structure of the Earth System

**MATH**

- Problem Solving
- Reasoning and Proof
- Numbers and Operations
- Geometry

## ⦿ *Objectives*

- Students will choose a good fruit or vegetable model of the earth and will explain their reasoning.

- Students will construct an accurate clay model of the earth, calculating or estimating the amount of clay needed for each layer.

- Students will effectively compare and analyze their various models of the earth's inner structure.

## ⦿ *Background Information*

The earth is composed of three layers (see Figure 36–1). The *core* has an inner solid portion surrounded by a liquid portion. The *mantle* is mostly solid rock, but also contains *magma,* or molten rock. The rocks of the *crust* create the continents and the ocean floors. The earth's materials have been distributed based on their *density,* with the heavier materials found near the planet's center (the core being composed mostly of nickel and iron) and the lighter materials in the crust. The deepest that humans have bored into the earth is at a geological test site in Siberia (more than 10 kilometers deep). Most of what we know about the composition of the inner earth is based on studies of *seismic waves* (i.e., earthquake waves moving through rocks and monitored by laboratory instruments as they travel through the various layers of the planet). The deeper you go into the earth, the warmer the temperature becomes. The heat comes from the original heat that was generated when the planet was formed and from *radioactivity. Plate tectonics* refers to the movement of the "plates" in the crust, driven by *convection* of the mantle (the plates are pushed about by the hot, shifting mantle underneath). The crust's plates are constantly, but very slowly (because the plates usually move only a few centimeters each year), being created and destroyed. Where plates diverge, new crust is created as magma rises from the mantle. Where plates diverge, the leading edge of the crustal plate is pushed down and lost into the underlying mantle. Most *earthquakes* occur along the boundaries of tectonic plates, as they slide against one another.

## *Main Activity, Step-by-Step*

1. Begin with a simple question: "What do you know about the inner structure of the earth? That is, what is the earth like on the inside?" Create a KWL (Know–Want to Know–Learned) chart by listing their response in the "Know" column of the chart. Fill in the next column of the chart by asking what they want to know about the earth's inner structure and recording their responses. Keep this chart up throughout the activity and refer to it, clarifying knowledge, adjusting factual misconceptions, and pointing out connections to the students' areas of interest.

2. The *exploration phase* of the learning cycle is as follows: Offer student groups a variety of types of fruits and vegetables (peach or nectarine, avocado, potato, orange, apple, grape, tomato, etc.) and ask them to choose the one that they think best represents the structure of the earth, especially considering what the planet is like on the inside. Be sure that they know they will be responsible for explaining their reasoning. Provide students with enough time to complete the task.

3. Now, to begin the *conceptual invention phase* of the learning cycle, ask each student group to present its fruit or vegetable choice and rationale. Because their explanations will be based on very limited knowledge, ask what they need to know about the earth to really pick the best piece of produce as an earth model. List their responses on the board. They should want to know more about what the inside of the earth is like.

   Recall that the purpose of the *conceptual invention phase* is to build on their thoughts and findings from the *exploration phase* (i.e., to connect appropriate and applicable concepts and terminology to their exploratory experiences). Therefore, during and after their fruit/vegetable model

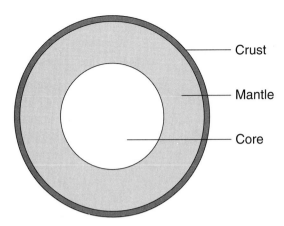

**Figure 36–1.** Earth's inner structure

presentations, explain the basics about the internal composition of our planet. Include the basic cross section (Figure 36–1) of core, mantle, and crust. For older grades, you could also include an explanation of the tectonic plates within the crust. (This conceptual information is found in the Background Knowledge section above.)

4. Proceed on to the *conceptual expansion phase* of the learning cycle by asking again which produce item is the best model of the earth, based on their new understanding of the facts. Ask each group to explain their answers in the light of the information about the earth's inner structure. Did they choose a different produce item this time? Why or why not?

    Have each student draw a cross section of the earth, labeling the core, mantle, and crust. Point out that this cross-sectional model is done in two dimensions (height and width). Also explain that they should base their drawings on the approximate diameters of each layer, which are as follows:

    Core = 3400 km; Mantle = 2900 km; Crust = 50 km

    Ask, "If you were going to make a three-dimensional, cross-sectional model of the earth, made from three different colors of clay (core = blue, mantle = red, crust = green), how much of each color would you need? That is, would you need more blue, red, or green, and can you decide just how much you would need to make your 'model earth' in cross section?" For older students, the answers can be found using the diameters of the earth's layers to calculate the proportions of clay, in grams, needed for the model. (They'll need to consider the relative proportions of the three layers, based on the layer's diameters, and then use those proportions to determine the relative amounts of clay, in grams, needed for the model.) If you want to add an extra challenge, direct them to make sure that the final model has an overall diameter of 15 cm. (Encourage divergent solutions to the problem, which should involve not only the relative proportions of the three layers, but also a determination of the mass of a 15 cm clay sphere, which must then be partitioned into the three colors.) For younger grades, simply have student groups estimate the approximate proportions of the three layers. In any case, be sure that each group can explain its rationale.

    As the student groups complete their calculations and/or estimates, offer clay and balances so that they might weigh out the proper amounts of each color and build their models. Groups can then compare and analyze their models for accuracy. Finally, ask students to determine and explain which is a better model of the earth's structure: the clay cross section or the piece of produce? Consider the sort of information each model offers, which model is most accurate, whether the model is practical (too small, too large, etc.) and any other considerations that come to mind.

5. Conclude with the "Learned" column of the KWL chart: Ask what students learned during this lesson and document their responses on the chart. What else do they want to know about the earth's interior?

## Questions for Discussion

1. Which fruit or vegetable was most like the earth? Which was least like the earth? How do you know?

2. How did your group determine the amount of each color of clay needed for your three-dimensional model of the earth?

3. How is your clay model like the earth? How does it differ?

4. What makes something a good model of something else? What are some things to consider when making a model of something?

## Assessment

1. Were students able to choose a good fruit or vegetable model of the earth and explain their reasoning? [embedded, performance, journal entries]

2. Were students able to construct accurate clay models of the earth, calculating or estimating the amount of clay needed for each layer? [embedded, performance]

3. Could students compare and analyze the different earth models, explaining what makes the difference between a good and a bad model? [embedded, journal entries]

## Other Options and Extensions

1. Find out more about the interior of the earth through research, either in the library or via the Internet. Students can find answers to their own questions.

2. For older grades, determine the scale of the clay earth model.

3. Make models of other planets (based on your research of their size and interior structure) and compare them to your earth model.

## Resources and Further Information

Gabel, D. L. (Ed.). (1994). *Handbook of research on science teaching and learning.* New York: Macmillan.

Gaylen, N. 1998. Encouraging curiosity at home. *Science and Children, 35* (4), 24–25.

Lightman, A., & Sadler, P. (1988). The Earth is round? Who are you kidding? *Science and Children, 25* (5), 24–26.

Trefil, J. (1992). *1001 things everyone should know about science.* New York: Doubleday.

Tolman, M. N., & Morton, J. O. (1986). *Earth science activities for grades 2–8.* West Nyack, NY: Parker.

Williams, D. (1995). *Teaching mathematics through children's art.* Portsmouth, NH: Heineman.

# The Tower Challenge

## Overview

This is an exciting and highly interactive opportunity for students in grades 3 through 8 to exercise their creativity and design skills. Working in cooperative groups, they are challenged to explore the geometry of tower design and construction, first by experimenting with possible designs, and then by choosing the most likely design candidate and building the tallest tower possible, using only paper and tape. This activity is easily connected to social studies via discussions of the world's tall towers, or to human anatomy, via the long bones of the body (which act like towers).

## Concepts

The construction of free-standing paper towers will require careful planning, trial-and-error problem-solving skills, an understanding of the geometry of a stable tower, spatial reasoning, and consideration of the architecture of towers.

## Processes/Skills

- Observing
- Measuring
- Describing
- Inferring
- Experimenting
- Communicating
- Developing spatial reasoning
- Construction
- Comparing
- Reflecting
- Recognizing shapes and patterns
- Problem solving

## Recommended for

| K–2 | Individual |
| 3–5 ✔ | Small Group ✔ |
| 6–8 ✔ | Whole Class |

## Time Required

1–2 hours

## Materials Required

- Standard 8.5 × 11 inch paper
- Masking tape
- Meter sticks
- Scissors

## Standards

**SCIENCE**
- Abilities Necessary to Do Scientific Inquiry
- Understanding About Scientific Inquiry
- Properties of Objects and Materials
- Abilities of Technological Design
- Understanding About Science and Technology
- Science and Technology in Society

**MATH**
- Problem Solving
- Reasoning and Proof
- Geometry
- Measurement

## Objectives

- Students will successfully design, construct, and evaluate free-standing paper towers.

- Students will measure accurately and will recognize geometric, shapes in their tower designs.

- Students will be able to compare their paper towers to famous or familiar towers of the world.

## Main Activity, Step-by-Step

1. Brainstorm with students: What towers have you seen or visited? Consider famous towers (e.g., Eiffel Tower, Watts Towers, Leaning Tower of Pisa), skyscrapers, radio transmission towers, and natural towers (e.g., Devil's Tower, Wyoming). Note: All "towers" are not necessarily architectural (e.g., the long bones of the body such as the humerus and the femur are essentially towers, too). What do towers have in common? How are they constructed? If you notice different tower "varieties," how would you categorize them? Leave the brainstormed list(s) on the board during the activity to prompt speculation, experimentation, and creativity during tower construction.

2. Tell the students that you are challenging them to build their own towers in class. The challenge is this: Build the tallest, free-standing tower possible from a single piece of paper and 30 cm of masking tape.

3. Discuss the following ground rules:

- Your final tower may only contain those materials (paper and tape) supplied by the teacher.

- The tower must not be attached at the base and may not lean against any other surface.

- You will have 30 minutes for official design and construction.

- Your tower must stand on its own for 10 seconds or longer.

- The height will be measured from the base to the highest point.

- You can have your tower "officially" measured as many times as possible within the 30-minute time limit; that is, you can keep adding to it as time permits.

4. The following scoring plan pits students only against gravity and eliminates any overt and unnecessary competition between groups:

Over 50 cm = Good

Over 80 cm = Outstanding

Over 100 cm = Spectacular

Over 150 cm = A Masterpiece of Engineering and Design!

5. Tower-building time will be broken into two sections: practice time and official time. Practice time will last for 30 minutes. Student groups receive several pieces of paper, scissors, 30 cm of masking tape, and a meter stick to check their progress. Ask and brainstorm, "What possible shapes or designs could you use?" They should be encouraged to test as wide a variety of tower designs as possible to find the one with the greatest potential. For younger students, allow more practice time and be willing to help with design ideas.

   Keep in mind that air conditioning, open doors, and/or open windows can create breezes that will topple towers and frustrate participants during this activity.

6. Official tower time begins when practice period ends, and lasts for another 30 minutes. Be sure that they surrender any extra paper and tape left over from practice time. You could take a break between the two periods to discuss practice efforts, likely structural candidates, etc. This discussion would allow students to hypothesize about the tower designs that are most likely to meet the chal-

lenge. Or, to encourage separate efforts by the student construction groups, you could dispense with that discussion, moving directly from practice into official time.

7. When official time begins, student groups receive a single sheet of paper and another 30 cm of tape. To make sure that practice paper is not accidentally incorporated into official towers (thus providing extra construction material), use two different colors of paper, one for practice and one for the official tower. With a list of student groups in hand, the teacher circulates and officially measures towers whenever students ask, documenting their progress on the list. They may continue to add to their tower throughout the time period, so that some groups may ask to be officially measured more than once.

8. Conclude with a classwide discussion and analysis of the activity, including a presentation of each of the towers constructed. What would they do differently next time? What did the students enjoy about this activity? What would they like to know about towers?

## Questions for Discussion

1. Which designs worked? Which didn't? How do you explain these results?

2. What geometric shapes do you see in the completed towers (consider the towers in cross section as well as in lateral view)? What other shapes did you experiment with? Why do you suppose that certain shapes work better than others in tower design?

3. How important were measurements in this activity? Explain your answer.

4. How did your completed towers compare with the real towers we listed on the chalkboard? How were your towers similar to those? How did they differ?

5. What sort of training do you think a person would need if she or he wanted to design and build real towers?

## Assessment

1. Were students actively involved in building and analyzing the design of free-standing paper towers? [embedded, performance]

2. Were they able to recognize geometric shapes in their tower designs? [embedded, journal entries]

3. Were they able to measure accurately? [embedded, performance]

4. Were they able to explain similarities and differences between real towers and their own paper towers? [embedded, journal entries]

## Other Options and Extensions

1. Homework: Ask students to identify towers or towerlike structures in their homes or in the community. Draw them, or construct three-dimensional models.

2. Build a paper tower model of a real tower (e.g., skyscraper, radio tower, Eiffel Tower, Washington Monument, Egyptian Obelisk, femur, Leaning Tower of Pisa, etc.). This could be done on an individual basis, by cooperative groups, or by the entire class.

3. Have students conduct research (e.g., library, Internet, interviews) into various towers of interest: strange towers, tallest towers, towers in history, most beautiful towers, etc.

4. Rather than building a tall tower, design and construct a beautiful tower, a functional tower, an intimidating tower, a fantasy tower.

## Resources and Further Information

Anderson, J. (1972). Aestheometry . . . Constructions in space mathematics. *Science and Children, 10* (1), 31–32.

Junior Engineering Technical Society. (1989). Engineering science in the classroom. *Science and Children, 26* (8), 20–23.

Kohl, M. A., & Potter, J. (1993). *Science arts.* Bellingham, WA: Bright Ring.

Ostlund, K. L. (1992). *Science process skills.* Menlo Park, CA: Addison-Wesley.

Pace, G., & Larsen, C. (1992). On design technology. *Science and Children, 29* (5), 12–15, 16.

Rezba, R. J., Sprague, C., Fiel, R. L., & Funk, H. J. (1995). *Learning and assessing science process skills.* Dubuque, IA: Kendall/Hunt.

Scarnati, J. (1996). There go the Legos. *Science and Children, 33* (7), 28–30.

# Designing and Constructing
# a Load-Bearing Structure

 ## Overview

We rely on many structures to bear loads. Examples such as bridges, chairs, shelves, tall buildings, and even our own legs must support weight consistently and effectively. But where do the human-designed examples come from? Who designs these structures and how do they do it? In this activity, students get to apply science and mathematics as they get a hands-on and process-oriented experience of engineering, architecture, and design. First, they explore the properties of wire as sculptural media, then they utilize some of that knowledge as they devise and build a load-bearing structure using nothing but ten pipe cleaners.

## Concepts

Students find out about the geometry of stable, weight-bearing structures as they are challenged to design and construct such an object using only ten pipe cleaners.

## Processes/Skills

- Observing
- Measuring
- Predicting
- Describing
- Inferring
- Experimenting
- Communicating
- Developing spatial reasoning
- Constructing
- Comparing
- Reflecting
- Recognizing shapes and patterns
- Problem solving
- Analyzing
- Creating

- Designing
- Inquiring
- Applying
- Cooperating

 ## Recommended for

| K–2 | Individual |
| 3–5 ✔ | Small Group ✔ |
| 6–8 ✔ | Whole Class |

## Time Required

1–2 hours

## Materials Required

**PRELIMINARY ACTIVITY**

- Various wiry materials: pipe cleaners and/or actual wire (copper wire, baling wire, galvanized wire, steel wire, thick wire, thin wire, etc.)
- Wire snippers (several pairs)
- Pliers (several pairs)
- Art books with photos of sculptures and/or actual pieces of sculpture

**MAIN ACTIVITY**

- Photos or illustrations of towers
- Lots of pipe cleaners of various colors
- Scissors
- Metric rulers
- Lots of pennies (or other small, standardized weights, e.g., washers, fishing weights)
- Plastic cups
- Balances/scales

##  *Standards*

**SCIENCE**

- Abilities Necessary to Do Scientific Inquiry
- Understanding About Scientific Inquiry
- Properties of Objects and Materials
- Abilities of Technological Design
- Understanding About Science and Technology
- Science and Technology in Society

**MATH**

- Problem Solving

- Reasoning and Proof
- Geometry
- Measurement

## *Objectives*

- Students will design and construct their own load-bearing structures out of pipe cleaners.

- Students will identify and communicate successful and unsuccessful strategies, shapes, designs, and patterns related to the construction of load-bearing structures.

## *Preliminary Activity*

This lesson begins with an open exploration of wire as a sculptural medium. Offer the students various wiry materials: pipe cleaners (of varied colors, if possible) and/or actual wire (of varied thickness, or gauge). If you do choose to include wire, you can find it in your hardware store in a wide variety of forms: copper wire, baling wire, galvanized wire, steel wire, thick wire, thin wire, etc. If you use wire, you'll also need some pliers and snippers. Pipe cleaners can be cut with scissors. Thin wire is easier (and therefore safer) to bend, cut, and manipulate. Demonstrate to students that by twisting the wire together it can be formed into nearly any shape. Ask them to use their imaginations to decide what it is they would like to create. Show some photos of sculpture to stimulate their imaginations. You might ask the entire class to sit with their eyes closed, take a few calming breaths, and visualize their sculpture. Then let everyone get busy making a boat, a car, a building, an animal, a tree, or whatever they wish. Some might enjoy sculpting their interpretation of an abstract concept (such as "knowledge" or "peace"), or a personal feeling. Compare and discuss projects when completed. What did they like about sculpting with wire? How do they feel about their creations?

## *Main Activity, Step-by-Step*

1. Ask, "Can you think of some structures that have to bear weight?" Possible answers might include the wooden frame of a house, a table, the human femur, a ladder, a column, the steel girders in a sky scraper, a tree trunk, and so on. Photos and/or illustrations would be helpful here. Students could even draw their own pictures of some of the structures. Generate and record as many responses as possible. Ask, "What characteristics do all these load-bearing structures have in common? How do they differ? What do you notice about their shapes? Are there any ways in which their shapes are similar? Different? How does the structure of something that must bear a relatively heavy load differ from that of something that must only support a light load?"

2. Explain that student groups will design and build their own load-bearing structures out of pipe cleaners. The challenge is this: Can your group design and build a structure that will hold a cup containing 50 pennies (or other small weights, totaling approximately 140 g) at least 10 cm off the table top, using nothing but 10 pipe cleaners? Explain that there will be a classwide competition for the structure that can hold the most pennies at least 10 cm off the table top. The following ground rules should be explained and discussed to make sure that the students understand:

- You may not use any materials other than the pipe cleaners, but you don't have to use all 10 if you don't need them.

- Your structure may not be attached to the table and may not touch or lean against anything but the table.
- The structure must support the cup of 50 pennies for at least 10 seconds, which the referee (the teacher) must time.
- You will have 30 minutes for trial-and-error "design time" and 45 minutes to construct the "official" structure. You'll get 5 trial-and-error' and 10 official pipe cleaners. (It's a good idea to make sure that the two sets of pipe cleaners are different colors to eliminate accidental mixing of extra materials into the official structure.)

3. Each group receives 5 practice pipe cleaners, a cup with a sealed bag containing pennies, a metric ruler, and a pair of scissors. Give them 30 minutes to plan their structure encouraging each group to brainstorm together and consider a range of possible designs. Remind students that in a brainstorming session the idea is to generate as many ideas as possible without judging them as good or bad. The final design is then chosen from that list of ideas. Suggest that they sketch potential structural plans on paper before actually building.

4. When the practice time is up, give each group the 10 official pipe cleaners and let them begin creating their final structure. Circulate among groups and offer encouragement, but only offer design suggestions to alleviate especially high frustration levels. Don't offer too much help; this exercise allows students to develop their own means of problem solving and too much teacher assistance will diminish that process. Test each group's structure for its 50-penny-supporting capability as requested. Be sure that each group has a structure to enter in the classwide competition.

5. When the 45-minute time period is up, ask all groups to stop work and to gather around for the classwide competition. Taking one structure at a time, test for its ability to support the cup of pennies. Keep adding pennies (in increments of 10) until only one structure remains. How many pennies could it hold before it collapsed? Weigh the pennies to find out how many grams they represent. Engage the class in a discussion of successful and unsuccessful shapes, designs, and patterns. What conclusions can be drawn about the effective design of load-bearing structures?

6. If time and student interest permit, allow groups to confer as you rechallenge them for a second try at building a strong load-bearing structure. Often, the second time around, using the same rules, procedures, and materials, is when many students really "get it."

## Questions for Discussion

1. Why do load-bearing structures need to be carefully designed?
2. How is mathematics important in designing/engineering load-bearing structures? For instance, what patterns or shapes were useful and how did you identify them?
3. Which load-bearing designs are also aesthetically pleasing? That is, is art important in designing/engineering load-bearing structures? Why? Under what circumstances would the aesthetic appearance of such a structure become important?
4. What else would you like to know about load-bearing structures? How could you find answers to your questions?

## Assessment

1. Were student groups able to successfully design and construct their own load-bearing structures out of pipe cleaners? [embedded, performance]
2. Could students identify and communicate about successful and unsuccessful strategies, shapes, designs, and patterns related to construction of load-bearing structures? That is, were they able to draw effective conclusions about designing load-bearing structures? [embedded, journal entries]

## Other Options and Extensions

1.  Try different but related challenges: Build a structure that elevates the load only to a 5 cm height (how does the maximum weight supported compare with that of the 10 cm version?), then build a structure that elevates the load to a 15 cm height (again, how does the maximum weight supported compare with that of the 10 cm version?). Graph "height" versus "maximum weight supported" and look for a relationship between these two variables.

2.  Homework: Make a list of load-supporting structures found in home, neighborhood, community.

3.  Make more wire sculptures: Consider working with a particular theme, making wire mobiles, and/or creating sculptures that go along with a favorite book or story, strictly geometric/arithmetic sculptures (e.g., all triangles, or using squares of increasing sizes).

## Resources and Further Information

Anderson, J. (1972). Aestheometry . . . Constructions in space mathematics. *Science and Children, 10* (1), 31–32.

Junior Engineering Technical Society. (1989). Engineering science in the classroom. *Science and Children, 26* (8), 20–23.

Kajander, A. E. (1999). Creating opportunities for children to think mathematically. *Teaching Children Mathematics, 5,* 480–486.

Kohl, M. A., & Potter, J. (1993). *Science arts.* Bellingham, WA: Bright Ring.

Ostlund, K. L. (1992). *Science process skills.* Menlo Park, CA: Addison-Wesley.

Pace, G., & Larsen, C. (1992). On design technology. *Science and Children, 29* (5), 12–15, 16.

Rezba, R. J., Sprague, C., Fiel, R. L., & Funk, H. J. (1995). *Learning and assessing science process skills.* Dubuque, IA: Kendall/Hunt.

Ritter, D. (1995). *Math art.* Cypress, CA: Creative Teaching Press.

Scarnati, J. (1996). There go the Legos. *Science and Children, 33* (7), 28–30.

# Your Very Own Museum: Making Collections

 **Overview**

Collections are fascinating! Much more than childish pastimes, collections form the basis for museums of natural history, found object art projects, and personal hobbies. Furthermore, many notable scientists—Charles Darwin, for example—began their lifelong investigations with childhood collections. In this activity, students collect a self-chosen category of specimens from the natural world. They will collect as wide a range of those objects as possible and will analyze and compare the specimens within their personal collection. Also, each will contrast the breadth, depth, and patterns of her or his collection with those of other students.

 **Concepts**

Students explore variety and depth when collecting specimens of interest from the natural world. They will also identify mathematical patterns and relationships among their collections.

 **Processes/Skills**

- Observing
- Describing
- Communicating
- Comparing
- Reflecting
- Recognizing shapes, patterns, and relationships
- Appreciating
- Creating
- Problem solving

 **Recommended for**

K–2 ✔     Individual ✔

3–5 ✔     Small Group ✔

6–8 ✔     Whole Class ✔

 **Time Required**

Open-ended; will vary depending on the nature of the collection

 **Materials Required**

**MAIN ACTIVITY**

- Will vary depending on the nature of the collection

**CONNECTING ACTIVITY**

- General art supplies

 **Standards**

**SCIENCE**

- Understanding About Scientific Inquiry
- Properties of Objects and Materials

**MATH**

- Numbers and Operations
- Algebra

 **Objectives**

- Students will make a self-chosen collection of objects or materials from the natural world.
- Students will make meaningful connections between their collections and math, science, and related careers.
- Students will identify and analyze patterns and relationships among their specimens and will reflect on the collecting process.

## *Main Activity, Step-by-Step*

1. This is a relatively simple activity. The value lies not only in the collecting, but also in the wondering, discovering, and extending. Therefore, the crucial aspects of collecting are (a) making sure that all students have *selected a subject of interest to them,* and (b) following up student collecting efforts with a variety of questions/inquiries/projects that prompt them to reflect meaningfully on their collections. These collections can be short term or ongoing throughout the school year. The possibilities are really endless! Several ideas are presented here, but teachers are encouraged to adapt to the children's concerns and directions.

2. Begin the activity by finding out which students already collect things. Responses are likely to be varied and enthusiastic. Next, have the class brainstorm objects from nature that can be collected. A class trip to a natural history museum will certainly raise interest and expand the range of student-generated possibilities. What sorts of objects or materials would they like to collect? How feasible are their ideas? (If the objects are not readily available, students are likely to quickly grow frustrated and bored.) The class may choose to all focus on a particular category of specimens, students may work together to form group collections, or individuals may gather objects on their own. Again, because of the simplicity of the activity, the possibilities are endless, and student choice is the key factor.

3. Students may choose a particular type of object for any of a number of reasons: interest, past experience, beauty, or curiosity. There is no "wrong" rationale. Again, it is important that they find a topic of personal interest to them. A variety of reference books, magazines, and so on the classroom may help reluctant children to identify a subject of interest. Possible collections include ants in a jar (or Ant Farm), photos/sketches of clouds, rocks, seashells, soil samples, water samples, algae, flying insects, flowers and vegetation (pressed or dried), recordings of environmental sounds, casts of animal tracks, recordings of bird songs, spiders, spider webs, fossils, fungi, insects found around the home, small pieces of tree bark, photos/sketches of geological formations, wood, eggs, or feathers.

4. Some collections will require special equipment (e.g., butterfly net), which can often be made easily and inexpensively at home). Others will require extra Internet or library research. This is an excellent opportunity for students to find out more about their topics, implement trial-and-error analysis, and begin to discover what it means to do scientific fieldwork. Special techniques will emerge from research and practice. For instance, spider webs can be collected on black paper by first spraying the web lightly with spray starch.

5. Some collections (e.g., bird eggs or pinned insects) will raise issues of ethical treatment of the living environment. Some students may oppose such invasive collections on moral grounds. Student perspectives should be respected and encouraged and developed in individual writing assignments, small-group discussions, and/or classwide, nonjudgmental dialogue. If any collections involve living specimens (whether plant or animal), you must be certain that the organisms are treated kindly and are cared for properly in terms of their unique needs, before returning them unharmed to their natural homes. Don't take webs, eggs, nests, and so on that are still viable and/or in use (students must check with an adult beforehand if there is any question). Challenge students to make as little environmental impact as possible when making their collections. This is an excellent opportunity for students to gain a first-hand experience of what *environmental impact* means.

6. Students can present, display, and discuss their collections with classmates. Focus discussions on the identification of mathematical patterns and relationships among collected specimens, within and between collections. How do various specimen measurements compare? What color patterns can you identify? How do the shapes compare? Count and compare the number of parts (e.g., the number of pistils in collected flowers). What percentage or fraction of the collection displays a certain property (e.g., what percentage of the seashells were spiral shaped?)? You may designate a special table or area in which collection samples may be displayed. Such a table would make a wonderful learning center for individual or group work.

## Questions for Discussion

1. Why did you choose to make this particular collection? What about it appealed to you?

2. What mathematical ideas do you see represented in your collection or the collections of other students? Consider number, shape, pattern, and statistical possibilities.

3. How does your collection compare with the collections of other students? Consider number of specimens, variety of specimens represented, difficulty of collecting these particular specimens, form of presentation, and so on.

4. What did you know about your specimens before you started the collection? What have you learned about your specimens and about collecting in general?

5. What jobs, careers, or professions might be associated with the specimens that you collected? Have you considered pursuing those careers? Explain.

## Assessment

1. Were the students able to successfully collect items? Were the collections wide ranging and innovative? [embedded, portfolio]

2. Were they able to make meaningful connections between their collections and mathematics concepts, science concepts, and related careers? [embedded, journal entries]

3. Did students identify, compare, and analyze patterns and relationships within and between collections and reflect appropriately on the collecting process? [embedded, journal entries]

## Connecting Activity

Allow students to create a sketch, drawing, painting, ceramic, collage, sculpture, mobile, or other art project based on some aspect or aspects of their specimens. Promote innovation and divergent thinking. Ask them to explain their project in a written journal entry. Display the projects when completed, gallery-style. Invite parents, administrators, other teachers, and students to visit the gallery. Collect visitor responses in writing (make pencils and paper available to all visitors) and post the comments on a bulletin board. Invite your students to consider the "public" reaction to their work.

## Other Options and Extensions

1. Students can conduct a mathematics-related investigation or project (individually, in small groups, or as a class) relating to their collections. Counting, averaging, identifying patterns/relationships, weighing/measuring, identifying geometric shapes, defining variables, problem solving, determining probabilities, and constructing charts/tables/graphs are all possible directions. Projects should include conclusive interpretations of any mathematical results/data obtained. The results and conclusions may then be generalized to other situations, collections, and experiences.

2. Write poems about collections or particular specimens.

## Resources and Further Information

Gaylen, N. (1998). Encouraging curiosity at home. *Science and Children, 36* (4), 24–25.

Kramer, D. C. (1989). *Animals in the classroom.* Menlo Park, CA: Addison-Wesley.

McIntyre, M. (1977). Collections. *Science and Children, 15* (1), 38–39.

Ritter, D. (1995). *Math art.* Cypress, CA: Creative Teaching Press.

Van Deman, B. A. (1984). The fall collection. *Science and Children, 22* (1), 20–21.

# 40

# Creating Art Projects From Recycled Materials

 ## Overview

So you've got your students recycling paper and plastic, but you want to go one better. Why not try this project, easily adapted to any grade level from K–8, in which students are challenged to design a collage, mosaic, or shadowbox entirely from "found objects," that is, recycled, natural, and/or discarded materials? Found object art has a history dating back to prehistoric times. The aesthetic nature of the art of salvage connects students not only to ancient, creative roots, but also to a future in which we must learn to reduce and recycle. As stated by Stribling (1970), "The Found Artist occupies a unique spot in the world of art for he [or she] is both a *collector* of things and a *creator* of things" (p. X). Stribling also noted that the collector/creator's "delight in finding treasures in unexpected places is compounded by the satisfaction of 'refinding' them in his [or her] mind and imagination" (p. X). As "refinders" of too often overlooked materials, students develop a deeper and very practical understanding of conservation and environmentalism. When we compound that experience by adding a mathematical theme to the art projects, we have a truly interdisciplinary lesson.

 ## Concepts

Students discover the value of discarded, recycled, and/ or natural objects as they use these "found" materials to create a variety of art projects, each containing algebraic, geometric, and/or arithmetic patterns.

 ## Processes/Skills

- Observing
- Comparing
- Describing
- Identifying shapes and patterns
- Collecting
- Enjoying

- Communicating
- Problem solving
- Reflecting
- Creating
- Recognizing mathematical relationships

 ## Recommended for

| | |
|---|---|
| K–2 ✔ | Individual ✔ |
| 3–5 ✔ | Small Group ✔ |
| 6–8 ✔ | Whole Class ✔ |

 ## Time Required

2–3 hours

 ## Materials Required

- A wide variety of discarded, recycled, and natural objects and materials (including empty egg cartons)
- Scissors
- Construction paper
- Glue/paste
- Paints, clay, and other basic art supplies as needed

 ## Standards

**SCIENCE**
- Properties of Objects and Materials
- Organisms and Environments

**MATH**
- Problem Solving
- Communication

- Numbers and Operations
- Algebra

---

## ◯ *Objectives*

- Students will select and collect a variety of usable "found" objects and materials and will use those materials to create imaginative collages, mosaics, and shadowboxes.

- Students will incorporate mathematical patterns (algebraic, geometric, and/or arithmetic) into their art projects.

- Students will expand their notions of the value of discarded, recycled, and natural objects and materials.

---

## *Main Activity, Step-by-Step*

1. This is a straightforward and organizationally simple activity, yet it encourages creativity in math, art, and science. Begin by showing the class a variety of discarded and/or recyclable materials (perhaps including empty milk cartons, magazines, newspapers, cloth, egg cartons, twine, aluminum foil, plastic containers, etc.). Ask them what these objects and materials have in common? What were they typically used for? What could they possibly be used for? (Encourage divergent and creative answers.)

2. Next, show the students a variety of natural objects and materials (perhaps a vacated bird's nest, colored pebbles, sand, feathers, shells, seed pods, leaves, bark). Ask them what these objects and materials have in common? What were they typically used for? What could they possibly be used for? (Again encourage divergent and imaginative, even playful, answers.)

3. Explain to the students, if they didn't already suggest the idea, that ether the discarded or natural materials could be used in art projects (materials and ideas might also be found in student's personal collections as explored in Activity 39). The first step will be to gather materials for use. Students should be encouraged to bring in cleaned recyclable/reusable objects and/or natural materials from their neighborhood or home. They will be able to use the materials they gather. Give them several days to amass an adequate collection. You may want to augment their collections with interesting materials that you find.

4. When a sufficient number of materials have been collected, show the students examples of collages, mosaics, and shadowboxes that you or past students have created. So that your students don't just mimic your examples, be sure to have them generate specific ideas about what they could do differently to make their art projects unique and meaningful to them. Be sure to draw their attention to the mathematical patterns represented in each project example. Inform the students that each of their projects—no matter its content, subject matter, or theme—*must* incorporate a mathematical pattern. Patterns can be geometric (spiral, square, circular, etc.), arithmetic (small to large, two-by-two, depictions of a particular number with different objects, etc.), or natural (bilateral symmetry of the colors in a butterfly's wings, or the radial symmetry of a starfish, etc.). An interesting pattern possibility for an egg carton shadowbox is algebraic: depict equivalencies for a particular number in each of the egg compartments (e.g., four: two plus two, or three plus one, or four plus zero, shown by types/colors of seeds in shadowbox holes, that is, two light and two dark in one hole, three light and three dark in another, three dark and three light in the next, and so on).

5. Collages and mosaics can be build on construction paper, cardboard, or even pieces of plywood. They could include written words, other media (such as watercolors or clay), or a background of magazine photographs. Cooperative groups could build large mosaics or collages. Shadowboxes can be easily made from the bottom half of egg cartons. Cut off the carton's top (and recycle it or use it as material for this or another project), paint the bottom half of the carton, and fill in the 12 holes with a depiction of a mathematical pattern, using small objects such as pebbles, seeds, buttons, magazine pictures, and so on. The sky is the limit with these projects. The only boundaries are time and materials. In addition to the mathematical pattern, the project could also include a science theme (such as cell division, evolution, plant growth and development, or environmentalism). Be sure that students can explain their mathematical patterns when asked.

6. When all projects are completed, hold a Found and Discarded Object Art Gallery showing in which students display and discuss their work with one another. Invite other school community members, including parents, administrators, other teachers, and students, to your room to view the projects. Obtain student/artist consent before showing any of their work; this should be entirely voluntary and fun, not coerced.

## Questions for Discussion

1. What normally happens to discarded/recycled and natural "found" materials?

2. If you were to create another collage, mosaic, or shadowbox, what would you do differently? Why?

3. What other mathematical patterns would you like to portray, and how would you portray them?

4. Make a list of other objects or materials that you would like to use in such a project.

5. Why do you think that so many objects and materials are thrown away or overlooked when they can be put to good use?

## Assessment

1. Were the students able to select and collect a variety of usable materials and objects, and did they use those materials to create imaginative collages, mosaics, and/or shadowboxes? [embedded, portfolio]

2. Did they create mathematical patterns (algebraic, geometric, and arithmetic) using the materials and objects collected, and could they explain their patterns? [embedded, performance, journal entries]

3. Did students expand their notions of the value of discarded, recycled, and natural objects and materials? [embedded, journal entries]

## Other Options and Extensions

1. Tie this activity into an expanded exploration of recycling, reducing, and reusing.

2. Investigate the ancient, multicultural origins and history of found object art.

3. Encourage students to learn about the work of well-known found object and natural materials artists, such as Marcel Duchamp, Robert Rauschenberg, and Andy Goldsworthy.

4. Encourage students to come up with their own artistic uses for discarded, recycled, and/or natural materials and objects.

## Resources and Further Information

Barrentine, S. J. (1991). Once around the paper route. *Science and Children, 28* (1), 27–29.

Gaylen, N. (1998). Encouraging curiosity at home. *Science and Children, 36* (4), 24–25.

Holly, K. (1998). The art of mathematics. *Teaching Children Mathematics, 4,* 266–267.

Jenkins, P. D. (1980). *Art for the fun of it.* New York: Fireside,

Lawrence, G. M. (1977). Project REUSE. *Science and Children, 14* (5), 25–27.

Sewall, S. B. (1991). The totem pole recycled. *Science and Children, 29* (5), 24–25.

Stribling, M. L. (1970). *Art from found materials.* New York: Crown.

# Useful Interdisciplinary Resources

*Science and Children* (journal)

*Teaching Children Mathematics* (journal; formerly *The Arithmetic Teacher*)

*School Science and Mathematics* (journal)

*Great Explorations in Math and Science* (GEMS)

*Project AIMS* (Activities Integrating Math and Science)

American Association for the Advancement of Science. (1993). *Benchmarks for science literacy.* New York: Oxford University Press.

Churchill, E. R. (1990). *Paper science toys.* New York: Sterling.

Cobb, V. (1979). *More science experiments you can eat.* New York: Harper & Row.

Cornett, C. E. (1999). *The arts as meaning makers.* Upper Saddle River, NJ: Merrill.

Craig, A., & Rosney, C. (1988). *The Usborne science encyclopedia.* Tulsa, OK: EDC.

Dubeck, L. W., Moshier, S. E., & Boss, J. E. (1988). *Science in cinema.* New York: Teachers College Press.

Ebeneezer, J. V., & Lau, E. (1999). *Science on the Internet.* Upper Saddle River, NJ: Merrill.

Gabel, D. L. (Ed.). (1994). *Handbook of research on science teaching and learning.* New York: Macmillan.

Ingram, M. (1993). *Bottle biology.* Dubuque, IA: Kendall/Hunt.

Jenkins, P. D. (1980). *Art for the fun of it.* New York: Fireside.

Kellough, R. D., Cangelosi, J. S., Collette, A. T., Chiappetta, E. L., Souviney, R. J., Trowbridge, L. W., & Bybee, R. W. (1996). *Integrating mathematics and science for intermediate and middle school grades.* Englewood Cliffs, NJ: Merrill.

Kellough, R. D., Carin, A. A., Seefeldt, C., Barbour, N., & Souviney, R. J. (1996). *Integrating mathematics and science for kindergarten and primary grades.* Englewood Cliffs, NJ: Merrill.

Kohl, M. A., & Potter, J. (1993). *Science arts.* Bellingham, WA: Bright Ring.

Kramer, D. C. (1989). *Animals in the classroom.* Menlo Park, CA: Addison-Wesley.

Larson, G. (1998). *There's a hair in my dirt!* New York: HarperCollins.

Lawlor, R. (1982). *Sacred geometry.* London: Thames and Hudson.

Mandell, M. (1959). *Physics experiments for children.* New York: Dover.

National Council of Teachers of Mathematics. (1989). *Curriculum and evaluation standards for school mathematics.* Reston, VA: Author.

National Research Council. (1996). *National science education standards.* Washington: National Academy Press.

Olshansky, B. (1990). *Portfolio of illustrated step-by-step art projects for young children.* New York: Center for Applied Research in Education.

Ostlund, K. L. (1992). *Science process skills.* Menlo Park, CA: Addison-Wesley.

Parker, S. (1988). *Eyewitness books: Skeleton.* New York: Knopf.

Rezba, R. J., Sprague, C., Fiel, R. L., & Funk, H. J. (1995). *Learning and assessing science process skills.* Dubuque, IA: Kendall/Hunt.

Ritter, D. (1995). *Math art.* Cypress, CA: Creative Teaching Press.

Stribling, M. L. (1970). *Art from found materials.* New York: Crown.

Strongin, H. (1991). *Science on a shoestring.* Menlo Par, CA: Addison-Wesley.

Terzian, A. M. (1993). *The kids' multicultural art book.* Charlotte, VT: Williamson.

Thompson, K. B., & Loftus, D. S. (1995). *Art connections.* Glenview, IL: Good Year Books.

Tobin, K. (Ed.). (1993). *The practice of constructivism in science education.* Washington: AAAS Press.

Tolley, K. (1994). *The art and science connection.* Menlo Park, CA: Addison-Wesley.

Tolman, M. N., & Morton, J. O. (1986). *Earth science activities for grades 2–8.* West Nyack, NY: Parker.

Trefil, J. (1992). *1001 things everyone should know about science.* New York: Doubleday.

United Nations Educational, Scientific, and Cultural Organization. (1962). *700 science experiments for everyone.* New York: Doubleday.

Van Cleave, J. (1989). *Chemistry for every kid.* New York: Wiley.

Walpole, B. (1988). *175 science experiments.* New York: Random House.

Williams, D. (1995). *Teaching mathematics through children's art.* Portsmouth, NH: Heineman.

# Index